LISIA

Vortigern's Island

GW00472346

Charles Parkinson

Armoricana Books
PO Box 552
St Peter Port
Guernsey
GY1 6HX

First published by Armoricana Books

ISBN: 978-0-9574732-0-1

Cover Artwork and Typeset by Shore Books, Blackborough End, Norfolk.

Printed and bound in the United Kingdom.

Introduction

This is the story of a remarkable corner of northwest Europe, set in its context, from the earliest times until the Norman Empire. It therefore covers periods when there was no writing at all, and periods, like the Dark Ages, when there was very little. This means that this book is as much a detective story as a history, but there is enough evidence from archaeology, place names, language, genetics and even simple navigation to allow us to fill in many of the gaps.

Herodotus, a Greek writing in about 440 BC, penned the first surviving text that could possibly refer to any of the British Isles. He wrote, *"that of the extremities of Europe towards the West, he cannot speak with any certainty. Nor is he acquainted with the islands called the Cassiterides, from which tin is bought."*

These words were written almost a century before any reference to 'Britain' is recorded. The first surviving mention of Britain occurs in reports of a voyage made by Pytheas (from Marseilles) in about 350 BC, in search of the source of Baltic amber. He is reported to have navigated much of the coastline of 'Brettaniai', but his own account of the voyage does not survive. However the state of knowledge of the ancient Greeks is clear from the work 'De Mundo', attributed in the Middle Ages to Aristotle, but possibly written up to 200 years after his death. That dates the text to the period 350 BC to 150 BC:

"Beyond the Pillars of Hercules [the Straits of Gibraltar] the ocean flows round the earth; in this ocean, however, there are two islands, and these are very large, called Brettanic [British Isles], Albion [Britain} and Ierne [Ireland], which are larger than those before mentioned, and lie beyond the Kelti [the Celtic people]...moreover, not a few small islands, around the Britannic Isles and Iberia [Spain], encircle this earth, which we have already said to be an island."

So what and where were the 'Cassiterides', which were known to the ancient Greeks, apparently before they were aware of the existence of

Britain and Ireland? Much academic research has been conducted over many centuries, but without reaching any satisfactory conclusion. The state of our knowledge in 1950 was summarised by RJ Fowler:[1]

"Though these islands were considered by Besnier to represent the islands off the Morbihan coast [southern Brittany], others have included Cornwall and the Scilly Isles (where tin ore is extremely rare!). Again the evidence of Diodor, who describes the Cassiterides as islands off the Spanish coast and distinct from Cornwall, has led others to believe them to be the Spanish tinfield. It is now generally accepted, however, that the "Cassiterides" stand for a general name of the tin localities in Western Europe (Haverfield, Hennig, Cary, Bailey) and later narrowed down in classical tradition...to certain islands which took part in the tin trade."

In short, the identity of the 'Cassiterides' was a complete mystery.

1 'Metallurgy in Antiquity'

ILLUSTRATIONS

The front cover shows part of Panel 1 of the Bailiwick of Guernsey Millennium Tapestry, which is reproduced by kind permission of the Trustees of the Millennium Tapestry Trust. The Tapestry comprises 10 panels, loosely illustrating the island's history in the second millennium, with one panel for each century. But the first panel records aspects of Guernsey's history since the Stone Age. The figure at the top left of the panel depicts the Celtic Warrior (c.100 BC), who was buried at the Kings Road village in St Peter Port. To the right of him are stone monuments, a dolmen and La Gran' Mere du Chimquiere, which now stands at the gate of St Martin's church. Below that is a reconstruction of the 3rd century AD ship, called the Asterix, which was found at the entrance to St Peter Port harbour. The lower section of the panel shows the chapel on Herm Island, dedicated to St Tugdual, which was originally constructed in the 11th century, and to it's right a traditional early Guernsey farmhouse. The figures in the foreground are local people of the 11th century, and Saint Sampson, who is said to have converted the island to Christianity in the 6th century. The kneeling figure is uttering the 'clameur de haro', an ancient form of injunction to restrain someone from doing something.

The photograph on the back cover is the author in the passage grave called Le Dehus, in the Vale, Guernsey. The dolmen, which is 33 feet (10 metres) long, was constructed c.3500 BC, and was excavated by the Lukis family between 1837 and 1847.

For more illustrations visit www.armoricana.com

ABOUT THE AUTHOR

Charles Parkinson is a son of the late Professor C Northcote Parkinson, the naval historian and author of 'Parkinson's Law'. The family moved to Guernsey In 1960 and Charles has had a home on the island ever since. He was educated in England, and read Law at Cambridge. After university, he qualified as a Chartered Accountant in London, and was called to the Bar, although he has never practised as a Barrister. During a successful career in the financial services industry, principally in Guernsey, he wrote a book called 'Taxation in France'. In 2004 he was elected a Deputy in the island's parliament. He served as Guernsey's Minister of Treasury & Resources from 2008 until he stood down at the 2012 general election, a term in which he led the development of the island's Strategic Plan. He speaks good French and a smattering of several other European languages, which has assisted him in the research for this book, and the knowledge he has gained from a lifetime of boating has informed the sections on navigation.

Contents

Chapter 1:

The Peoples of Britain and Gaul in Pre-Roman Times

1.1   Ethnic Background

Man has occupied the British Isles for a very long time. The earliest surviving relics of human activity in Britain are 32 worked flints found on the Suffolk coast in 2003, dating from about 700,000 BC, and the oldest human remains, a shin bone found in West Sussex, date from about 480,000 BC. Neanderthal man appeared around 130,000 BC, and disappeared around 30,000 BC, when the species was displaced by the Cro Magnon people.

The last Ice Age began about 20,000 years ago and lasted for 10,000 years during which it is likely that Britain (and most of northern Europe) was depopulated. So much water was stored in the polar ice caps that sea levels were 120 metres lower than they are today, and Britain was joined to Ireland. It was further connected to Denmark and the Netherlands by a strip of low-lying land (now the Dogger Bank in the North Sea).

When the ice receded, Britain was recolonised by Stone Age hunter-gatherers from the European Continent, presumably from the North Sea area. No more than a few thousand individuals crossed the land bridge, but these pioneers account for a large proportion of all the genes found in the indigenous population of Britain today. As the climate gradually warmed, sea levels started to rise, and the land connection to Ireland disappeared about 8000 BC. The land connection across 'Doggerland' was broken about 6500 to 6200 BC, and the British have been an island race ever since. In the Channel Islands, Guernsey and Alderney were cut off from mainland France at about the same time as England, but Jersey remained connected for a few thousand more years, probably being severed from Normandy in about 4000 BC.

North-west France was originally populated by people arriving from the south-east of the Continent, but around 6000 BC there was a very large scale migration of peoples, originally from the eastern Mediterranean or

1

beyond, who moved around the north coast of Africa and up the Atlantic seaboard of Europe. It is convenient to call these people Celts, although that term has acquired political and cultural overtones, since the beginning of the 18th century, which narrows the meaning of the word. These peoples, who reached Britain by sea, made a significant contribution to the gene pool of the British Isles.

A study by Brian Sykes[1] suggested that the original post Ice-Age immigrants and the Celts between them account for about 80% of the DNA of the poopulation of Britain today. Subsequent studies have suggested lower figures for this influence, for example Heinrich Härke estimates the aboriginal contribution to the Y chromosome (male line) DNA of the population of England today at between 27.5 and 75.6%, depending on the region (with larger indigenous contributions in the west and smaller ones in the east).[2] The genetic influence of the aboriginal population in the DNA of females is greater.

The greater part of the non-aboriginal genes in the Caucasian population of Britain are of Germanic or Nordic origin (the two sources being practically indistinguishable), and much of this influence is attributed to the Anglo-Saxon invasions of the 5th and 6th centuries. In fact, the Germanic influence in the DNA of Britain today is greater than the archaeological evidence of the first millennium would lead us to suppose. The population of late Roman Britain has been estimated at 3.7 million, and even allowing for a substantial reduction during the 5th century, it is hard to see how the immigration of 100,000 – 200,000 Anglo Saxons could have had such a large genetic impact. There is an evident 'mismatch' between the archaeological and the genetic evidence, notwithstanding that the DNA of the British population today also reflects the impact of subsequent immigrations.

Two main theories have been advanced to explain this. The first holds that the Anglo-Saxons practised a form of 'apartheid', and that the privileged Anglo-Saxon minority were able to 'outbreed' the indigenous Britons (a view held by Härke among others), and the second is that there was already a significant Germanic influence in the British DNA before the Anglo-Saxons arrived (a view advanced by J E Pattison)[3] As will become apparent, I believe there is significant support for the latter interpretation

1 'Blood of the Isles: exploring the genetic roots of our tribal history', (2006)

2 Heinrich Härke, 'Anglo-Saxon Immigration and Ethnogenesis', (2011)

3 'Integration versus apartheid in post-Roman Britain: a response to Thomas et Al.', (2008)

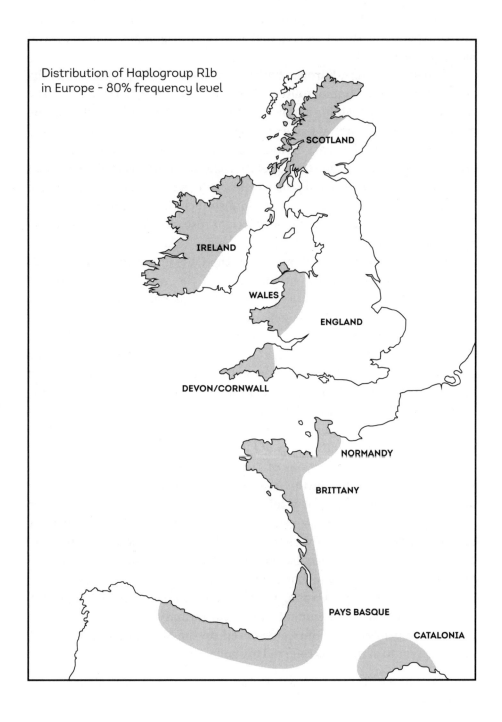

Distribution of Haplogroup R1b
in Europe - 80% frequency level

in the development of the English language.

But significantly, no modern studies suggest that there is any evidence of a substantial migration into Britain from central Europe, and this contradicts earlier theories that the Celts originated from a Central European heartland

A map of western Europe showing areas where the proportion of the population with the Haplogroup R1B gene exceeds 80%, corresponds very closely with the distribution of people that we now regard as Celtic, in the modern and more narrow sense of the word – i.e. Scotland, Ireland, Wales, Cornwall, Brittany, the coast of Aquitaine and the north coast of Spain.[4]   In France the area covered by this population extends north-east of the present borders of Brittany, to include the western side of the Cotentin peninsula in Normandy. And by inference, it would also include the native population of the Channel Islands, although insufficient research has been done in this area to prove the point.

For a long time it was thought that the Celts emerged from a Central European heartland, partly on the basis of the writings of Herodotus, who we met in the Introduction. Herodotus has been called 'the Father of History', and is regarded as generally objective, a man of integrity and intellectual discipline. But he could only record what he knew, and, living as he did in what is now Bodrum in southern Turkey, unfortunately his geography of Western Europe was rather vague. He evidently thought that the source of the Danube lay in the Pyrenees, and that the river bisected the European peninsula in an east-west direction. He wrote: *"[The Nile} starts at a distance from the mouth equal to that of the Ister;[5] for the river Ister begins from the Keltoi and the city of Pyrene."*

From this text, generations of historians have assumed that the Celts (the 'Keltoi') originated from the area around the source of the Danube, rather than from the Pyrenees (for a full discussion see Stephen Oppenheimer, 'The Origins of the British: a genetic detective story" 2006). The genetic evidence tells us that the Pyrenees would be a far more probable point of origin of the Celts in France, because they had been established along the Atlantic seaboard for many thousands of years.

In terms of culture, it was again thought for a long time that the pottery and metalworking skills evident in Central Europe in the 1st millennium BC were associated with the Celts, based on the misapprehension of the migration route of the Celts referred to above. There were Central European

---

4 This is a relatively modern concept. Before the 18th century, the peoples of Scotland, Ireland, Wales and Cornwall never considered themselves to be Celts.

5 *the Danube*

cultures in this period which archaeologists have banded into three broad groups – the 'Urnfield Culture' of about 1200 BC, the 'Hallstatt Culture' which started in the 8th century BC and lasted until about 500 BC, and the 'La Tène Culture' into which the Hallstatt seamlessly evolved.

The Urnfield culture, which derives its name from the practice of burying the cremated remains of the dead in urns, spread over modern Germany, eastern France and north-east Spain, and a variant of it existed in what is now Belgium and Holland. The Hallstatt culture derives its name from a town in Austria in which a pre-historic cemetery was found in the 19th century, which produced a rich haul of pottery and metalwork of distinctive and highly developed styles. The La Tène culture is associated with an area on the north shore of Lake Neuchatel in Switzerland, where remains of an Iron Age culture was found in the 19th century.

On the basis of the genetic evidence, many scholars now think that the development of these cultures was unrelated to the migration of the Celts, who were concentrated along the Atlantic seaboard in the earlier of the relevant periods. But nothing is certain in terms of the history of the period and others, disputing the reliability of the genetic evidence, hold to the view that the Celts migrated across mainland Europe. However there is support for the coastal migration theory in early literature, because Pausanius, writing in the 2nd century BC, tells us that the Gauls *("originally called Celts")* live on *"the remotest region of Europe on the coast of an enormous tidal sea"*. While this statement was no longer entirely true in the 2nd century BC, because the Celts had by then colonised most of Gaul, it is likely that it reflected the historical reality, and the Celtic heartlands were probably still located along the coast.

From their Atlantic coast settlements, the Celts seem to have spread north and eastwards to become the dominant ethnic group in France by the middle of the first millennium BC. In about 500 BC, the pre-existing trade routes down the Rhône valley were disrupted, and these developments are thought to be connected to the arrival of the Celts in that region. It appears that by then the Celts occupied northern France, west of the Seine. The southwest of France was always rather different, having been occupied by man since very ancient times, as shown by the evidence of cave-dwelling peoples to be found in the Dordogne. In particular, the Basque people are of a very ancient stock, and their language is unrelated to the other Indo-European languages of the Continent.

So Gaul, as Caesar famously said, was divided into three parts. The Gauls themselves mainly occupied the central band, south and west of the Seine and the Marne, but north-east of Aquitaine. The people of Aquitaine became a mixture of Celts and the indigenous population, who were some of the oldest ethnic groups in Europe, going back 400,000 years. To the north-east of the Gauls were the people called the Belgae, who Caesar tells us were Germans who had crossed the Rhine 'a long time ago', and settled east of the Seine.

We really only have Roman sources to allow us to form any view of the size of the populations of pre-Roman Britain and Gaul, and the picture we get is a confusing one, with an impression of greater population density in the eastern regions. In terms of Britain, Caesar tells us that *"The population is exceedingly large, the ground thickly studded with homesteads, closely resembling those of the Gauls, and the cattle very numerous."* But then he was able to mount an incursion with two legions (up to 11,000 legionaries, plus auxiliaries), which the British were unable to repulse. Even allowing for the fact that the Romans tell us that the British tribes were never able to coordinate their forces, and that they were poorly equipped, this suggests that the population cannot have been very large.

Certainly, Roman towns in Britain were very small by modern standards – London had a population of possibly 35,000 and Colchester and St Albans, the next largest towns, had populations of possibly 10 - 12,000. By way of comparison, the population of Rome was probably around one million by the end of the 1st century BC. It is impossible to measure the size of the total population of Britain in Roman times, but published estimates are of the order of 3 to 4 million.

In eastern and southern Gaul, Caesar faced some really substantial armies – of possibly up to 300,000 men. In his 'Gallic Wars', he recounts that, of the tribes from the east, the Bellovaci could provide 100,000 men, and the Suessones and the Nervii could each provide 50,000 men to fight against his forces in 57 BC. And at the Battle of Alesia in 52 BC, the largest tribes, such as the Héduens and the Arvernes, together with their allies, provided 35,000 men each.

But on the other hand it seems that he faced little opposition in Brittany. The tribes of Brittany provided 20,000 in total at the Battle of Alesia (admittedly after the largest of them had been destroyed in battle and by enslavement). It has been estimated that the total population of Brittany in the Bronze Age was something between 100,000 and 200,000 people (plus or minus 50%), and that this had increased in the Iron Age to 150,000 to 300,000 (with the same margin of error).[6]

---

6 Pierre-Roland Giot, Philippe Guigon and Bernard Merdrignac, 'The British Settlement of Brittany' (2003).

1.2   Ancient Architecture and Technology

On both sides of the English channel, in the 'Megalithic Age' (5000BC to 2000BC), the Celtic people erected massive stone monuments. In Brittany, these monuments are called 'menhirs' (standing stones) or 'dolmens' (passage graves), after their names in the Breton language, and more than 500 menhirs are still standing. Similar monuments are found on the northern side of the Channel, most famously at Stonehenge in Wiltshire, which was constructed in several phases from about 3000 BC to 1500 BC. This amazing site is at the centre of the largest group of Stone Age and Bronze Age monuments in England, and like others of its ilk, it appears to have been laid out in relation to the position of the sun at the solstices and equinoxes.

One of the oldest surviving stone structures in Europe is the passage grave called Le Cairn de Barnénez (c. 4600 BC) at Plouézoc'h, in the Bay of Morlaix, which has been described as the 'Megalithic Parthenon', and another of similar vintage is the burial mound called Les Fouillages at L'Ancresse in Guernsey (c. 4500 BC). By 'structure', I here mean stones placed on top of each other to form a shelter or tomb. In fact, 59 megalithic sites are located on Guernsey and its sister island Jersey, but as many as 130 have been destroyed since the 17th century[7] . These standing stones and passage graves are known in the Channel Islands as 'pouquelayes', a term unknown anywhere else, and it has been suggested that the name derives from a Celtic word 'pwca' meaning fairy and 'lieux' meaning 'places' in Norman French. Almost all of the megalithic sites in Alderney were destroyed by quarrying in the 19th century, but it is clear that the Channel Islands, as a group, were home to one of the largest concentrations of megalithic monuments anywhere. Of course we do not know the reason for this focus of early human activity, and nor can we tell whether the megaliths were constructed by people living on the islands or by visitors arriving in boats, but the scale of their efforts is certainly impressive.

This culture died out about 2000 BC, at about the time that the people of north-west Europe learned about metals. The acquisition of metalworking skills seems to have diverted human endeavour into the making of better weapons and tools for working wood. But, whatever the reason, the descendants of the builders of the megaliths did not build in stone, so we must suppose that the religious imperative, which had previously inspired the massive effort required to construct monuments, had for some reason

7 Paul Driscoll, 'The Past in the Prehistoric Channel Islands' (2010)

waned. In fact, the oldest stone building in Europe, after the Megalithic Era, is the Parthenon in Greece (447 – 432 BC), and after that the next oldest surviving buildings in Europe are the stone houses located in the Shetland Islands, north of Scotland. These date from about 200 BC, and no other buildings in Europe survive from the pre-Roman era. But fortunately Iron Age man did re-use old megalithic sites, so these sites have proved to be vauable sources of later objects.

'The Bronze Age' describes the period between 'the Stone Age' and 'the Iron Age', but it was not the period when man first started to use metals. Copper has been used for at least 10,000 years, but somewhere around 3000 BC, the peoples of the Near East discovered that copper was stronger if alloyed with tin to make bronze. This technology reached Western Europe in about 2000 BC, and the Bronze Age in the West then lasted until about 600 BC, when bronze started to be replaced by iron.

The metal bronze was not, of course, the only distinguishing feature of the Bronze Age. The making and use of metals required a far greater degree of social cooperation and trade – even international trade – than had ever been seen before, and it therefore transformed human societies. And metal tools made achievable advances in agriculture and the production of goods for both utilitarian and ornamental purposes, which had never before been possible.

The term 'Bronze Age' refers to different periods in different regions, because Western Europe lagged considerably behind the Mediterranean and the Near East in cultural development. In the Mediterranean, the Bronze Age came to an end in about 1200 BC, when 'barbarians' burned every major town in the eastern Mediterranean to the ground. Only Egypt had the strength to stave off the predators, and we are largely dependent on Egyptian hieroglyphics for our knowledge of what happened. But in Western Europe the Bronze Age continued for another 600 years.

Of course, production of bronze did not cease at the end of the Bronze Age, and the metal is still blended in large quantities today. Indeed, for a long time after the method of smelting iron had been discovered, bronze was regarded as the better metal, because it was easier to work and less brittle than iron. So for example officers in the Roman army had swords made of bronze, while the ordinary soldiers had swords made of iron. Only later did swordsmiths discover that reduction of the carbon impurities in iron to a level of about 2% or less (they did not of course know the precise figure), resulted in a much stronger metal (i.e. steel). It is clear nevertheless that the bronze production industry was in secular decline in the centuries before the Roman era, as iron gradually replaced the use of bronze in many objects.

Bronze is an alloy of copper and another metal, and originally arsenic was used (copper and zinc is called 'brass'). However the ancients soon became aware of the dangers of using arsenic, and tin was substituted to produce an alloy that was a lot stronger and a lot harder than pure copper. Copper is in reasonably plentiful supply: it is the 26th most common element in the Earth's crust, so it was not very expensive. And in the ancient world, copper was found in Iran, Oman and, most especially, in Cyprus, from which the name of the metal was derived, so it was conveniently available in places close to where the bronze was required.

Tin, on the other hand, is comparatively rare: it is the 50th most common element in the Earth's crust. And worse still, while the quantities required to make bronze were comparatively small (the ideal mixture was approximately one part of tin to seven to ten parts of copper), the sources of tin were very remote. Tin was first found in India, and indeed, the metal was known to the Greeks under its Sanskrit name, Kastira. It is principally obtained from the mineral cassiterate, which was found by panning in rivers and then by mining the source lodes from which the river deposits arose. For a long time, India was the only known source of tin, but then supplies were found on the western borders of the then known world, in Cornwall, in Brittany and in north-west Spain.

Tin mining had begun in Cornwall about 2150 BC, and it is clear that fairly early on, a trade had grown up between Cornwall and the Mediterranean. Objects found in Cornwall, such as the Billaton Cup and the Pelynt Dagger, prove that the Cornish had direct or indirect contact with the Mycenaean Greek world (1900 – 1200 BC, i.e. before the great catastrophe which overtook the eastern Mediterranean in 1200 BC). By 1600 BC, Cornish tin and other metals were being exported across Europe, and bronze products were being sold into Britain in return.

1.3   The Celtic Tribes

On both sides of the Channel, the Celtic peoples formed themselves into tribes. In southern Britain, the Dumnonii occupied Devon, Cornwall and the western part of Somerset; the Durotriges occupied Devon (to the east of the River Axe), Dorset, South Wiltshire and South Somerset. The Atribates and the closely related Regneses occupied central southern England including Hampshire and West Sussex. The extreme southeast of England was occupied by the Cantiaci, or Cantii, who were a Belgic, or possibly even

Baltic tribe. Caesar records that their land was divided into four areas, each ruled by its own king.

The boundary between the Durotriges and the Atribates was the Bokerley Dyke, southwest of Salisbury, which was clearly built by the Durotriges because the ditch is on the east side. The border extended down through the New Forest to the coast, east of Hengistbury Head, which was in the territory of the Durotriges. Indeed tribes related to the Durotriges may have occupied the land as far to the east as the Solent, and there is evidence in the distribution of coins that the Isle of Wight was linked to them. Hengistbury was well located for trade not only with the Continent, but also between the Atribates and the Durotriges in times of peace.

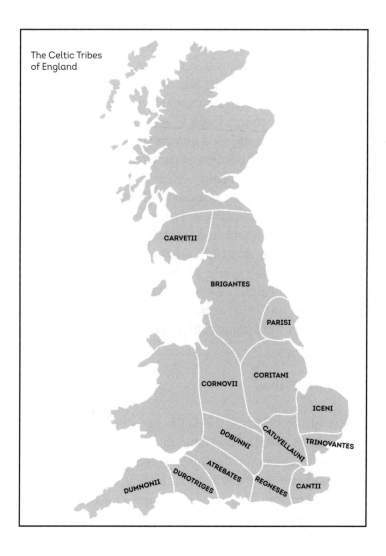

The Celtic Tribes
of England

The Celtic Tribes of Northern Gaul

MENAPII

MORINI

ATREBATES

CALETES

UNELLI

ABRINCATUI   LEXOVII

OSISMES

CORIOSOLITES   BELLOCASES

VENETI

REDONES

NAMNETAE

RIVER LOIRE

There were three main tribes in the Brittany peninsula: the largest, before the Roman invasion, was the Veneti, who were a seafaring tribe based around the city now known as Vannes; the western extremity of the peninsula was occupied by the Osismes, based around the city now known as Brest; and to the north-east of the Veneti were the Coriosolites, whose capital city was Corseul, and who controlled the major port of Alet, at the mouth of the River Rance (now called St Servan).

To the east of the Veneti were two tribes, the Redones who were based around the city now known as Rennes, and the Namnetae, who occupied the region around Nantes. At the south-east corner of the Bay of St Malo, there was a tribe called the Abrincatui, based around modern Avranches, and the Cotentin peninsula of Normandy was mainly occupied by the Unelli, whose capital was at modern Coutances. To the east of them there were several tribes between the Unelli and the lands of the Belgae to the east of the Seine, of which an important one was the Lexovii.

1.4   Cultural Influences and Language

It has long been hypothesised that the majority of European languages share a common ancestor, long extinct, which has been called 'Proto-Indo-European' and which is assumed to have developed on the Eurasian Steppe, north of the Black Sea in the 4th millennium BC. However, in the early 20th century, fragments of manuscripts written in an unknown language were found in the Xinjiang province of western China. This language, which is now called Tocharian B, was subsequently deciphered to reveal, among others, the following words:

Tocharian B	English	Old Irish
pacer	father	athair
macer	mother	mathair
procer	brother	brathair
ser	sister	siur
yakwe	horse	ech
ku	dog (cur)	cu
okso	cow (ox)	oss
ap	river	ab

The similarities to English, and even more so to Old Irish, are astonishing. Tocharian B, which died out in the 9th century AD, is the only known language which represents an eastwards migration of Proto Indo European, but it also gives us a great deal of additional information as to what that language looked like.

It appears that the branches of this language were exported along three general routes, which were reunited in north-western Europe. The northern route, along the river valleys of central and Eastern Europe, brought the Germanic languages to the west. The central route, through the Balkans and along the northern shore of the Mediterranean, brought the Romance languages, and the southern route, down through the Caucuses, through Anatolia, around the southern shore of the Mediterranean and up the Atlantic coast of Europe, brought the Celtic languages. And it can be assumed that the migrations of the languages reflected the migrations of peoples.

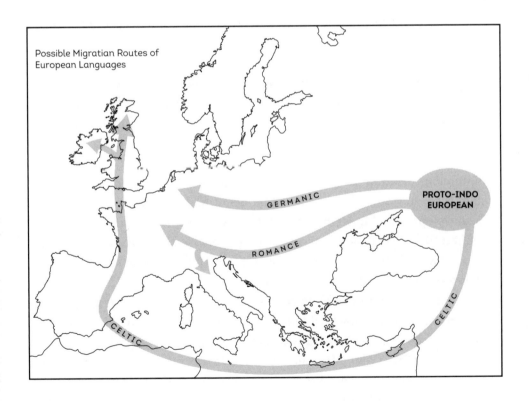

Possible Migratian Routes of European Languages

This pattern of movements receives some corroboration from the patterns of later migrations from east to west across Europe. It seems to have been repeated down the ages, as the northern route to the west was followed by successive waves of invaders, eg the Visigoths, Alans and Huns, the central route was exploited by peoples like the Ostrogoths, and the southern route around the Mediterranean was followed by the Phoenicians, the Vandals and the Arabs of the Ummayad Caliphate. All of these episodes will be explored in greater detail in this book.

The three language families were to some extent reunified when they reached the far north-west of Europe. The Germanic and Celtic languages had a common border in France, especially in the region east of the Seine which was occupied by a mixture of Celtic, Belgic and German tribes, and a largely Germanic language which I have called Belgic was a result of the fusion. The Celtic languages reached the west of Britain without this Germanic overlay. And the Romance influence, which became the dominant ingredient of French, came to England with the Romans and, to an even greater extent, with the Norman French.

Caesar tells us that the Belgae and the Galli spoke different languages, and that *"the greater part of the Belgae were sprung from the Germanic peoples, and that, having crossed the Rhine at an early period, they had settled there, on account of the fertility of the country".* But he also tells us that there were German tribes in Gaul, the Condrusi, the Eburones, the Caeroesi and the Paemani, so it seems clear that at least three languages were spoken in northwest Gaul. In this book I refer to the language of the Belgae as 'Belgic', a Germanic language that now survives only as a component of other languages. Speculation on the existence of such a language is not novel, but I believe that Belgic had a far larger influence on the development of English than is generally recognized (as will be seen in Chapter 9). The language was also a component in other ancient languages of northwest Gaul, such as Old Walloon and Old Franconian, and it was, therefore, indirectly a source of French.

Moreover, we can infer from Caesar's comments that the peoples of Britain living on the coasts of England across the Channel from the Belgae were closely related to them and may even have lived under common chieftains. In his 'Gallic Wars', he tells us *"The Suessiones had very extensive and fertile territory, bordering on the Remi themselves. Within living memory their king had been one Diviciacus, the most powerful ruler in the whole of Gaul, who had control not only of a large area of this region but also of Britain"*.[8] He then goes on to say that the leaders of the Bellovaci fled to Britain in 57 BC, which again indicates pre-existing cross-Channel relationships.

And there are other clues that the tribes at the eastern end of the Channel were related to their counterparts across the water. Before mounting his first incursion into Britain in 56 BC, Caesar sent a leader of the Atribates (a Belgic tribe living in the area around the Pas de Calais) to negotiate with the British leaders. The same tribe seems to have had a presence in West Sussex, based around Chichester, and the eastern part of Hampshire. The city of Winchester was known to the Romans as Venta Belgarum ('the market of the Belgae'), so it appears that the people living in south-east England were related to, and may well have spoken the same language as, the Belgae in north-east Gaul.

This area of 'Belgic' connections, before the arrival of the Romans, is likely to have included Hampshire, Sussex, Kent, Surrey, Middlesex and Essex, but also the land of the Catuvellauni in Hertfordshire, Bedfordshire, Northamptonshire and southern Cambridgeshire (it is thought that the Catuvellauni were related to the Catalauni tribe in Belgic Gaul). It has also been speculated that the Parisi, who lived in what is now the East Riding of Yorkshire, could have been related to the Continental tribe of the same name, but there is little hard evidence for this. Certainly, the commercial practices of the tribes of south-east England were similar to those of the tribes of Gaul in that they issued their own coins, usually with images, or the names, of their 'kings'.

However Caesar records that the tribes of the north and west of Britain were different. *"The interior of Britain is inhabited by people who claim on the strength of oral tradition, to be aboriginal; the coast by Belgic immigrants who came to plunder and make war....nearly all of them retaining the names of tribes from which they originated....and later settled down to till the soil."* The commercial customs of these people were different, because with one exception, the tribes of the 'interior' did not mint coins. And that one exception was the Durotriges, who appear to have had strong trading relationships both with the 'Belgic' tribe to their east, the Atribates, and with the Coriosolites of northern Brittany. The coins of the Durotriges are however distinctive because they did not feature written inscriptions, which suggests that they did not read or write.

I therefore conclude that the tribes of southeast England were ethnically and linguistically 'Belgic' when the Romans arrived, and I believe

8 Translation by Anne and Peter Wiseman – 'The Battle for Gaul'. (1992)

that their influence spread over most of modern England during the period of Roman rule. Stephen Oppenheimer argues that the scarcity of Celtic loan words in the English language suggests that the later Angles and Saxons settled in an area that was not Celtic speaking, and I think this was the case. We know that the British had to use translators to communicate with the Anglo-Saxons, but if the language spoken by the peoples of England was a Germanic language, it may have been distantly related to Anglo-Saxon and some words may have been mutually comprehensible.

The languages spoken by the Celts of the 'interior' of Britain and the language of the Gauls were all members of the family of Celtic languages, which were very ancient and which had evolved into several different branches. On the Continent, the principal Celtic languages were Gaulish, spoken throughout Gaul, and Celtiberian, spoken in the Iberian Peninsula. But in the British Isles, two families of 'Insular Celtic' had emerged, 'Goidelic' (the ancestor of Gaelic) was spoken in Scotland, Ireland and the Isle of Man, and 'Brythonic' was spoken in Wales and western Britain. So we can assume that when the Durotriges traded with the Coriosolites, as we know that they did, they spoke related, but not necessarily very similar, forms of Celtic. Unfortunately, although Brythonic has survived, the Continental Celtic languages are long extinct, and since they had a remarkably small influence on modern European languages, we know little about them. We therefore cannot tell, for example, how easy it was for Brythonic speakers to converse with Gaulish speakers.

1.5 Lifestyle

Whatever their linguistic differences may have been, the Celts of northern Europe all appear to have lived fairly similar lifestyles, and indeed their general circumstances seem to have been similar to those of other tribes of northern Europe. The Celts lived in wooden 'round houses', which naturally only survive, where they survive at all, as post-holes. They wrote very little, and very few tribes (certainly in Britain) produced coins. So the only descriptions we have of them or their culture are those of Roman or Greek commentators, some of whom were not complimentary. But enough evidence is available to allow us to gain at least some understanding of their societies.

In pre-Roman times, the Celtic people on both sides of the Channel were essentially peasant farmers, living in scattered farmsteads, villages or hamlets, who brought their surplus produce to local markets to exchange with other farmers. Similarly there were small-scale industries producing pottery, woodwork, metalwork, and specialty foods (like garum, a fish sauce made with anchovies and salt, produced in what is now Douarnanez in Brittany) and the artisans and craftsmen would also have brought their goods to market for barter. The markets were held in local towns (sometimes referred to under the Latin term 'oppida', which is not really appropriate to the large fortified camps of Brittany), which may have been controlled by a local lord.

Areas equivalent to one or two modern counties were occupied by specific tribes, who were presumably, to a greater or lesser degree, extended families. And in some cases these tribes had 'kings', but in others the society seems to have operated with a looser constitutional structure. They worshipped a variety of gods of a natural or astronomical origin, and religious leaders called Druids ministered to the spiritual needs of the people.

Caesar described the tribes as hierarchical. He wrote: *"Everywhere in Gaul there are only two classes of men who are of any account or consideration. The common people are treated almost as slaves, never to act on their own initiative and are not consulted on any subject...The two privileged classes are the druids and the knights".* The 'knights' were ranked according to the number of attendants they brought with them to the battle.

Which brings us to the subject of war. In ancient times there was little for farmers to do between the planting of the seeds in the spring, and the harvesting of the corn in the autumn. This was the fighting season, and men would band together to go to war. Caesar observed that: *"the Gallic states used to fight offensive and defensive wars almost every year".* However, it is not clear whether they waged war indiscriminately on their neighbours, or whether the borders between the Gallic and Belgic tribes were a particular zone of friction and conflict. It appears that the men were well built – Caesar tells us that they would mock the Romans for their diminutive size - and no doubt years of practice made them confident in their fighting abilities. But they wore no body amour, and their weapons were inferior to those of the Romans.

Many of the Roman commentaries present an unflattering view of the Celtic people, but these probably need to be taken with the proverbial pinch of salt. The Celts were portrayed as headhunters, who engaged in human sacrifice, and who were sexually licentious. It is certainly clear that some of the Celtic tribes in southern Gaul collected heads as trophies of war, but there is very little archaeological evidence of human sacrifice, at least in north-western Europe. As for their sexual mores, we cannot know what the truth is: but according to the Romans the women gave their sexual favours freely, and were often in relationships with several men from the same family. The men, Caesar tells us, often preferred male sexual partners.

Some of the Celtic tribes went into battle naked, apart from helmets and shields, and with their bodies painted blue with woad. They made a fearsome noise, both by shouting and the use of horns. The nobles, we are told, shaved their cheeks, but let their moustaches grow freely – certainly from the surviving images, the moustache was de rigueur for the fashion-conscious Celtic warrior. They used swords and slings as weapons, but the bow and arrow were used mainly for hunting.

Children often lived with foster parents, and a system of hostage taking operated between tribes. This was not quite what we would associate with the term. As Barry Cunliffe describes it *"The taking of hostages...was equally widespread. It should not, however, take with it the connotations of the modern world. Among the Celts, hostages were usually young men of noble families from one tribe who lived and served with another as a guarantee of agreed behaviour: it was, in fact, a bonding mechanism."* ('The Ancient Celts' 1997).

They ate meat (cattle, sheep, pigs, red deer, rabbits etc), fowl and fish. They grew crops of grain, and ate fruit. And they drank beer ('cervesa' – one of the few Continental Celtic words that has come down to us, in Spanish, unchanged) and wine. Salt was a valuable commodity, produced by natural evaporation or boiling of seawater, or by mining rock salt. And the Celts of north-west Europe bought spices from the Mediterranean region.

Most clothes were made of wool, and the British tribes in particular were noted for a long hooded cloak called the 'birrus britannicus' by the Romans. A Celtic warrior's grave found in St Peter Port, Guernsey, and dating from about 100 BC revealed that he wore a coarse outer cloak and a shirt or tunic made of finer threads. The Romans were horrified that the men wore trousers, as indeed the St Peter Port warrior did, at a time when men in Rome wore togas. Cotton from Egypt or silk from China were luxury commodities available to the elite in the Roman world, and may have been acquired by Celtic nobility.

Horses were used for transport, and in time of war they were employed to mount light cavalry or to draw chariots. The utility of horses was limited until the stirrup and solid saddle made their way to Europe in the 6th and 7th centuries, because without stirrups a warrior did not have a particularly stable platform from which to wield his weapons. The stirrup in turn requires a solid saddle, designed to bridge the spine of the horse so as not to cause the horse discomfort, and the technology that developed into the medieval 'knight in armour' did not reach Western Europe until the 8th century. In the Roman era, horsemen had only soft saddles or rugs, without stirrups, and cavalry were primarily deployed as scouts or spies, and to harass stray infantry, for example after an army had been routed. Nevertheless officers 'of equestrian rank' rode horses as a form of transport, and to give them a good view of the battlefield. A wooden tablet by an anonymous author found at the Vindolanda Roman fort in Britain records that *"The Britons are unprotected by armour. There are very many cavalry. The cavalry do not use swords nor do the wretched Britons mount in order to throw javelins"*.[9] So it is unclear what these apparently unarmed horsemen were supposed to achieve in battle.

Some of the British Celtic tribes used horses to draw chariots, which was a technique of warfare regarded as obsolete by the Romans (although it survived in the form of chariot racing for entertainment purposes). Each chariot had a driver and a knight, and the objective of the charioteers was to break up the enemy ranks and deposit the knight in the most advantageous spot for the battle. The driver would stand by to rescue the fighter if necessary. Caesar was impressed by the skill of the British charioteers:

"Their mode of fighting with their chariots is this: firstly, they drive about in all directions and throw their weapons and generally break the ranks of the enemy with the very dread of their horses and the noise of their wheels; and when they have worked themselves in between the troops of horse, leap from their chariots and engage on foot. The charioteers in the meantime withdraw some little distance from the battle, and so place themselves with the chariots that, if their masters are overpowered by the number of the enemy, they may have a ready retreat to their own troops. Thus they display in battle the speed of horse, (together with) the firmness of infantry; and by daily practice and exercise attain to such expertness that they are accustomed, even on a declining and steep place, to check their horses at full speed, and manage and turn them in an instant and run along the pole, and stand on the yoke, and thence betake themselves with the greatest celerity to their chariots again."

9 Tablet in the British Museum.

Chapter 2:
Trading Patterns in the Region

2.1   Road system

Although the Romans have been credited with creating the road systems in Britain and Gaul, we know that both countries had road networks before their arrival. For example, Watling Street in England connected Dover, Canterbury, London, St Albans and Wroxeter, where there were onward links to Holyhead in Wales, to Chester and onwards to Scotland. Some of these roads may have been little more than tracks beaten down by years of use, but any notion that the Celtic roads were not suitable for heavy traffic needs to be re-examined after the recent discovery of an Iron Age road near Shrewsbury, which was metalled a century before the Roman invasion. It is now unclear how many of the roads, which we regard, as 'Roman roads' were in fact constructed before the Romans arrived.

Similarly, roads in pre-Roman Gaul were not insubstantial. Major roads were five to ten metres wide, and they provided a network of communication over most of France, but as no maps of the road system survive, we cannot be sure where they went. However it is a reasonable assumption that the Roman road builders would have adopted the Celtic roads whenever they served a useful purpose, and we do have a map of the Roman road system. The 'Peutinger Table' is a schematic map (i.e. not intended to be accurate in terms of precise locations – rather like a map of the London underground), so the perspective is highly distorted and the then known world is compressed into a long, thin strip, like a roll of wallpaper. The surviving copy is in the Austrian National Library in Vienna (where it is not on public display).

The Peutinger Map covered the whole of the known world, from Iberia in the west to India in the east. The map was originally made in 12 sections, but the first of these, which included part of the British Isles, is lost. However the missing section was reconstructed from other copies and fragments in 1916 by Conradus Miller. The map is in total 22 feet (6.75 metres) long and 13 inches (34 cm) high.

The surviving copy is a reproduction of several earlier generations of the map, and reflects a number of editorial changes over time. In 1265, an anonymous monk in Colmar, eastern France wrote in the 'Annales Colmariensis' *"Anno 1265 mappam mundi descripsi in pelles duodecim pergameni"* (*"In the year 1265, I drew a map of the world on twelve skins of parchment"*), and it is assumed that he was referring to the surviving copy of the Peutinger Table.

Dating the original source documents is difficult: the map shows the city of Campania, which was destroyed by Vesuvius in AD 79. But it also shows the Roman road network in Dacia (Germany), a province that was annexed in the early 2nd century and abandoned in the 270s. Richard Talbert discusses this question in 'The Peutinger Map; Rome's World Reconsidered' (2010), and explains why he would ascribe a date of c. AD 300 to the underlying source material. In any event, what the map describes in terms of Gaul is basically the Via Agrippa, the Roman Road system developed by Marcus Vipsanius Agrippa (63 – 12 BC).

The map shows one route in particular which was very important in the Bronze Age because it provided an overland route from Brittany to the Mediterranean. Starting at Reginca (the former Alet) at the mouth of the River Rance, the road passed through Condate (Rennes), Juliomago (Angers), Casaraduno (possibly Tours), Avaricum (Bourges), and then Degetia, and either Aquis Bormonis or Augustodvro, Poerinio (Perigny?), Ariolica, Roidomna (Roanne), Mediol, Lugduno (Lyon), Viqenna (Vienne), Valentia (Valence), Arelate (Arles) and Massilia (Marseilles). The identification of some of the towns is obscure.

We can assume that this route, or something like it, had existed from the beginning of the first millennium BC, because as we have seen, tin from Cornwall was reaching the Mediterranean from early times. However, the route was sometimes disrupted by wars and the resulting changes in territorial sovereignty. The millennium was dominated in Western Europe by the expansion of the Celts, and their territorial gains had a significant effect on the routes across the continent.

By about 500 BC, the Celts had made their way across France to the Danube and into Provence, and archaeological evidence from Heuneberg, Malpas and Le Pègue shows a wave of destruction and burning which attended their progress. Jean-Jacques Hatt writes (in 'Celts and Gallo Romans' 1970): *"To this Gallic invasion of 500BC and its consequences – the destruction of the network of trading posts in the Rhône and Saône valleys and the Jura and the establishment of Gallic settlements in Cisalpine Gaul –*

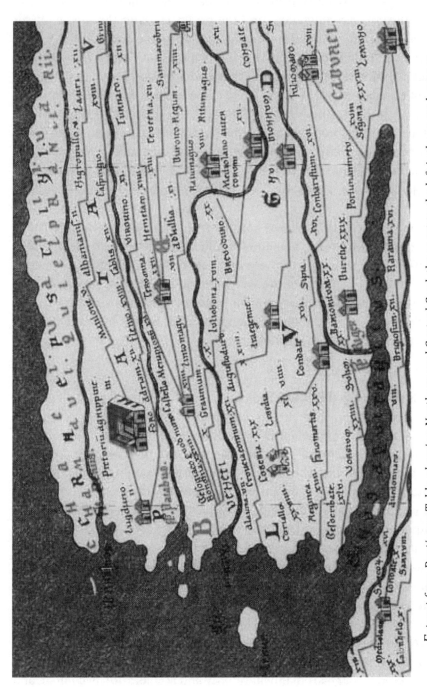

Extract from Peutinger Table, showing Northern and Central Gaul. the coast to the left is the coast between Gesocribate (Brest?) and Lugduno (Leiden in the Netherlands). The large island to the left is thought to be marked I. Lenur

can be attributed the profound changes which took place after this date in the patterns of trade between the Mediterranean countries and the Celtic world. Spina now supplants Marseilles, and the routes through the Alpine passes superseded the roads along the valleys of the Rhône and Saône."

The economic connection between Britain and Brittany on the one hand and the Mediterranean on the other, had previously been based on the export of metals, but as the Bronze Age came to an end and the commonly available iron increasingly replaced bronze, the pattern of trade within Europe became less dependent on the supply of scarce metals and more concerned with the distribution of agricultural surpluses. Nevertheless, metals continued to be exported, food and wine was increasingly traded across borders and the road system remained a vital network of communication.

However, travel by road was not risk-free, and robbery was a constant threat. The road from Brittany to Marseilles passed through the territory of many different tribes, which were often at war with each other, and even after the Celts had control of the whole length of the road (say, from 400 BC), the risk of hijack, or demands for 'tribute', remained significant. For the early traders in commodities, the option of transport by sea must have been attractive, despite the obvious perils.

2.2 Ships and Sea Routes

Probably no other achievements of the ancient world more clearly demonstrate the technical skills of the peoples of that time than the ships which they built. These were the most advanced form of transport technology of the period – the ancient equivalent of the moon rocket today. We know quite a lot about the ships of antiquity from contemporary records and illustrations, but also from the surviving archaeology of shipwrecks, shipyards and the cargoes carried by sea. It is important for us to understand the limits of the available technology, so that we can appreciate the influence this had on the development of early trading routes.

Ships were developed for either of two purposes: as weapons of war or as cargo vessels. And the designs of both were determined by the conditions in the region in which the ships were to operate. Warships were long and thin for speed, with a length to breadth ratio of, typically, 10 to 1. They were powered by oars, for manoeuvrability and acceleration in combat, and they mounted a ram on the bow to inflict damage on enemy ships. They were double-ended, meaning the stern and bow were the same shape, so they could reverse, increasing their tactical options. In the Mediterranean these vessels were called 'galleys' ('long ships' to the Greeks), but designs similar in principle were later developed in northern Europe, where they were all called 'long ships'. They typically had a single mast and a square sail for auxiliary power, but were powered primarily by their oarsmen, who doubled up as fighting troops once an enemy ship was closely engaged.

The Phoenicians, who originated in the area which is now the Lebanon, and who dominated the Mediterranean Sea from about 1550 to 300 BC, produced a double-deck design of galley called the 'bireme', which had emerged by 750 BC. This was the dreadnought of its day, being about 24 metres long and 3 metres wide, and powered by 120 oarsmen. The ship also carried some marines, as well as its officers. Later on, from about 540 BC, a design with three banks of oars was produced, called a 'trireme'. This was not notably faster than a bireme, but it carried 180 rowers, and therefore a larger fighting force. Contrary to popular myth, the oarsmen were freemen and not slaves, and indeed in the Phoenician navy they were Phoenicians (unlike some of the troops in their polyglot army). (The danger of employing slaves to do the rowing was vividly illustrated at the Battle of Lepanto, the last great battle between galley fleets in Europe in 1571, when the Christian galley slaves in the Turkish fleet broke their chains and turned on their oppressors, contributing to the victory of the Christian allies).

Sailing ships were called 'round ships' by the Greeks, or 'ships of burden' ('navis oneraria') by the Romans, and the main type used in the Mediterranean was called the 'corbita', which means basket. These were slower than galleys, being powered by sails made of flax, but able to carry substantial cargoes. In 500 BC, ships capable of carrying 100 to 150 tons were common in the Mediterranean, and ships capable of carrying 350 to 500 tons were far from unknown. These ships were typically 18 to 30 metres long, and 7.6 to 10 metres wide. Some were as big as 40 metres long and 10 metres wide. 500 years later they had grown to 3 masted, 3 deck vessels, capable of carrying enormous loads. The ship that brought the obelisk now standing outside St Peters, Rome, from Egypt, carried an estimated weight of 1300 tons.

There were also many types of merchant galleys, with a length to breadth ratio typically of 5.5 or 6.5 to 1, which had fewer oarsmen and more room for cargo than a galley built for war. But most cargo ships were powered by sails.[10] The construction of ancient ships is another interesting

10 For a full discussion of the history of ancient ships, see Lionel Casson's 'Ships and Seamanship in the Ancient World' (1995).

topic which we do not need to cover in detail, but suffice it to say that ships had evolved from the earliest dug-out logs, via simple boats made of planks stitched together (as in the three ferries found at Ferriby on the Humber River in northern England, which date from 2000 – 1680 BC), to the elegant and well-built vessels of the first millennium BC.

All ships have an outer skin and an inner reinforcing structure, but these evolved in quite different ways in the Mediterranean and Scandinavia (on the one hand) and north-west Europe (on the other). In the Mediterranean, ships were built by constructing the outer skin first, using mortise and tenon joints to connect adjacent planks to each other and to the keel, with the hull probably supported in a jig during construction. Then, when the outer skin and keel had been assembled, an inner reinforcing framework of ribs and crossbeams was built into the hull, and in Phoenician galleys the whole structure was tensioned by a rope running the length of the ship that was wound tight. In Scandinavia, the same 'shell first' approach was taken, but the planks of the hull were laid with each one overlapping the one below it (now called 'clinker' construction), and joined with iron nails driven through the overlap and clenched on the inboard side ('clinken' in Norse). The reinforcing framework in Scandinavian long ships was relatively light, so the vessel was intended to flex in the waves.

In north-west Europe, the construction order was reversed. The keel, stem and stern were laid and then the ribs of the vessel were constructed. Only then was the outer skin of planking attached to the skeleton of the boat, with the planks laid side-by-side (now called 'carvel' construction), leaving gaps between the planks which were filled with a flexible natural sealant, probably tar.

Galleys were not designed for over-night accommodation, and were designed to be hauled out of the water when not in use. They were therefore lightly constructed, and could be lifted out of the water by their crews.

The galley was fundamentally unsuited to the sea conditions of north-west Europe, so all sea-going vessels of the British and the western Gauls were sailing ships. The Gallic vessels were known to the peoples of the Mediterranean as a type of ship called the 'gaulois', a term adopted by disparaging Greeks for the bathtub. In the Semitic language of the Phoenicians, the gaulois became the 'golah'.

While galleys could be remarkably fast *("Aemilius Paulus' record 8-knot dash from Brindisi to Corcyra is quoted again and again"* – Lionel Casson), the recorded voyages of sailing fleets achieved no more than 4.5 knots, and typically perhaps 2.5 knots on average. When Caesar mounted his first raid on Britain, he left port in France at midnight, and arrived off the white cliffs of Dover (23 miles away) at 9.00 am, so travelling at an average 2.5 miles per hour.

Caesar was very struck by the design of the Gaulish ships, and records them in some detail: *"The Gauls' own ships were built and rigged in a different manner from ours. They were made with much flatter bottoms, to help them ride shallow water caused by shoals or ebb tides, and the hulls were made entirely of oak, to enable them to stand any amount of shocks or rough usage. The cross-timbers, which consisted of beams a foot-wide, were fastened with iron bolts as thick as a man's thumb...."*

A Gallo-Roman cargo ship, dating from 280 AD, found in St Peter Port harbour in Guernsey was built of oak, with a flat-bottom, a keel, stem and sternposts and carvel planking. The ship, which has been nicknamed 'Asterix', is of immense archaeological significance, not only for the information which it provides to corroborate Caesar's description of the construction of Gaulish ships of the period, but also, as we shall see later, because of the preserved remains of its cargo. One difference noted by Caesar was that the Gaulish ships had sails made of hide, not flax, either because the Gauls were ignorant of the uses of flax or to withstand stronger winds.

All ships were steered by an oar on the starboard side ('the steer board side') at the stern, and while this worked up to a point, the arrangement cannot have been nearly as efficient, and the leverage of the helmsman cannot have been nearly as great, as with a rudder operated by pulleys and ropes. The idea of attaching a rudder to the sternpost, with a system of tackles to pull it to one side or the other, was an Arab invention that did not reach the Romans until the middle of the 1st century AD.

The remains of ships similar to the Asterix in Guernsey have been found in the river Thames, so the basic design concept was clearly common to the vessels of the English Channel. The so-called County Hall wreck was 18 to 21 metres long. Strabo, a Greek writing in 24 AD, also provides quite a lot of detail on their construction: *"they do not bring the joints of the planks together but leave gaps, they fill the gaps full of sea weed, however, so that the wood may not, for a lack of moisture, become dry when the ships are hauled up."*

The British and Irish also developed a kind of sailing vessel unique to their waters, the sailing curragh, a relative of the Welsh coracle. This was constructed with a frame of bent osier (willow tree), covered by stitched hides, and sealed with tar. Being light, it was relatively fast. Ocean-going curraghs were 15 to 20 metres in length, and could carry up to 10 tons. The Romans were very surprised to see these boats, but they are still in production in Ireland today, albeit now with some solid planking and with canvas in place of hides for the outer skin.

So by the middle of the first millennium BC, we know that the ancients had effective warships powered by oars, and used exclusively in the Mediterranean, and sailing ships capable of carrying hundreds of tons of cargo, with designs called corbitas in the Mediterranean and gaulois in the Atlantic. The range of the galleys was restricted by how far the crew could row in a day (thought to have been typically 50 to 60 miles), while the range of the sailing ships was only restricted by their slow speed and the limitations of early navigation. The British curragh would have been capable of making an overnight voyage, but it does not sound like the sort of vessel that anyone would want to have travelled a long distance in. I think we must assume that a Channel crossing would have been at the outer limits of its capabilities under normal circumstances.

The Phoenicians established various trading posts around the Mediterranean, of which the most important was Carthage on the coast of modern Tunisia. Indeed, after King Nebuchadnezzar had forced the Phoenician city of Tyre to accept the authority of Babylon in 575 BC, Carthage became the dominant power in the western Mediterranean, with a navy of 300 – 350 warships. From there the Phoenicians ventured through the 'Pillars of Hercules' (the Straits of Gibraltar) into the Atlantic, and established a trading post at Cadiz in southern Spain. And from there they established further trading posts along the coast of Portugal as far as Santa Olaia, near Lisbon. A scattering of Phoenician coins and artefacts further north demonstrates that they were engaged in trade with the peoples of northern Portugal and north-west Spain, including the Celtic Galicians.

But there is no evidence to suggest, as many do, that the Phoenicians traded directly with Britain and Ireland. Such a journey would have been very difficult for a merchant galley, because the Atlantic seaboard of France is not the sort of coast on which anyone would want to put ashore at night. And sailing across the Bay of Biscay would have been a daunting task for a sailing ship designed for the Mediterranean. It would have been far better for the Phoenicians to trade with the Celts in north-west Spain, and to leave them to handle the Bay of Biscay in their own ships, which were designed for the task.

2.3   The Phoenician Myth

The Phoenicians came from the cities of Tyre and Sidon in modern Lebanon. They wrote, and indeed gave us most of our alphabet (with the exception of the vowels, which the Greeks added later). And given their sea-faring prowess, they must also have made charts, but few records of their sea journeys survive, probably due to the destruction of Carthage by the Romans in 146 BC. In any case, the Phoenicians had a commercial interest in not disclosing their trade links beyond the Straits of Gibraltar, in which they enjoyed a monopoly, and, far from publicising their forays into the Atlantic, they were motivated to peddle lurid tales of sea monsters and demons beyond the 'Pillars of Hercules'. The charts which they made and logs which they kept were probably trade secrets, which they themselves would have destroyed rather than divulge.

In about 500 BC, the Carthaginians sent out expeditions to explore beyond the Straits of Gibraltar. One went southwards under the command of Hanno, and accounts of this voyage survive, so we know that he set out with 60 ships and sailed to a point on the coast of Africa south of the Equator – probably off Senegal – his crew becoming the first people from north of the Sahara to encounter gorillas!

A second expedition was sent out under Himilco at the same time, but no contemporary account of this voyage survives. The earliest reference to it is contained in the work of Pliny the Elder, probably written around the middle of the first century AD: *"When the power of Carthage flourished Hanno sailed round from Cádiz to the extremity of Arabia, and published a memoir of his voyage, as did Himilco when he was dispatched at the same date to explore the parts beyond Europe."*

So we know next to nothing about where Himilco went, or what he saw. The primary surviving record is a poem called the 'Ora Maritima' (the 'Sea Shore') written in about 350 AD, by a Roman author Rufus Festus Avienus. This was based on an earlier Greek story, but the translation of the earlier Greek prose into Latin poetry has reduced the content to largely incomprehensible ramblings. What interests students of ancient British and Irish history are references to Britain, Ireland and some islands called 'the Oestrymnides'. 'Oestrymnis' was an ancient name for 'the western extremity' of Portugal, but the text makes it clear that Avienus was not describing Portugal:

"The orb of the spreading seas lies extensively,
and a wave in turn surrounds the earth. But in
the area from the Ocean where the deep salt
water inserts itself so that here the swell of our
sea extends far, there is the Atlantic gulf. Here is
the city Gadir [Cadiz], formerly called Tartessus. Here

*are the columns of the persistent Hercules, Abila and
Calpe. The latter is on the left of the mentioned land;
Abila is near Libya. They resound with the harsh north
wind, but remain firmly in their positions. Here rises
the summit of a projecting ridge, which a more ancient
age called Oestrymnis, and the lofty mass or rocky height
faces directly the warm south wind.*

*Under the head of this promontory, the
Oestrymnic bay lies open for the natives. In it
the islands called Oestrymnides stretch themselves out.
They lie widely apart and are rich in tin and lead. There
Is much vigour in the people here, a proud spirit,
an efficient industriousness. They are all constantly
concerned with commerce. They ply the wide troubled
sea and swell of the monster-filled ocean with skiffs of
skin. For these men do not know how to make keels with
pine or maple. They do not build boats, as the custom is,
from fir trees. Rather they always marvelously make boats
with joined skins and often run through the vast salt waters
on leather[11]*

For reasons that will become clear, I believe that this part of the poem needs to be split into two sections, as I have done in the layout of the text above. The first section describes the Straits of Gibraltar, and the second describes part of a very different geographic region – the British Isles. And it is far from certain that the second part was based on any account of Himlico's voyage. This appears to have been drawn in part from 'Caesar's Gallic Wars'. Barry Cunliffe, in 'Europe Between the Oceans' (2008), says that he does not believe that Himlico travelled north at all, but rather probably sailed west into the Atlantic: *"We learn of a voyage lasting three months during which time Himilco encountered only sluggish windless seas and masses of seaweed which impeded progress. The text is sometimes interpreted as suggesting that he sailed north to Britain and Ireland but this is wrong; it is more likely that his intention was to sail west."* Cunliffe notes that the discovery (in 1749) of a hoard of eight Carthaginian coins of the 3rd century BC on the island of Corvo on the Azores, suggests that the Carthaginians were trying to discover the limits of the Atlantic.

11 Translation by J P Murphy

Whatever the truth behind the poem, archaeology provides little support for a theory that there were any Phoenician voyages to north-west Europe. Five ancient coins of Phoenician and Sicilian origin were found at Le Yaudet, near Lannion on the North Brittany coast, in 1869, but it is possible that these were brought to Brittany in modern times by French soldiers returning from North Africa. That at least was the finding of the Commission de la Topographie des Gaules at the time. (The only way we would know when the coins were brought to Le Yaudet would be to date the strata in which they were found, and that could not be done in 1869). As we shall later see, Le Yaudet was a significant port, and my view is that the most likely explanation for these coins is that they were brought to Le Yaudet in ancient times, but that they are evidence of the trade that was being conducted up and down the Atlantic coast of Europe, between successive regions. While it is not impossible that Phoenicians reached northern Gaul, I believe it is unlikely.

Only one object has been found in the British Isles that (a) is of Mediterranean origin, (b) dates from the pre-Roman era and (c) is not likely to have arrived via a cross-Channel supply route. This is a lead stock of a Graeco-Roman anchor, dating from the late 2nd century or early 1st century BC, found at Porth Felen in north Wales. It was found underwater near a low cliff, and must represent the last remains of a ship that was wrecked on the rocks. Hundreds of these anchors have been found in the Mediterranean, and a dozen or so off the coast of southern Portugal, but none anywhere else.

The following points need to be considered here. Firstly the anchor dates from the period after the end of the Phoenician Empire (which came to its end in c. 300 BC). Secondly, lead anchor stocks do not 'wear out' or corrode, and it could already have been an old object when it was deposited in the sea off north Wales. And thirdly it could have been a second-hand object, carried by a Gaulish or British ship. It cannot, therefore, be taken as proof that a ship from the Mediterranean was plying a trade off the coast of north Wales in c. 100 BC.

So, if anything, this is the 'exception that proves the rule'. The fact that this is the only anchor of its type found anywhere along the Atlantic coast of Europe, north of central Portugal, tends to prove that the Mediterranean peoples of the pre-Roman world did not sail to north-west Europe, or at least not on a regular basis. In fact Phoenician finds are very scarce north of the river Minho in Portugal, and there is no reason to think that they ventured further north, except perhaps on a few very special voyages of discovery.

We have found no pots, tools, ornaments or buildings of Phoenician origin anywhere in Brittany or Cornwall, and no shipwrecks offshore. If there was a direct sea route from the Mediterranean to Cornwall before the Roman era, we have found no trace of it. As Peter Fowler succinctly puts it *"There is absolutely no evidence whatsoever that any Phoenicians came to Cornwall, trading for tin or anything else, at any time."* ('The Past in Contemporary Society: Then, Now' 1992).

Finally, the old fable that the standing stones of Brittany and southern England were erected under the influence of the Phoenicians pays no respect to the chronology of events. The stones were standing thousands of years before the civilisation of Tyre and Sidon developed. But, despite the total lack of supporting evidence, the 'Phoenician Myth' has become established as an historical 'fact'. As Jean Cocteau said *"L'histoire est du vrai qui se deforme et la legende du faux qui s'incarne"!* ("History is truth which becomes deformed, and legend is falsehood which is made flesh!").

While there is no evidence that the Phoenicians ever visited Britain, there is a large stone at the mouth of the Rance River, where St Servan (formerly Alet) is situated, which is marked with a Greek cross. Local legend has it that this mark was made by Phoenician navigators to mark the entrance to the river. It is certainly true that crosses, whether simple, Greek or Maltese, were symbols used widely before the Christian era, so it is not necessary to attach any religious significance to this one. The second point to note is that such crosses are found on ancient stones and menhirs over quite a wide area of France. There are a number of them in the Hautes Corbières region of southern France, in the valleys of the Sals, Agly and Verdouze rivers. And there are others in Brittany, for example at Plouharnel, near Carnac. Clearly these were not all made by 'Phoenicians', and if the mark has any navigational significance at all, it was probably placed there by Gallic seamen.

Ships may not have been sailing directly from the Mediterranean to the English Channel in pre-Roman times, but it is clear that peoples all along the length of the Atlantic seaboard of Europe traded with each other. And there is also clear evidence that the Phoenicians traded with the western coast of the Iberian Peninsula in the first millennium BC. So an indirect sea connection between Britain and the Mediterranean almost certainly existed, albeit one monopolised by the Phoenicians towards the end of their ascendancy.

Avenius tells us that the Tartessians (from Andalusia, in southern Spain) visited the Oestrymnides for trade, but here Avenius is probably referring to the western fringe of the Iberian Peninsula, or at most, the islands off the coast of Gaul. We know that the British and Irish were trading with Galicia in north-west Spain through the distribution of archaeological finds, and this means it is likely that they connected indirectly with the Phoenicians. As Kristian Kristiansen ('Europe Before History' 2000) puts it: *"Detailed study of bronze products does however show that there was extensive and regular exchange of goods between southern England, Ireland, north-western France and north-west Spain from the 11th century BC onwards."*

In particular the Iberian Peninsula produced a series of bronze axes with two rings, which could be used either as axes or hoes. The most widespread were massive palstaves (a special type of axe), but socketed axes with two rings are also found. These objects are found all along the Atlantic coast, and offshore finds of bronze articles at Salcombe and at Dover suggest that Britain was part of the trading system.

2.4   Ports of the English Channel

When it came to cross-Channel trade, there were a small number of alternative routes. Clearly a direct voyage from Ushant to the south coast of Devon or Cornwall would have been a major undertaking in 500 BC, when ships did not have compasses or weather forecasts, and progress was very slow. The distance of a typical voyage across the western end of the Channel would be about 120 miles, which could have meant 48 hours at sea – not impossible, but inadvisable in anything but settled weather or in any conditions which prevented astronomical observation.

Julius Caesar tells us that the ports on the Gallic side of the Channel were few and far between, but we know from archaeological evidence that there was Iron Age occupation of Nacqueville, near Cherbourg, at Alet at the mouth of the River Rance and at Le Yaudet at the mouth of the river Léguer.

On the British side of the Channel, the main ports of the western Channel were Mount Batten in Plymouth, especially before the first century BC, and Hengistbury Head, near Christchurch in Dorset, which enjoyed its heyday between 120 and 60 BC. Hengistbury was formerly known as Hynesbury, and was presumably renamed by the Saxons (Hengist means 'stallion' in Anglo-Saxon).

Nearly all the surviving Roman amphorae of the period when Hengistbury was at its peak (120 – 60 BC), were found in Hampshire and the Isle of Wight, which strongly suggests that there was no other port of arrival before the Roman conquest of Gaul. It seems curious to us now that the trade links at the eastern end of the Channel appear to have been so under-developed, but activity on the route from Boulogne and the ports of the Belgae in Gaul significantly increased later on.

For the reasons discussed above, a direct route from, say, Mount Batten to Le Yaudet would have been challenging for navigators in the pre-Roman era, but Barry Cunliffe believes that a recent find of a shard of British pottery at Le Yaudet suggests that it was a route that was used at least occasionally. However, the only shipwreck found in the area is that of a much later vessel (from the end of 4th century), which is likely to have sailed from East Anglia (see 4.7), so there is little tangible evidence of a route directly across the western end of the Channel. It is of course possible that the British pottery found at Le Yaudet did not arrive there directly.

Archaeological research undertaken by Sir Mortimer Wheeler in 1938-9 demonstrated that Alet was involved in cross-Channel trade with Britain, but it did not produce a great wealth of evidence. Alet was a principal port of the Coriosolites, the tribe that controlled the Breton coast from the bay of St Brieuc to Mont St Michel. And we know that the Coriosolites traded with the Durotriges tribe in Dorset, around Hengistbury, because the only Armorican coins found in southern Britain have been those of the Coriosolites and their neighbours, the Unelli. These are found mainly in the Hampshire area.

Philip de Jersey has argued that Alet may not have played as significant a part as this evidence, and the Peutinger Table, might lead us to suppose, based on the navigational hazards around the entrance to the river Rance and an insufficiency of evidence from the site itself. Certainly, the Coriosolites could have used other ports to trade with Britain, for example Plérin at St Brieuc or Binic just a little to the north of St Brieuc.

"It may, therefore, be that the main passage to Hengistbury began in the Baie de Saint Brieuc and made use of Guernsey as a stopping off point en route. This would be consistent with the evidence for the main pottery producing area being on the east flank of the Baie and for the presence of imports, including wine amphorae, in Guernsey. Jersey at this time appears to have been largely avoided, possibly because of the navigational problems posed by shallows and reefs to the north and south of the island" (Barry Cunliffe; 'Armorica and Britain: Cross Channel Relationships in the late first millennium BC' 1997).

2.5   The Tin Road

We saw in 2.1 that there were roads from the coast of the English Channel to the Mediterranean in early times, and we know that some of the traffic on these roads was the transport of tin. Diodorus Siculus, a Greek historian writing between 60 and 30 BC tells us:

"And tin is brought in large quantities also from the island of Britain to the opposite Gaul, where it is taken by merchants on horses through the interior of Celtica both to the Massalians and to the city of Narbo, as it is called. This city is a colony of the Romans, and because of its convenient situation it possesses the finest market to be found in those regions.

Strabo tells us, on the authority of Polybius (c. 200 – 118 BC), that the route passed through the town of 'Corbilo', which he thought was on the Loire, but says that the town no longer existed in his day, and that Polybius and his contemporaries had been unable to find out where it was: *"The Liger,[12] however, discharges its waters between the Pictones[13] and the Namnitae.[14] Formerly there was an emporium on this river, called Corbilo, with respect to which Polybius, calling to mind the fabulous stories of Pytheas, has said: "Although no one of all the Massiliotes[15] who conversed with Scipio was able, when questioned by Scipio about Britain, to tell anything worth recording, nor yet any one of the people from Narbo[16] or of those from Corbilo, though these were the best of all the cities in that country, still Pytheas had the audacity to tell all those falsehoods about Britain."*

It is clear that Strabo was not an admirer of Pytheas (whose account of his visit to Britain Strabo frankly disbelieved). But it is not clear, contrary to the general assumption, that Corbilo was near the mouth of the Loire. Strabo may have described the place where the Loire discharges into the sea merely to identify the river. Some have suggested that Corbilo was the modern Coueron, near Nantes. Others have suggested it was at modern St Nazaire, which is at the mouth of the Loire, and it is said that archaeological evidence of an ancient port was found when the modern docks were constructed there in 1856. However, this evidence was dispersed and not recorded, so we do not know how strong it was.

What we do know is that when St Nazaire was first surveyed in the

12 The Loire

13 *a tribe on the south bank of the Loire*

14 *a tribe living on the north bank, between Nantes and Angers*

15 *people of Marseilles*

16 *Narbonne*

mid-18th century, it was a village of 600 inhabitants on the southern edge of the second largest swamp in France. It was not directly connected to the system of main roads in France, although the presence of dolmens in and around the town indicates that it had been occupied since Neolithic times. On the basis of the known facts, it seems an unlikely candidate to have been one of the three most important cities in France in 200 BC, but we must allow that much can change over two millennia. All that we can really conclude from Polybius' account, via Strabo, is that Corbilo was a town on the Loire - at over 620 miles, the longest river in France.

In fact, the Peutinger Table gives us a great deal of assistance in resolving this conundrum. The Table shows that there were only four ports on the Channel coast of France that were connected to the Via Agrippa: Brest (Gesocribate), St Servan (Reginca), Boulogne (Gesogiaco) and 'Coriallo', the identity of which is uncertain. On the Peutinger map, Coriallo appears to be a short distance from the coast, but various academics have speculated that it may have been Cherbourg, or the nearby Tourlaville. In addition, we also know that on the southern coast of Brittany were the ports of Vannes and Nantes (a short distance inland from the mouth of the river Loire). And as we have seen, it is often suggested that 'Corbilo' was St Nazaire, at the mouth of the Loire, despite the fact that this town does not appear on the Peutinger Table.

In effect, any tin from Cornwall must have been coming into France through one or more of these ports, and we can rule out Boulogne, both because it is so far out of the way for a traffic in tin originating in Cornwall, and because it does not appear to have been of any significance before the Roman era. That allows us to fix the latter part of the road journey from the port of arrival, because all of the candidate ports would connect to the Roman roads to the Mediterranean at Angers.

There were only two main roads into Brittany in Roman times: the one from St Servan ('Reginca'), passing through Rennes ('Condate' (meaning 'confluence') – renamed by the Romans 'Civitas Redonum') and onwards to Angers (named 'Juliomagus' by the Romans); and the other from Brest, passing though Vannes, Nantes and again arriving at Angers. This road passes within 12 miles of St Nazaire, but does not run through it. There was also a road from Coriallo to Angers. We do not know for certain where Coriallo was, but we do know how far it was from other places on the map, including Angers. From Angers, the obvious route to Marseilles was by the road to Tours, Bourges and then via either of two possibilities to Lyon and down the Rhône valley.

Once it is accepted that the tin passed along the Loire valley from the area of Angers, through Tours and Bourges, the route from Angers to the coast speaks for itself. The object of any shipper of heavy cargo in ancient times would have been to minimise the road journey. Once a cargo was on board a ship, it was relatively easy to move it a great distance, and probably at a reasonable speed, but the road journey would have been slow and arduous. Of the ports connected to Angers, Brest and Coriallo were about double the distance by road, compared to the other two, and therefore not feasible.

Vannes to Angers is about the same distance as Alet to Angers, so there would have been no saving in time on the road for the extra sea miles sailed to get to Vannes. St Nazaire was about 12 miles closer to Angers than Alet, but to get there involved a lengthy and perilous sea voyage around Finisterre. The risk-to-reward ratio simply would not have supported this choice. So the alternative to Alet was Nantes, where the extra miles sailed would have resulted in a much shorter road journey. No doubt some ships did sail from Britain to Nantes, but this journey involved not only the voyage around Finisterre, but also a tricky passage through Quiberon Bay and a crawl against the current up the River Loire.

The route round Finisterre is no easy journey, even today. After perhaps a 120 mile passage across the western Channel (for many hours out of sight of land), the alternatives for the Gaulish or British ships would have been to pass outside Ushant and the Ile de Sein, exposed to all that the Atlantic could throw at them, before turning south-east for the Loire; or to take the more sheltered route inshore of the Plateau de la Helle (which speaks for itself), through the Chenal du Four ('the Channel of the Oven') and the formidable Raz de Sein, one of the most violent stretches of water on the Atlantic coastline in anything but perfect conditions. And on either route, the unwieldy Celtic ships, steered by oars, would have been sailing on a lee shore (in other words, in prevailing wind conditions, if forced downwind they would have run ashore).

We know that the Celtic ships were capable of making this journey, at least by Roman times. The question is: why would they want to if they could unload their cargo on the north coast of Brittany without greatly extending the road journey to Angers? Fortunately, the town of Corbilo furnishes us with another clue, which may help to narrow the options. But to identify this town, we need first to try to translate its name.

Chapter 3:
The Evidence of Language

3.1   Continental Celtic and Insular Celtic

It is a theme of this book that place names and language provide us with a lot of useful information about events and patterns of life in early times. Place names can identify the geographic areas occupied by different tribes, and can even describe the place for us. However, we are working with a family of related languages, and it is sometimes different to distinguish the words of one vocabulary from those of another. The languages of the Celts and the Germans (as well as Greek and the Italic languages) show similarities to the now extinct West Tocharian language of the Tarim basin in western China, and it is believed that this language and most European languages came from a common ancestor, which academics call 'Proto-Indo-European', which arose in the Pontic Steppe on the northern shore of the Black Sea before the 4th millennium BC.

The route by which this influence came to the west is much debated and the evidence for any theory wafer thin. Some believe that it came to Europe via Anatolia in eastern Turkey and the Mediterranean coastline, and some believe that it migrated westwards from the Black Sea into central Europe overland. One of the branches of this language became the Celtic languages, and the evolution of these is also much debated. But for our purposes we can assume that the languages spoken in the British Isles (which we can refer to as the Insular Celtic languages) evolved away from the languages spoken on the Continent (Gaulish and Celtiberian, for example) and that the Insular Celtic languages further evolved away from each other to produce the Goidelic (or Gaelic) languages of Scotland, Ireland and the Isle of Man, and the Brythonic languages of Wales and Cornwall.

The Continental Celtic languages are extinct, but provide a few hundred 'loan words' to French and Spanish. There is rather more evidence of Continental Celtic in the ancient language of the Catalans in north-eastern Spain, but none of the Celts were literate before the Roman era and the Latin influence extinguished Continental Celtic before very much of it could be recorded. The Insular Celtic languages have, however, survived (apart from Manx and Cornish, which some people are attempting to revive). To add some confusion to the scene, Brittany was populated during the 5th and 6th centuries by people from Wales and Cornwall, and thus became Brythonic speaking. But the language they spoke was by then very different from the Continental Celtic language which had previously been spoken throughout Gaul, and the two languages can hardly have been spoken contemporaneously in Gaul.

For the purposes of unravelling the mysteries of the Tin Road, I want to focus on the word 'cor', which I believe was a noun from the Continental Celtic language. This was imported into Britain and then evolved into different forms in the Brythonic and Goedelic languages. 'Cor' is obviously the common factor in the names of Corbilo and the equally mysterious Coriallo, and it appears in the names of a large number of other places. In France, there are more than 240 communities with names beginning with 'cor', so this was clearly a word that was quite commonly used. And it is also found all over Celtic Britain.

Examples from the British Isles include Corwen, and Corlannau (Wales), Corcrain (Ireland), Cornaa and Corrany (the Isle of Man), Corfe, Corscombe and Coryates (Dorset), Corston (Somerset), Corsley (Wiltshire), Cory (Devon), Corgee (Cornwall), and numerous places in the Highlands of Scotland, eg. Corgarff, Cornaigbeg, Cortachy and Corpach). And if one goes back to the Domesday Book,[17] there were others – for example Corselle in Shropshire (now Cross Hill) – which have since been renamed. However the 'Cor-' stem is virtually unknown in the areas of England occupied by the Belgic tribes of the southeast, suggesting a distinct linguistic boundary.

The 'Cor-' element is also rare in Devon and Cornwall, compared to other Celtic areas, for reasons that I will discuss later. Incidentally, the name 'Cornwall' is unrelated because it is known that this derives from the Celtic 'kernow' (peninsula) and the Anglo-Saxon 'wealah' ('foreign' or 'strange') – so it means 'the foreign peninsula'.

In France there has been a tendency to assume that 'cor' derives from either the French word describing a horned musical instrument (eg the Cor Anglais) or the Latin word for 'heart'. But these explanations are plainly absurd. In addition to the more than 240 'cor-' place names in France, there are a great many beginning with 'cour-', which in some cases appear to have the same root, so it appears that 'cor' is a lost Continental Celtic word that was in fairly common use.

---

17 The Domesday Book is a survey of much of England and Wales undertaken in 1086 for King William I, the first of the Norman kings of England

The 'cor' place names, both in Britain and in France, all appear to relate to hills, and it is my contention that the word meant 'hill'. There are so many examples that it would be tedious to set them all out here, but as a random selection, we find the following names: Corancy (Nievre, Burgundy), Coray (Finisterre), Corbara (Corsica), Corbarieu (Tarn-et-Garonne), Corbas (Rhone Alpes), Corbehem (Pas de Calais), Corbel (Savoie), Corbelin (Isere), Corbenay (Haut-Saone), Corbeny (Aisne), Corbere (Pyrenees-Orientales), Corbieres (Alpes-de-Haut-Provence), Corbigny (Burgundy), Corbon (Calvados) etc

And one that I would particularly mention is Corseul (on the Côtes d'Armor), which was the capital city of the Gallic tribe I have already mentioned, the Coriosolites. Although the 'cor' names are distributed widely over most of France, they are not found in lowland areas such as the coastal plain of Aquitaine. And where the 'cor' element is found otherwise than as the first element in French place names, such as in the Vercors, a plateau of hills in the Drôme and Isère regions, it also appears to be associated with uplands. The 'cor' place names in Britain are also hills (eg Corfe), so I believe that the translation of 'cor' as 'hill' is reasonably secure.

In addition there are many places in France with names starting with a 'Cour-' prefix. These need to be considered with great care, because they may well derive their names from the French word 'cour' (meaning 'court') or from other etymology. But if we assume that 'Cor' means hill, a fairly large group of 'Cour-' place names can be identified as potential candidates for the same meaning, by virtue of their locations. In any case, since the Celtic languages were unwritten, we should not attach too much weight to the spellings of the names. Examples of 'Cour-' place names that may also be based on 'cor', meaning a hill, include Courchevel (in France) and Courmayeur (in Italy), both well-known ski resorts.

The Continental branch of the Celtic language is long extinct, but the nearest living relative of Continental Celtic is the Catalan language of Catalonia, in north-eastern Spain. The 'Cor-' element appears in the Catalan word 'corbera', which is used in the names of many ranges of hills. Similarly, the Catalan word for the region called the Corbieres in southwest France is Corberes. So it seems certain that 'corbera' meant a range of hills in Continental Celtic.

3.2   Corbilo and Coriallo

Armed with this information, we can now start to decipher 'Corbilo'. 'Bilo' is the pronunciation of the Catalan word 'vila', meaning 'town', so 'Corbilo' probably meant Hill Town. (Incidentally this suggests that the Continental Celtic 'bilo', rather than the Latin 'villa' (meaning house) is the true ancestor of the modern French word 'ville', having the same, rather than just a related, meaning).

If Corbilo meant Hill Town, it clearly did not refer to St Nazaire, Nantes or even Tours, all of which are built on the estuary or flood plain of the Loire. The search for Corbilo can be narrowed to a hill town on the Loire, which could plausibly have been one of the three most important cities in France at the time. And the obvious candidate is Angers.

As we have seen, it is inevitable that the tin passed through Angers, wherever it was unloaded, or even if it was mined in Brittany. When one considers that Strabo specifically refers to the Namnitae, the people who lived in the area between Nantes and Angers, the suspicion that Angers was Corbilo is strengthened. Angers is a strategically located hill fortress, not only at the junction of the two main roads into Brittany, but also at the confluence of the Maine and Loire rivers. The area around Angers has been occupied since the Neolithic era, and bronze artefacts found there link the city with the trade in bronze objects from Spain and the rest of the Atlantic region. Greek and Etruscan objects have been found at the crossing points of both the Maine and the Loire.

A decent outside bet would be the plateau between the current villages of Distré, Rou-Marson and Verrie, on the left bank of the Thanet river (near Saumur) which is now uninhabited but which is littered with Bronze Age objects, some of which are now in the museum of Saumur.

If the town of 'Corbilo' still exists, but under another name, why would the name have changed? Clearly a lot of place names changed as a result of the Roman or Frankish conquests. Few pre-Roman Continental Celtic place names survive in France, thousands having been displaced either by the names of saints, or by Frankish names (brought from the east) or by Insular Celtic names (arriving from the west). Corseul owes the survival of its name to the fact that it was not of sufficient significance that the Romans or Franks saw any benefit in renaming it. Incidentally, one can only wonder if 'seul' meant single, or sole.

We can then turn our attention to Coriallo. If Coriallo was also a hill town, it is unlikely that it was Cherbourg or Tourlaville, both of which are built on the coastal plain. The hill behind Cherbourg, however, is called the Montaigne du Roule, and this may well be a French translation of Coriallo (possibly meaning 'The Royal Hill?). This hill was occupied in the Gallo-Roman period (but not before or afterwards), and it may therefore have been known to the original cartographers on whose work the Peutinger Table was based.

The legend is that the Montaigne du Roule got its name in 1379 when du Guesclin rolled large stones down the hill in the hope of breaching the ramparts of Cherbourg. But, regardless of whether this event occurred, the suggested toponymy sounds unconvincing. The site is at archaeological risk, so it is to be hoped that further work will be undertaken there before it is lost forever.

If Coriallo was the Montaigne du Roule, and it was therefore occupied only during the Roman era, that would tie in with the name of Cherbourg ('Caesar's Town'), and it would tell us that Cherbourg played no part in the trade in British tin, which had by then all but dried up. The Tin Road, in pre-Roman Gaul, started at Alet.

Before leaving this topic, it is worth taking a look at the use of 'cor-' in Channel Island place names, partly because of what this tells us about the cultural influences on the Channel Islands in pre-Roman times. The 'Cor-' stem (or the very similar 'Gor-') is found in the names of several hills in the Channel Islands, usually vital navigation points on the route from Alet towards Britain, namely La Corbière (the south-west point of Jersey), La Corbière (on the couth coast of Guernsey), Cornet (the islet, and now castle, which guards St Peter Port), Les Cornus (an area in the south of Guernsey), Gorey (the hill, now surmounted by a castle, on the east coast of Jersey) and Port Gorey (a bay under the peninsula of Little Sark).

It may be observed that Cornet (possibly 'small hill') is today an islet (albeit connected to the land by a breakwater), and not a hill. But before the breakwater was constructed, it was possible to walk to the islet at low tide, and when the sea was 6 – 8 metres lower (as it was in Roman times) than the present level, Cornet was almost certainly a hill at the extremity of a peninsula of land or rocks.

The conventional view in Jersey is that the name 'La Corbière' means a place where crows gather, but this is founded on a mistaken association with the Norman-French word 'corbin' ('crow'). This is clearly wrong, both because the Norman-French name for a place where crows gather is known ('la corbinerie'), but more importantly because crows do not gather on cliffs – and for a very good reason. They would be eaten by seagulls.

So the Jersey and Guernsey Corbières almost certainly share their etymology with the Corbières of southwest France, meaning a range of hills. And that is exactly what the south coast of Jersey between La Corbière and Noirmont looks like from the sea, and exactly how the south coast of Guernsey appears.

3.3 The Insular Celtic languages

The Continental version of Celtic had been slowly growing apart from the versions in the British Isles (the Insular Celtic languages) long before the arrival of the Romans in Gaul, but the Roman conquest of Gaul meant that for a century, links between the British Isles and Gaul were much reduced. The Romans very effectively forced their language and culture onto the people of Gaul, and Latin or a Gallo-Roman hybrid language largely displaced Continental Celtic during the Roman era. In Britain, the Romans never conquered Scotland or Ireland, and Wales and Cornwall remained largely independent in practical terms, so the Insular forms of Celtic survived.

However, when the Romans conquered England, taking control of the crossings over the River Severn and building Hadrian's Wall, they effectively severed the land bridges between Wales, Scotland and Cornwall. As a result, the Insular Celtic languages became quite distinct, both from each other and from the Continental versions. With no written form to standardise vocabularies or pronunciation, words evolved over time.

One example of this is the evolution of the word 'cor'. In Devon and Cornwall, and some parts of the west and north of England this became 'tor'. For example, in Devon and Cornwall we find Torbay, Torquay, Sheepstor, Hawk's Tor, and Helman Tor. In the west we find Glastonbury Tor, familiar to festival goers. Back Tor and Dovestone Tor are found in Derwent, Great Tor, Higger Tor and Over Owler Tor in the Peak District and Tor Raynor in Sheffield. In north Wales we find Tor Bay, but Tor does not appear in Scotland where the word in the Lowlands for a hill was 'law' – a further shift away from the Continental language.

Anglo-Saxon England retained the word 'tor', but with the more specialised meaning of a hill, the top of which has been weathered to reveal bare rocks. It is possible that it had a similar meaning in the original Celtic. But over much of England the Anglo-Saxon word 'dun' or 'down' has displaced the 'cor' or 'tor' names. In France, 'cor-' was later replaced with 'colline' (not 'col', meaning 'mountain pass', which derives from the Latin word 'collum' meaning 'neck').

The point is important when we come to consider the Celtic language spoken in Brittany, because, for reasons that we shall see, this is essentially an insular form of Celtic (specifically a form of Cornish, or 'Brythonic'). By the time of the main influx of Britons into Brittany, Continental Celtic had either died out entirely or it was on the verge of extinction (it is estimated to have died out by the 5th century AD – though some sources suggest the extinction came earlier, perhaps as early as the end of the 2nd century.

3.4   The Influence of Continental Celtic in the Channel Islands

The surviving traces of Celtic in Channel Islands place names take the Continental form, not the Brythonic form. Although several words of Continental Celtic origin are found in Channel Islands place names, most of these are Celtic words that were adopted into French, and it is possible that their existence in the Channel Islands is due to the influence of French rather than Celtic. Examples are 'bec' (point of land), 'grève' (bay), and 'lande' (a clearing in woodland). So names like 'Bec du Nez', 'Grève du Lecq' and 'Albecq' all derive ultimately from Continental Celtic, but have possibly arrived in the Islands via French.

But there are Continental Celtic words that are found in the Channel Islands that have come to us directly and not via French. One example that is beyond dispute, because it is not used in French, is the name of a bay in Guernsey called 'Cobo' (which meant victory[18]). Another example is the word 'rock' which is the same word in Catalan and English, and clearly of Celtic origin. It forms the base of the French word 'roche', where the last consonants have been softened, but has come to the Channel Islands in its original form with a hard 'ck' ending, for example in La Rocque in Jersey, and in Rocquaine Bay and Les Rocquettes in Guernsey. Rocquaine is also interesting because it tells us that 'aine' must have been the Celtic word for 'bay' ('ainse' in French). So Rocquaine means 'bay of rocks' in Celtic – which is entirely appropriate.

Indeed, it is a reasonable assumption that any place name in the Channel Islands that cannot be explained otherwise (eg by French, English or Norse) is of Continental Celtic origin. In particular, there is a distinctive feature of Catalan that is noticeable in some Channel Islands place names, a hard 'z' between vowels. This suggests that Rozel (as in the Câtel de Rozel, a large promontory fort with Iron Age earthworks in Jersey), and Vazon (like Cobo, a bay on the west coast of Guernsey) (possibly meaning 'big cup' – the ancestor of 'vase') are probably of Continental Celtic origin. (The same influence is found in French place names like La Chèze in Brittany and Azay-le-Rideau and Mézerey in the Loire region). Rozel is also a family name, which is known from Norman times, but the origins of the name may go back a long way before that period.

So it is not surprising to find the Continental 'cor', rather than the Insular 'tor' in the names of hills in the Channel Islands. The Islands were culturally part of Celtic Gaul.

18 'Dictionnaire de la Langue Galoise', Xavier Delamarre

3.5   'Cor' as a Key to Celtic Personal Names

The Celtic personal names that were preserved by being recorded in writing – either as inscriptions on monuments or in the Roman histories, are invariably the names of people of high social standing, such as Celtic chieftains.   Examples of names recorded on monuments are Moricus, Rextugenos, Smertulitanus, and Vertros.   Examples of the names of chieftains are Boudicca, Vercingetorix, Guorthigern (or Vortigern in the Latin form) and Cassivellaunos

Many names in the latter group appear to be titles, rather than personal names. For example Vercingetorix seems to mean 'great warrior king' ('rix' certainly meant 'king'). Similarly 'vellaunos' meant 'commander'. 'Budeg' meant 'Victory' (so Boudicca probably meant 'Victoria').

' Tigern' is reported to be a Brythonic word for 'kingly', so it has been suggested that Vortigern may have meant 'great king'. But this interpretation is undermined by the fact that several other 'tigern' names are recorded, for individuals who were not necessarily kings- eg Kentigern, Catigern, Ritigern and Tigernmagius. However 'tigern' in Gaulish means 'house', so 'Vortigern' (or Guorthigern) possibly meant 'great house' and 'Tigernmagius' may have had a similar meaning in a more Latinized form. 'Cata' is known in the first part of Gaulish names, meaning 'against or 'with', and 'cet' or 'cait' in Gaulish meant 'wood', so 'Catigern' could either mean 'with house' or may have meant 'woodhouse'. 'Rix' meant 'king', so 'Ritigern' may have meant 'King's House' and 'Kent' may have meant 'border' (or possibly 'hundred' – 'cent'), so a possible translation of Kentigern is 'border house').

What is interesting about the possible Gaulish explanation for the 'tigern' names, which are found in Britain, is that it suggests that Gaulish and Brythonic still shared a part of their vocabulary into the Christian era, indeed until the demise of Continental Celtic. Or at least it can be argued that the Continental Celtic influence in the names of people living in Britain endured, even after the languages had diverged.

But whatever the connection between the languages, the Celtic names for people of high status have all, self-evidently, died out. In contrast, the names of ordinary people seem to have been much more durable. Corcondray, Corfelix, Corgengoux, Corgoloin, Cormenon, Cormeray, Corneilhan, Corneilla, Corquilleroy, Corribert, Corrobert, Corronsac and Cortambert are all places in France, the names of which reveal personal names of the first millennium AD or earlier. And it is these names, the names of ordinary people, which have survived.

Ronsac is the name of a village near Toulouse, from which a family name is derived, and Ambert is a village in the Puy-de-Dôme, so presumably in this context also a family name (there is also a Questembert in Brittany, which may reflect the same personal name).

Felix is clearly Latin. Condray, Menon, Meray, Neilhan, Neilla, and Quilleroy (Kilroy) are Celtic and Gengoux (Gengoul), Goloin, Ribert (Richbert) and Robert are Germanic. (So, we go back 1500 years and find that Kilroy was already there!).

The etymology of Corneilla is uncertain. It could derive from the Latin name Cornelia, which in turn is associated with a cliff top town in Italy called Corniglia. A family called Cornelia owned this in Roman times, and it is generally assumed that the town got its name from the family, rather than the other way around. (Niglia is a surname in Italy, so this is not certain). But Corneilla looks more like the feminine form of Corneilhan. The similar Cordelia also has roots in both Latin and Irish, so it seems that the Latin and Celtic versions, although very similar, may derive from separate sources.

The survival of the names of the common people supports the theory that, when a territory is subject to a wave of immigration or an invasion by a foreign army, the consequence is typically a displacement of the ruling elite, rather than the genocide of the subjected population. And in the context of Britain, this is consistent with the DNA evidence discussed in Chapter 1.

3.6   The Demise of Continental Celtic

Since the personal names found in the 'Cor' context are a mixture of Celtic, Latin and German names, this strongly suggests that 'cor' was in use in Gaul in the middle of the first millennium AD, after the arrival of the Burgundians and the Franks.

And a great many other 'cor' place names in France are a mixture of Celtic and Latin, for example: Corbas, Corbel, Corbon, Cormont, Cormontrieul, Cormoyeux, Corpeau, Corroy, Corsaint, Corsept, Corseul, Cormatin, Courbette, Courboin, Courchevel (and incidentally Courmayeur in Italy), Courcival, Courcuire, Courmangoux, Courmas, Courmont, Cournois, Courpiere, Corseulles-sur-Mer and Courzieu.

This demonstrates that Continental Celtic was in use, at least in remote and hilly regions, throughout the Roman period and indeed into the period after the arrival of the Germanic tribes from the east in the 5th century.

Chapter 4:
The Cassiterides

4.1   The Ancient Writings

For most of pre-Roman history, the British Isles were shrouded in mystery for the ancients, and the geography of the region was the subject of some speculation. The earliest surviving reference to any of the British Isles was written by Herodotus, who tells us *"that of the extremities of Europe towards the west, he cannot speak with certainty. Nor is he acquainted with the islands called the Cassiterides, from which tin is bought."*

Clearly we need to understand how the Cassiterides fitted into the trade route for tin. Pliny the Elder tells us that the first person to buy tin from the Cassiterides was a Greek trader called Midacritus, and although he was writing several centuries after the trade in tin started, the comment is revealing in that it suggests that the demand for British tin came primarily from the Greeks. The Cassiterides were clearly a place where lead and tin (and possibly silver) were bought and sold.

Strabo, a Greek writing in 24 AD, certainly knew about these islands. He describes the Cassiterides as *"ten in number, lying near each other in the ocean, towards the north from the haven of the Artibri".* He writes *"one of them is a desert, but the others are inhabited by men in black cloaks, clad in tunics reaching to the feet, and girt about the breast, walking with staves, and bearded like goats. They subsist by their cattle, leading for the most part a wandering life".* And he notes that *"they have metals of tin and lead."*

4.2   The Traditional Candidates

The candidates suggested over the years for the identity of the Cassiterides have been wide-ranging to say the least. Indeed some of them scarcely merit serious consideration, but for the sake of completeness, they need to be eliminated from the search. The main suggestions have been the Scilly Isles, the Azores or 'islands off the north coast of Spain'. None of these are plausible, for reasons that I will now discuss.

Firstly, the Scilly Isles are not a source of tin, but further there is no obvious logic to the transportation of tin from Cornwall to the Scilly Isles for onward export to Continental Europe. The idea really depends on the Phoenician Myth, for which, as we have seen, there is no supporting evidence. And secondly, there is clear evidence that until about 400 – 500 AD, the Scillies were one island, earlier named Ennor and not an archipelago. At that time, with rising sea levels, the sea broke through the outer ring of hills and flooded the central plain of Ennor, leaving a series of small islands around the edge, five of which are inhabited today. The first literary mention of the Scilly Islands (plural) is in the 12th century Orkneyingsaga, written in Old Norse. And finally, as we shall see in 4.7, there is ample archaeological evidence that the tin from Cornwall was exported eastwards.

The Azores would fit the bill, insofar as there are nine main islands and some smaller islets, and because tin is found there. They may even have been discovered by the Phoenicians in the 3rd century BC, but they do not appear to have been 'rediscovered' until the 14th century AD, and then they were found to be uninhabited. A further problem is that there is nothing to the south of the Azores except Antarctica, and therefore no 'haven of the Artibri'. (Incidentally, the Portuguese name for the Azores is Açores, allegedly after their word for the goshawk – 'açor' – a bird that is not found in the islands. In view of their mountainous topography, it seems more likely that the name derives from the Continental Celtic word 'cor').

Finally, there is the argument that the Cassiterides were located off the coast of northern Spain. This is based on two factors, the similarity of the names of the Artibri with the tribe called the Arrotrebae who lived around the area of modern La Coruña in north-west Spain, and secondly a reference in Pliny the Elder's 'Natural History', Book 4: *"Opposite to Celtiberia are a number of islands, by the Greeks called Cassiterides, in consequence of their abounding in tin."* Celtiberia was the land of a Celtic tribe that occupied an area of central Spain roughly to the east of modern Madrid. This area is entirely landlocked and therefore cannot have been near any islands.

As for the similarity of the name of the Arrotrebae to the Artibri, this does at least suggest the identity of a coastline because the Arrotrebae were definitely a tribe living on the coast of north-west Spain. But a glance at a map of northern Spain will confirm that there are simply no significant islands off the coast. There are three small islands near to Malpica de Bergantriños, and that is it. Which is why later writers have had to adapt this idea, to say that the concept of the Cassiterides embraced the Spanish tin mines themselves (see the Introduction). While Galicia was certainly part of the trading and cultural network of the Atlantic Celts, and therefore linked strongly with Brittany and the Celtic regions of the British Isles, the absence of islands to the north is simply crushing to this interpretation.

We are forced to conclude that Pliny was wrong. His geography of Western Europe was generally vague, and he has allowed himself to be seduced by the similarity of the names of the Arrotrebae and the Artibri into forming a conclusion that is unsustainable. And the fiction is betrayed by his total ignorance of the location of the Celtiberians, with whom he seeks to associate these islands. To cap it all, he also contradicts his own opinion by quoting a much more accurate account from a historian called Timaeus, as we shall shortly see.

4.3   What was the Trade Route?

To discover the Cassiterides we need to go back to first principles. We know that, from about 1100 BC, tin from Devon and Cornwall was reaching the Greeks via their colony in Marseilles. This book has sought to show the route of the famous 'Tin Road' across Gaul, from the Channel port of Alet, so if we can trace the route of the tin to Alet, we have a good chance of finding the Cassiterides.

Diodorus Siculus (a Greek born in Sicily and working in 60 – 30 BC), (probably basing his account on the records of Posidonius, a Stoic who travelled to Britain in about 90 BC), described the first part of the journey thus: *"The inhabitants of that part of Britain which is called Belerion[19] are very fond of strangers, and, from their intercourse with foreign merchants, are civilised in their manner of life. They prepare the tin, working very carefully the earth in which it is produced. The ground is rocky, but it contains earthy veins, the produce of which is ground down, smelted, and purified. They beat the metal into masses, shaped like astragali[20] , and carry it to a certain island lying off Britain called Ictis. During the ebb of the tide the intervening space is left dry, and they carry over into this island the tin in abundance in their wagons."*

The next stage is described by Timaeus, a historian, as reported by Pliny the Elder (whose own faulty identification of the Cassiterides we have already considered). The text is reproduced here in full in the original Latin, because it has generally been mistranslated, to the point of inventing

---

19 *Cornwall*

20 shaped like an ankle bone – to make it easier to transport on a horse

an island called 'Mictis', which is not in fact mentioned at all: *"Timaeus historicus a Britannia introrsus sex dierum navigatione abesse dicit insulam Ictim, in qua candidum plumbum proveniat; ad eam Britannos vitilibus navigiis corio circumsutis navigare"*. This means: *"The historian Timaeus sailed six days inwards from the island called Ictis, where tin comes from; to which Britons sail in boats made of wicker covered with hides"*.

I have translated Ictim as Ictis, because it seems obvious to me that these were one and the same island. So the Cornish tin embarked on a six-day sea journey to the Continent in curraghs. The timeline and the detail of the boats used are both very helpful. There has been much debate about where Ictis was, the traditional view being that it was the islet off the Cornish coast near Penzance called St Michael's Mount. This corresponds to the description inasmuch as the foreshore between the islet and the coast dries at low tide. But the eminent archaeologist Barry Cunliffe has argued that there is no archaeological evidence of a trade in tin at St Michael's Mount, in contrast to the wealth of finds at the Mount Batten site in Plymouth, which he has excavated. Mount Batten is a peninsula in Plymouth harbour, which may in the past have been cut off from the land on some high tides. However it is not thought that the link to the shore was persistently flooded, especially when sea levels were markedly lower than they are today.

In fact, the 6-day timeline tells us is that it is unlikely that Ictis was in Plymouth, because it is very hard to conceive of a route to Alet which would have taken 6 days. Of course, the navigators of the time would not have sailed for 6 days continuously, but the obvious route from Plymouth would have taken a maximum of 5 days of sailing.

In the tidal English Channel, any journey up or down Channel would have been sailed in 6-hour stages, to take advantage of the favourable tide during daylight hours. (There are two tides a day, so about 6 hours of rising tide, followed by approximately 6 hours of falling tide etc, and in general only one rising tide and one falling tide will be completed entirely during daylight hours). For a boat making an average of 2.5 miles an hour, with the benefit of say 1 mile per hour of tide, that means that each stage of the journey needs to be about 20 miles. In the stronger tides of the Channel Islands, 30 miles would be achievable in a single leg, given the favourable tide.

The shortest Channel Crossing at the western end of the Channel is the journey from Prawle Point, or the nearby Start Point, in Devon, to Guernsey. This is 65 miles, and would have taken a whole day. To some extent, the effects of the tide cancel out when sailing across the tidal stream, because the boat is simply swept from left to right for six hours and then from right to left for six hours. After about 12 hours the boat is back in the position it would have been if it had been sailing for 12 hours in non-tidal waters. But nevertheless, the cross-Channel part of the journey would have been by far the most daunting stage, and would have required careful planning.

On the assumption that the navigator would have planned approximately 20 mile stages on the UK side of the Channel, and up to 30 mile stages on the French side, with a longer haul across the Channel at the shortest crossing point, a possible journey from Plymouth to Alet would have been: Plymouth - River Erme – Salcombe – Guernsey – Jersey – Alet. That is five days' sail, and it is difficult to see how it could be stretched to six.

I conclude that Ictis must have been further west than Plymouth. But the absence of any archaeological evidence for the use of St Michael's Mount as a port argues against St Michael's Mount as the port of embarcation, and the voyage around the Lizard Point would have been a daunting one. Moreover, most of the tin in Cornwall was found east of Mounts Bay, so it is far from clear what the logic would have been in carting it west to load on a ship which, as the archaeological evidence shows (see 4.7) then sailed east.

An island in the estuary of the River Fal would be a possible candidate, and Pendennis at Falmouth is certainly believed to have been an Iron Age cliff castle. There is also a great deal of evidence of occupation in the Roman era of the country around Falmouth (eg several defended farmhouses and hordes of Roman coins found at Pennance Point and Turnaware).

But I think there is a stronger candidate for 'Ictis'. Looe and Looe Island have been occupied since the Bronze Age. Indeed Looe is where the famous Pelynt Dagger (1400 BC) was found, proving that this area was at least indirectly linked by trade to Mycenaean Greece. A stone circle at Bin Down, above East Looe, dates from about 1000 BC, and the Duloe stone circle also dates from the Bronze Age. Looe is near the silver and lead mines of Herodsfoot, and within easy reach of the tin producing areas.

The obvious objection to Looe Island as Ictis is that it is not connected to land at low tide. But sea levels in the Bronze Age were significantly lower than they are today (they were still 6 to 8 metres lower in Roman times), and it may well have been possible to walk to the island at low tide at the start of the 1st millennium BC. One final point to note is that, in local legend, Joseph of Arimathea arrived at Looe Island with Jesus as a young boy. We do not need to speculate on the historicity of this story, but we can note that, to those passing on the legend and their audience, Looe Island was a credible port of arrival for a visitor from the Continent.

4.4   Who Were the Atribri?

In the search for the Cassiterides, one clue, which we have already touched on, may be the identity of the 'Artibri'. However it would be wrong to place too much emphasis on the details of the name, because the names used by the Romans may have been approximations of the names used by the tribes themselves, and it would be even more wrong to attach significance to the spelling of the name, when the Celtic people did not write.

As Martin Papworth puts it (in 'The Search for the Durotriges' 2011): *"The classical authors who wrote about the British were alien to the societies they were describing.   Therefore, the tribal names may only have been convenient Roman administrative divisions that masked many sub-groups, and not the names the British people personally identified with."*

As we have seen, there were Celtic tribes called the Artibrates on both sides of the Channel in Roman times, but the Artibrates in Artois were an inland tribe (Artois is the inland part of the Pas de Calais region). Those Artibrates had access to the sea by rivers, but there are no islands off the coast of the Pas de Calais.

On the other hand the Artibrates of West Sussex are known to have traded with the Channel Islands, because ballast stones of Jersey and Guernsey origin have been found at Fishbourne in Chichester harbour. They are also known to have been the most Roman tribe in Britain (their leader Commius brokered a peace agreement at the end of Caesar's second campaign in Britain). They were one of the few tribes in England that minted their own coins, suggesting that they were involved in trade with other tribes. Further, it is known from their mosaics (at Fishbourne) that they were keen on wine and good living. And therefore it is reasonable to conclude that they are very likely to have had trading links with the Continent through the Channel Islands and Alet.

In my view, the Artibri were the Artibrates, and their haven was Alet.

4.5   The Suggested Solution

If the 'haven of the Artibri' is Alet, Strabo's description of the Cassiterides suddenly makes sense.   There were ten islands north of Alet: Jersey, Guernsey, Alderney, Sark, Herm, Jethou, Brecqhou, the Ecrehous, Chausey and the Minquiers.

Sea levels in the pre-Roman era were 6 – 8 metres lower than the present level, and this would have had dramatic effects on the geography of the Bay of St Malo. Jersey would have been about twice its present size, extending far to the southwest of the present shoreline. The Ecrehous, Minquiers and Chausey would all have been significant islands, and Iron Age pottery found on the currently uninhabited Ecrehous and Minquiers shows that there have been settlements there at some times. But it would not be at all surprising to learn that the Minquiers were uninhabited (i.e. a 'desert') in Strabo's day, as indeed they are now.

Of course, the Channel Islands do not produce any tin, but Herodotus wrote that the Cassiterides were islands *"from which tin is bought"*, not where it was mined. And the Channel Islands make logical staging posts on any voyage under sail from the south coast of England to Alet.

In other respects, Strabo's description is remarkably apt for the Channel Islands, even down to the reference to cattle. Today, Jersey and Guernsey have world-renowned breeds of dairy cattle. The reference to the 'wandering lifestyle' of the herdsmen is consistent with the fact that, before the Norman era, there is hardly any evidence in the Channel Islands of enclosures. The pattern of farming was of scattered hamlets with free-range animals. And the description of men wearing long cloaks and sporting 'beards like goats' accords entirely with people wearing the birrus britannicus, and sporting Celtic style beards and moustaches.

Diodorus Siculus continues with his account of the tin trade as follows: *"Now there is a peculiar phenomenon connected with the neighbouring islands, I mean those that lie between Europe and Britain; for at the flood-tide the intervening passage is overflowed, and they seem like islands; but a large space is left dry at the ebb, and then they seem to be like peninsulas. Here, then, the merchants buy the tin from the natives and carry it over to Gaul; and after travelling overland for about thirty days, they finally bring their loads on horses to the mouth of the Rhône."*

Anyone familiar with the near-10 metre rise and fall of tide around the Channel Islands (some of the biggest tides in the world) will recognize the description of the change in the landscape between high tide and low tide. To a traveller from the Mediterranean, not used to significant tides, the alteration must have been amazing. And given that sea levels were 6 – 8 metres lower than at present, the expanse of rock unveiled at low tide in 90 BC must have stretched for miles in some directions.

Clusters of rocks that are now barely above water, such as the Minquiers, Chausey and Ecrehous, would have been substantial islands, and the other islands would have been significantly bigger. Most dramatically, Herm would have extended northwards to include most of the islets and rocks known as the Humps, and westwards to include the rocks as far out as the Brehon Tower, Jethou would have extended southwards to include the rocks stretching down to Demie Ferrière, and the two islands would have been connected, at least at low tide. So what are now two fairly small islands would have been one predominantly low-lying island, about 6 miles long. It would have been bigger, in fact, than Sark or Alderney. Moreover there would have been very little water between this 'super-Herm' and Guernsey,

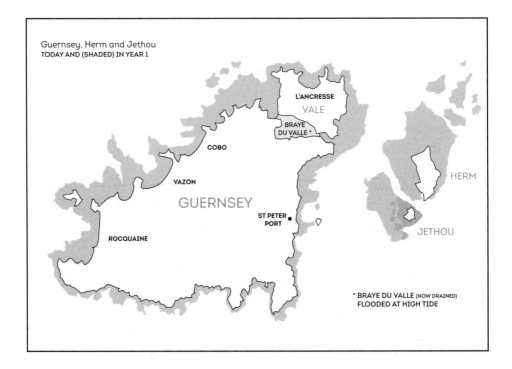

4.6   A Triangular Trade Route

On navigational logic, I take the view that the cross-Channel trade would have followed a classical triangular trade route. Assuming that tin and other metals reached Alet from Ictis via the Channel Islands, the prevailing westerly winds would have taken the boat travelling from Ictis downwind, along the coast of Cornwall and Devon and then diagonally across and away from the wind, on a 'broad reach' to Guernsey. It would have sailed to Guernsey rather than another Channel Island because Guernsey is the nearest of the Islands to Prawle Point (about 65 miles), and it has by far the best harbour in the Islands. The boat would have sold its cargo in Guernsey and Gaulish boats from Alet would have visited the Island to buy metals, probably stopping at Jersey en route. They would have brought wine, olive oil, garum (fish sauce) and pottery to the market to trade.

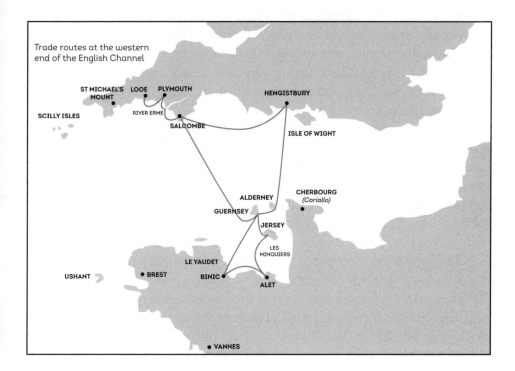

Trade routes at the western end of the English Channel

In the prevailing winds, the Gaulish boats would have generally sailed a 'reach' across the wind, in both directions, although they may have had to sail close-hauled (i.e. diagonally towards the wind) to reach the western side of the Minquiers. All of the points of sail involved are straightforward, and the journeys should not have involved too much tacking towards the wind. This would have been helpful to the crews of unwieldy boats laden with metals, some of them very heavy.

It is possible that the Gaulish boats also sailed a triangular route, connecting Alet with St Brieuc or Binic and onwards to Jersey and Guernsey. If Philip de Jersey is correct that the Armorican pottery that found its way to the Channel Islands and southern Britain mainly came from the east side of the Bay of St Brieuc, this would help to explain that fact.

The British boats, having stocked up with wine, olive oil, etc, would then have sailed to Hengistbury to the north, which again is a reach across the prevailing wind from the west. The boats may well have travelled via

Alderney, which would have reduced the Channel crossing to 80 miles, but at the cost of making a passage either through the Alderney Race or the Swinge (to the west of Alderney), both very fast tidal races which can be unpleasant when the wind is against the tide.

From Alderney, the navigators would have set sail in the evening, and, given good visibility, would have steered towards the North Star. Landfall in the morning would have enabled them to locate their position in the approaches to Hengistbury, taking care not to fall foul of Christchurch Ledge, a reef extending about 3 miles offshore. Again, in the prevailing westerlies, this course would have been a reach.

Once the heavy cargo of wine etc was unloaded at Hengistbury, the boat would have carried coins, pottery and high-value tradable objects back, to pay the miners of Devon and Cornwall. On many occasions this would have involved a beat into the wind, but fortunately their boats would by now have been lightly laden, and by choosing the west-bound tides, and taking shelter (eg in Torbay) when necessary, the crew would have made their way to Devon or Cornwall, possibly to Looe Island.

To support the theory that the Channel Islands were the Cassiterides in the Late Bronze Age, we must next turn to the subsequent history of the Islands, in the Roman era, to see if there is evidence of the trade route described above. If commerce in the Roman era used the Channel Islands as an entrepôt for trade between Gaul and Britain, it would be strong circumstantial evidence to support the theory that the same route was earlier used to transport tin.

The Greek author Strabo gives us an amusing tale of industrial espionage, which also sheds some light on the sea-borne trade route for tin:

"Formerly the Phœnicians alone used to ply this trade from Gadeires [Cadiz], keeping the way thither a secret from all. And on the Romans following a shipmaster, in order that they too might find out the marks, the shipmaster through rivalry purposely cast away his ship on a shoal, but having enticed likewise those who followed him into the same destruction, he himself escaped by means of the wreck, and received back at the public expense the price of the freight which he had lost. The Romans, nevertheless, by making frequent attempts, succeeded in finding out the way. But when, moreover, Publius Crassus crossed over to visit them, and found the mines being worked at a shallow depth, and the people peaceful, he made it known to those who were already exceeding willing to ply on this sea, although it is greater in extent than that which divides off Britain."

It seems that this text combines two unrelated stories: (1) that the Phoenicians had a trade route from Cadiz (possibly for tin, possibly not), and that the Romans eventually succeeded in discovering it and (2) that Publius Crassus visited some place on a tin trade route from Cornwall. In other words, there should be a paragraph break after the sentence that explains that the Romans found the route.

The first trade route was explicitly a route from Cadiz in southern Spain, possibly only as far as Portugal but conceivably direct to southern Brittany (or, very implausibly, further afield). For reasons already discussed it seems unlikely that the Phoenicians reached Cornwall, or anywhere north of the Minho River. In any event, the story of the Phoenician captain deliberately wrecking his ship to lead the Romans astray sounds like a bit of fast-talking from someone who had some explaining to do!

If the text is read as one continuum, the second story suggests that Publius Crassus, who, as we shall see in Chapter 6, was one of the Roman commanders who defeated the Gauls in 56 BC, crossed over to Cornwall to inspect the tin mines. This is literally incredible, because when Julius Caesar came to Britain in 55 and 54 BC, he was violently opposed and the Romans fought several bloody battles to gain a foothold in the country. The idea that a Roman general could have just 'popped over' to Cornwall, on his own, a year earlier, to have a look at the Cornish tin mines beggars belief. This was one of the men who had just defeated the Celtic cousins of the Cornish, in Brittany, resulting in the enslavement of the major tribe of the peninsula.

Moreover, the comment that the sea crossing was *"greater in extent than that which divides off Britain"* makes no sense if Crassus crossed direct to Britain from Gaul. On both counts, it is not possible to believe that Crassus visited Cornwall. It seems obvious that he visited somewhere on the route to Cornwall, which he estimated to be nearer the British end of the journey than the Gallic one.

There has been some speculation that Crassus crossed the river Loire on this journey, but clearly this could not have represented a distance *"greater in extent than that which divides off Britain"* (even allowing for the fact that the Loire was then about twice its present size). The story is, however, entirely consistent with a visit to one of the Channel Islands by Crassus, except that he was reported to have visited the mines. Since it is obviously very unlikely that he visited the mines, this piece of the story has to be reinterpreted – he may well have visited the merchants who traded in tin, and learned about the production of the tin.

The question then is: which Channel Island could he have visited? I have already suggested that the tin was traded in Guernsey. And wherever he went, it was clearly, in the opinion of Crassus, nearer to Britain than to

France. None of the Channel Islands is actually nearer to Britain than to France, although the distance sailed from Alet to Guernsey could be longer than the distance from Guernsey to South Devon, depending on how close the navigator sails to the Minquiers. So Guernsey is the best fit. In any case, Crassus may have been motivated to emphasise the proximity of his destination to the hostile British mainland, to underline his daring!

So a plausible explanation of the story is that Crassus visited Guernsey. And if he had, he would have claimed it for Caesar (and not for Rome, with which Caesar was at loggerheads, to the extent that he marched on Rome in 49 BC and overthrew the government). We will later see that, when the Romans governed England, one of the islands in the sea around Britain was called Caesarea.

4.7   Archaeological Evidence

Having set out my hypothesis that the Channel Islands were the Cassiterides, and that they were engaged in a triangular trade route with Hengistbury and 'Ictis' (possibly Looe Island), it is now time to test this theory against the known archaeology.

There is ample evidence of trade at Mount Batten, and Hengistbury (Barry Cunliffe, 'Europe Between the Oceans' 2008, 'Hengistbury Head' 1978 etc), and there is plenty of evidence in Guernsey too: a site at Kings Road in St Peter Port has yielded high quality Breton pottery together with shards of Dressel 1A amphorae and Kimmeridge shale vessels – typical of the goods found at both Hengistbury and Alet. Smaller finds of Armorican pots in Jersey, dating from the 2nd and 1st centuries BC, demonstrate that some of the goods passing through the Channel Islands ended up there. Bronze age axes of Armorican origin, dating from about 1100 BC have been found in a horde at St Lawrence in Jersey, and other hordes found in Jersey and Alderney include Carp's Tongue swords (typical of the Hallstatt period – 8th century BC), axes, decorated buttons and buckles, spear heads and wood-working tools.

The Jersey and Alderney hoards also include later bronze axes which appear to have been widely used as a currency. Many of these contain such a high lead content that they could not have been intended for use. Fewer metal objects of this period have been found in Guernsey. As Barry Cunliffe puts it: *"Bronze socketed axes of Breton types found in hoards at St Helier and St Lawrence in Jersey, at Longis Common in Alderney and scattered elsewhere in the Islands are sufficient to demonstrate that in the middle of the first millennium BC, ships were transporting bronze from Armorica (Brittany) to the Islands, probably en route to the coasts of central southern Britain, where concentrations of Breton axe types are found."* [Barry Cunliffe, 'Hengistbury Head' 1978]

And there is evidence of Bronze Age occupation of Looe Island. A survey of Looe and Looe Island by Wessex Archaeology in 2009 reported that *"A number of late prehistoric or Romano-British finds have been made in the vicinity of the two sites, including a large bronze ingot found by divers south of Looe Island, which has led a number of people to suggest the island is possibly Ictis".*

The 'smoking gun', to prove that the trade in British tin was conducted via the Channel Islands, in pre-Roman times, would be a horde of metal ingots on the islands, or a shipwreck, either around the Islands or on the route to Alet. No horde has been found on the Islands, but three wreck sites have been found off south Devon. The locations are consistent with the trade route postulated above, but of course do not prove the cross-Channel element, being on the northern shore.

The first is a find of 'ankle shaped' tin ingots at the mouth of the River Erme in south Devon. The boat itself has entirely disappeared, which is unsurprising (especially if it was a curragh), and the metal is simply the raw material, so it is impossible to date the wreck with any precision.

The second is a site off Salcombe, found in 2009, which has so far yielded 259 copper ingots and 27 tin ingots along with other objects including a gold torc (solid necklace). This probably dates from around 1000 BC. Again, this find is consistent with the suggested supply route for raw metals, and a ship about to head south across the Channel. As would be expected, no trace of the vessel survives.

Possibly the oldest is a site at Moor Sand, off Prawle Point, the southernmost point of the Devon coastline just to the east of Salcombe. The finds here were eight bronze weapons (six swords/daggers and two palstaves) of northern Gallic origin, dating from about 1300 BC. This is entirely consistent with the theory that high value manufactured products were shipped from France to Cornwall to pay for raw materials. And all of these sites are located east of all of the candidate locations for Ictis, which proves that the tin was not exported to the Scilly Isles.

Remarkably, only one ancient wreck site has been found on the Atlantic or Channel coasts of France. (A few items from other ancient ships have been trawled up or washed up on beaches, but the locations of the wrecks from which they came are unknown). The evidence of the wreck which has been found is a cargo of 271 ingots of lead (weighing 22 tonnes) originating from northern and eastern Britain and dating from the late 4th century, which was found in the Sept Îles in 1983. The Sept Îles lie five miles offshore from Perros Guirec, on the Côtes d'Armor, close to the ancient port of Le Yaudet. Presumably this ship, of which nothing else survives, was bound for Le Yaudet, and since the lead came from the east coast of England, it is likely that the ship was loaded in East Anglia.

This obviously tells us nothing about shipments of metal from the West Country, so we have not yet found archaeological evidence of the port at which British tin was unloaded in Gaul. And sadly, we have not found any hordes of tin or other raw metals in the Channel Islands. But that is perhaps not so surprising: the Islands clearly were not the ultimate destination of the metals, and transhipments would have been passed down the supply chain fairly quickly. However, I think it can only be a matter of time before we find a wreck site, somewhere between Prawle Point and St Servan, which contains ingots of metal from Cornwall.

4.8   The Fortunate Isles

The literature of the ancient eastern Mediterranean contains several accounts of islands found at the western edge of the Earth, to which the bodies of the dead were taken. It is more than usually difficult to distil any factual base from the purely fanciful in these stories, but this book would not be complete if these references were disregarded entirely. In some accounts the destination in the story is described as Elysium or the Elysian Fields and in some it is described as a group of islands called the Fortunate Isles or the Islands of the Blessed.

The early sources talk of Elysium as an identifiable place on the Earth, whereas in the later texts it formed a part of the underworld, and we therefore do not need to concern ourselves too much with these later poetic references. Even when considering the earlier sources, the interest in this topic is the possible light it sheds on early funerary rites, and we cannot realistically hope to identify with certainty a 'land of the heroes'.

Homer, the Greek poet who probably lived about 800 BC, but who worked from an earlier oral tradition, wrote of Elysium or the Elysian Fields as a place where heroes and the righteous went if they had chosen to be reincarnated three times, and had been judged as especially pure. The Elysian Fields were, according to Homer *"located on the western edge of the Earth, by the stream of Oceanus"*.

And the legend of Elysium was still alive in Virgil's day (70 – 19 BC), as illustrated in the Aeneid: *"Night speeds by, And we, Aeneas, lose it in lamenting. Here comes the place where cleaves our way in twain. Thy road, the right, toward Pluto's dwelling goes, And leads us to Elysium. But the left Speeds sinful souls to doom, and is their path To Tartarus th' accurst."* (Tartarus was in southern Spain).

So, viewed from Greece, and looking west, hell was to be found to the left in southern Spain (plus ça change!), and the road to Elysium was to the right (presumably to Gaul or beyond). But to obtain a detailed description of the location of these islands, we have to wait until Plutarch (c. AD 46 – 120), who describes the 'Islands of the Blest' in his 'Life of Sertorius': *"These are two in number, separated by a very narrow strait; they are ten thousand furlongs distant from Africa [1250 miles], and are called the Islands of the Blest. They enjoy moderate rains at long intervals, and winds which for the most part are soft and precipitate dews, so that the islands not only have a rich soil which is excellent for ploughing and planting, but also produce a natural fruit that is plentiful and wholesome enough to feed, without toil or trouble, a leisured folk. Moreover, an air that is salubrious, owing to the climate and the moderate changes in the seasons, prevails on the islands. For the north and east winds which blow out from our part of the world plunge into fathomless space, and, owing to the distance, dissipate themselves and lose their power before they reach the islands; while the south and west winds that envelope the islands sometimes bring in their train soft and intermittent showers, but for the most part cool them with moist breezes and gently nourish the soil. Therefore a firm belief has made its way, even to the Barbarians, that here is the Elysian Field and the abode of the blessed, of which Homer sang."*

Considering what the islands around Guernsey looked like, before the rise in sea levels of the last two millennia (see map at 4.5), it is impossible not to think that Guernsey and the 'Super-Herm' of that period answer the description of the 'Islands of the Blest' (a synonym for the Fortunate Isles), provided by Plutarch – two in number and separated by a very narrow strait. The Roman Pliny the Elder (23 – 79 AD), in his 'Natural History', portrays the islands in stereotypical terms as places which *"abound in fruit and birds of every kind"*, but then adds an unusual detail: *"These islands, however, are greatly annoyed by the putrefying bodies of monsters, which are constantly thrown up by the sea".*

It should be noted that the practice of ferrying the bodies of the dead to an offshore island is reported many times in the ancient culture of Gaul. In Tréguier, on the north coast of Brittany, the traditional route of the dead to their grave was a boat voyage across the Baie de l'Enfer ('Bay of Hell'). At the Baie des Trépassés ('the Bay of Dead Men'), near the point of the Raz in Finisterre, the legend has it that the dead embark on their final voyage to the Île de Sein.

Procopius of Caesaria (AD 500 – 565), in relation to his description of Brittia, relates a similar story: *"They imagine that the souls of the dead are transported to that island. On the coast of the continent there dwell under Frankish sovereignty, but hitherto exempt from all taxation, fishers and farmers, whose duty it is to ferry the souls over. This duty they take in turn. Those to whom it falls on any night, go to bed at dusk; at midnight they hear a knocking at their door, and muffled voices calling. Immediately they rise, go to the shore, and there see empty boats, not their own but strange ones, they go on board and seize the oars. When the boat is under way, they perceive that she is laden choke-full, with her gunwhales hardly a finger's breadth above water. Yet they see no one, and in an hour's time they touch land, which one of their own craft would take a day and a night to do. Arrived at Brittia, the boat speedily unloads, and becomes so light that she only dips her keel in the wave. Neither on the voyage nor at landing do they see any one, but they hear a voice loudly asking each one his name and country. Women that have crossed give their husbands' names."*

It may be that these legends have a basis in fact – that the inhabitants of Gaul made a practice of ferrying the bodies of the dead to offshore islands for burial. But it is hard to imagine anyone rowing for a day and a night, and it is hard to believe that anyone would row from Gaul to Britain if a sailing boat were available. Boats powered by oars were used in the English Channel, at least from Roman times onwards, but they were used as warships where speed and manoeuvrability were of the essence – not for ferrying corpses.

Many suggestions have been put forward for the identity of the Fortunate Isles, or the Islands of the Blessed, ranging from the Canary Isles to Bermuda, but the descriptions in the earlier Greek legends do not permit any convincing conclusion. The later Plutarch may have based his story on the navigational knowledge of his time, and the distance from Africa, which he quotes, is certainly intriguingly precise. Assuming that we are still talking about islands *"at the western edge of the Earth"* (and it should be noted that some commentators have looked towards the east from Africa), the options become rather limited – the Canary Islands are visible from the coast of Africa, and Bermuda is about 3000 miles out into the Atlantic.

The Azores would be a better fit, being about 1160 miles from Western Sahara – and there is some archaeological evidence that these were discovered by the Phoenicians in the 3rd century BC – but this is still long after Homer. The Cape Verde islands have been suggested, but they are about 360 miles off the Senegalese coast, and were not discovered until the 15th century. Madeira was not 'officially' discovered by the Portuguese until the 15th century, although it is likely that it had been discovered by the Phoenicians before then (still too late to be the Fortunate Isles). But it is only 323 miles from the coast of Africa. So although several of these islands have their supporters none actually fits the geographical description.

It is a fact that the Channel Islands are about 1250 miles by sea from Africa. It is also a fact that there are several Channel Islands, which could be described as a pair of islands, separated by a very narrow strait, and that Guernsey and Herm would have been a perfect example (see 4.5). Moreover, as we shall see later, we know that Guernsey's name in Roman times was Lisia (see 5.8), and some have speculated that this was a corruption of Elysium. It also seems clear that the Channel Islands enjoyed a special religious status in Normandy from early times: in Gustave Jules Dupont's 'Le Cotentin et ses Iles', of 1870, we read that *"Jersey, Guernesey, Aurigny, Serk et Herm furent, pour notre contrée, ce que Sein était pour l'Armorique, et Mona pour la grande île bretonne".* ('Jersey, Guernsey, Alderney, Sark and Herm were, for our country (Normandy), what the isle of Sein was for Armorica and Mona (Anglesey) was for Britain.")

It is also the case that the northern part of Guernsey was a largely uninhabited area, which contains several ancient burial sites. These include the tomb at Les Fouillages, one of the oldest surviving man-made structures in the world, dating from 4500 BC and found to contain more than 35,000 artefacts. Another example is the Dehus passage grave, a 10 metre (33 foot) long burial chamber, which was found to contain skeletons and other objects dating from 3500 to 2000 BC. And a large number of megalithic tombs are to be found on Herm, one of which has been the subject of an archaeological investigation led by Professor Chris Scarre of Durham University, supported by specialists from Cambridge, Oxford and Guernsey. This tomb was in use until c.1000 BC, but it was found to contain a shard of Roman ceramic in its upper levels, so the tombs of Herm were clearly known to the Romans.

So there is some evidence that the Channel Islands may have been the Fortunate Islands, and that Guernsey may have been Elysium. Some later writers (mainly those who promote the Scilly Isles as the Cassiterides), link the Fortunate Isles with the Cassiterides. Pliny placed the two groups in the same category, albeit as two separate archipelagos. In Book IV, Chapter 36, 'The Islands in the Atlantic Ocean', he writes:

"Opposite to Celtiberia are a number of islands, by the Greeks called Cassiterides, in consequence of their abounding in tin: and, facing the

Promontory of the Arrotrebæ, are the six Islands of the Gods, which some persons have called the Fortunate Islands."

So what can we make of all this? In my opinion, the stories of the Cassiterides and the Fortunate Isles (or Islands of the Blest) are separated by a significant period of time, and I would analyse the position as follows:

- I regard it as virtually certain that the Channel Islands were the Cassiterides, and that tin and other metals were traded in Guernsey. I think this trade flourished from the second half of the second millennium BC, until the Iron Age, but continued at decreasing levels of activity until Roman times, by which time the traffic had been replaced to some extent by trade in other commodities.

- The legends of Elysium or the Fortunate Isles are much older. Indeed they were probably ancient history to Homer (800 BC), and may have their origins in the Minoan folklore of ancient Crete (2700 – 1500 BC). Anyone listing the Channel Islands today would probably name the larger inhabited islands of Jersey, Guernsey, Alderney, Sark, Herm and Jethou, which would accord with Pliny's description of an archipelago of six islands. There are no groups of six islands off the Atlantic coast of Spain, and although it is possible to identify groups of six islands off the coast of Brittany (eg the uninhabited Sept Îles to the north, or any selection of the scattered islands in the Bay of Biscay to the south), none of these possible groupings look convincing. In my view, an ancient reference to a group of islands must mean a group of islands that are within sight of each other.

- It is possible that the Channel Islands were used as burial grounds by the peoples who inhabited Gaul. The concentration of megalithic monuments on the Islands (nearly 200 in Jersey and Guernsey and unknown numbers in Alderney and Herm), and the evidence of their intensive use (35,000 objects found at Les Fouillages alone), is certainly impressive, especially given the small population of the islands. Although many of the monuments were not constructed as graves, those that were date from 4500 to 1500 BC, and re-use of the tombs continued until about 1000 BC (eg at Les Vardes Passage Grave in Guernsey and at Roberts Cross in Herm).

- The Channel Islands may even have been the Oestrymnides (see 3.2), since the description in the Ora Maritima closely matches the probable trading activity on the Islands. But, while the description was apt for the Channel Islands, the name probably did not refer to them. I believe that it referred to the islands off the western extremity of Brittany, such as Ushant and Île de Sein, although it possibly also embraced the islands at the northern end of the Bay of Biscay (the Île de Groix, Belle Île etc).

4.9   Summary

As we approach the Roman era, we can see that the Channel Islands, and Guernsey in particular, had a long-established and significant role in the export trade route for British metals. And they were also engaged in the reciprocal trade in agricultural products (particularly wine) and pottery.

Jersey's involvement was more limited, consisting mainly of a traffic in artefacts and produce to serve the local market, probably imported through Bouilly Port in St Brelades. This was the most accessible port on the route from Alet to Guernsey, and we will later see that there is evidence that the south-west corner of Jersey had stronger cultural links with Brittany than the rest of the island. But even this more limited trade gave the island close social and cultural connections with the Coriosolites, for whom Jersey appears to have served as an offshore repository for valuables.

St Peter Port, in contrast, had trading links with both Britain and Armorica, and had developed into an international commodities market in the depths of antiquity. The resulting creation of a sophisticated mercantile class gave the town a character which was distinct, both from the other Channel Islands and indeed from the hinterland of Guernsey itself. Avenius' account may be based partly on Caesar's, but it also includes a character sketch which is very illuminating: *"There is much vigour in the people here, a proud spirit, an efficient industriousness. They are all constantly concerned with commerce. They ply the wide troubled sea and swell of the monster-filled ocean with skiffs of skin".*

Because of their trading links with the Continent, we know quite a lot about these people, in their long dark cloaks and tunics and their goatee beards.

In fact, we know more about them than about the pre-Roman populations of any other part of the British Isles. And in Chapter 5 we will discover what they wore and ate in the Roman era. But it cannot be assumed that their lifestyle and habits were typical of other parts of the British Isles, because we know that they were not. Virtually the only places in pre-Roman Britain where wine amphorae are found are Hampshire and the Isle of Wight. The rest of the country drank beer.

Meanwhile, the prosperous commodity traders of the Channel Islands enjoyed a diet of fresh produce and locally brewed beers, enriched by Italian wines and olive oil, spices from the eastern and southern shores of the Mediterranean and fish sauce from Brittany. They were fortunate indeed.

Chapter 5:
The Roman Empire until AD 250

5.1   The Scheme of this Chapter

The Roman Empire is by far the best-documented period covered by this book, and there is a wealth of literature on the subject. So I will try not to dwell on the general history of the period, but rather to focus on what the Empire meant for the people living in the Channel Islands. Inevitably, this will require a wider perspective, because events even as far afield as Constantinople had an impact in the Islands, but I will try not to stray too far away from the central focus.

This is such a vast topic that I have broken the material down into more digestible chunks, firstly by splitting the Roman era into two chapters, one covering the period from the rise of the Romans in approximately 300 BC until the plateau of the Empire's peak influence, ending in about AD 250, and the second covering the disintegration of the Western Empire from AD 250 to AD 500. And within each of these chapters, I have taken a thematic approach to the material, to highlight certain key factors or developments that particularly impacted on the Channel Islands.

This chapter covers the following topics:

a)   The Rise of the Roman Empire: the developments that resulted in the Roman Empire absorbing Gaul, if not the Channel Islands themselves.

b)   What Did Roman Rule Mean in Practice?: The extent to which the Empire depended on the acquiescence of its subjects and the evidence of any Roman administration in the Channel Islands.

c)   The Implications for Trade: particularly the effects on trade through the Channel Islands.

d)   The Roman conquest of Britain.

e)   The Channel Islands in the Roman World.

f)   The Roman Era Settlement in St Peter Port

g)   The Roman names of the Channel Islands.

5.2   The Rise of the Roman Empire

The Celts were gradually driven out of northern Italy in the third century BC, and the Romans simultaneously secured control over the Mediterranean Sea by defeating Carthage in two 'Punic Wars', the first between 264 and 241 BC, and the second between 218 and 201 BC. Carthage continued as a much reduced power until given the 'coup de grace' in a Third Punic war, between 149 and 146 BC, but Roman regional hegemony was established by the start of the second century. The new Rome was a militaristic power, in which citizens were expected to serve in the army, and social standing depended on valour and martial achievement, so expansionism was at the core of its nature.

The Romans embarked on a series of military campaigns to expand their Empire, starting with the invasion of Spain in 201 BC, which led to control of the Iberian Peninsula by 133 BC. Perhaps more importantly it made a battle-hardened force out of their army, and proved ideal preparation for the campaign that followed in Gaul. One of the strengths of the Romans was that they learned from their enemies, so by the end of the Iberian campaign they had acquired a great deal of expertise in warfare, on land and at sea. In 121 BC, the Romans crossed the Alps and conquered the tribes in 'Transalpine' Gaul, the rather inapt term to describe what are now the regions of Languedoc-Roussillon and Provence-Alpes-Côtes d'Azur in the south of France. For the next 70 years, the area of Gaul under Roman control expanded slowly, to the shores of Lake Geneva in the east, up the Rhône valley in the centre and to Carcassonne and Toulouse in the south-west.

In 59 BC, when his term of office as a Consul expired, Julius Caesar was made governor (Proconsul) of Cisalpine and Transalpine Gaul, initially for a period of five years. Somewhat unusually, he was also given an army, because of the tensions in the region. This instability was caused by a wave of German invasions from the east, and a threatened migration of the Helvetii (from Switzerland), heading for the south-west of Gaul. Caesar took action, ostensibly to maintain order, but in reality for personal aggrandisement and enrichment.

Having driven the Helvetii back into Switzerland and then having defeated the Germans in 58 BC, Caesar moved immediately against the most powerful of the tribes in Gaul, the Belgae, who occupied the north-east corner of the territory. Despite the fact that these tribes offered no real threat to Roman power or security, Caesar marched into their lands and defeated them in 57 BC. Caesar then sent a young and inexperienced officer with no official rank, called Publius Crassus, to subdue Armorica (north-west Gaul), at the head of the 7th Legion. The tribes of the western peninsula were described in Chapter 1, where we saw that the most important of them were the Veneti, based around Vannes.

The size of the force at Crassus' disposal is instructive. A legion consisted of up to 5,500 men, and Caesar expected Crassus to be able to bring all the tribes of the north-west of France to heel with this unit. Nor was he disappointed, because, initially, the tribes were cowed into submission. They pledged to pay tribute to the Romans and gave hostages as surety of their compliance. Caesar then gave orders for the construction of a fleet of galleys on the Loire, in preparation for an invasion of Britain.

However, in 56 BC, the Veneti revolted, forcing a change in Caesar's plans. Crassus had camped at Angers for the winter, and needed supplies of corn to feed his troops. So he sent two 'ambassadors' to the Veneti, and one each to the Coriosolites and the Esubii, to demand supplies. The 'ambassadors' were all detained, and the Veneti demanded the release of their own hostages in return for the freedom of the Romans they held. Caesar considered that he had no choice but to confront this challenge to his authority with force, and to punish the Gauls for their crime of detaining Romans *"of equestrian rank"*.

Caesar himself took charge, and sent Crassus to Aquitaine to prevent that region sending any reinforcements to join the revolt. He similarly sent Quintus Tiberius Sabinus with three legions to the territory of the Unelli, the Coriosolites and the Lexovii in northern Armorica. He put a young Decimus Brutus in charge of the fleet that had been built on the Loire, together with the Gallic ships which Caesar had ordered the Pictones, the Santani and the tribes of the other pacified districts of Gaul to supply.

The fortified camps of the Veneti were built on headlands, which made them difficult to attack. Even though the Romans sometimes managed to break down the defences with the sheer scale of their siege works, or in some cases by building dykes to keep the sea out, so that they could attack the Gallic defences from the rear, the Veneti could always respond by evacuating their entire defensive force by ship. The tribe were notable seafarers and there are more than 50 islands in the Morbihan, the inland sea near Vannes, so it seems that they may have retreated in orderly fashion from island to island across the bay.

Caesar decided that the only effective course of action was to destroy the naval power of the Veneti, and he began planning for a battle at sea. He recognised at once that the Gaulish ships were immune to ramming, and that their considerable extra height above the water gave the Gauls an advantageous platform from which to throw down javelins or other projectiles onto the soldiers in his galleys. He saw immediately that the Romans' only advantages lay in the speed and manoeuvrability of the galley, and its autonomous power source. So he planned his attack for June, when light winds could be expected.

The Roman fleet approached the base of the Veneti, probably arriving outside the Morbihan in Quiberon Bay, but in any case within sight of Caesar and his land forces on the shore. The Veneti, with reinforcements from neighbouring tribes and from Britain, had gathered a fleet of over 200 ships to confront Caesar's navy.

The Romans had supplied themselves with sharpened hooks, attached to long poles, and they adopted the tactic of rowing up to the Veneti ships and grappling these hooks into their halyards (the ropes that held up the cross-spars from which the sails were hung). The halyards were then severed by a sudden spurt of rowing, causing the yards and sails to collapse on deck and rendering the ships helpless.

With greater mobility, the Roman galleys had the initiative and were able to surround the ships of the Gauls, one by one, and overwhelm their defenders. The Veneti were defeated, and when the outcome of the battle became clear, their remaining ships tried to sail away from the scene. But at that point the wind dropped entirely, and the Romans were able to capture most of the fleet. Only a few escaped, and some have speculated that they may have sailed north to the Channel Islands or Britain. Certainly we do know that the Veneti had ships that could cross the Channel, because Caesar tells us so.

Caesar decided to make an example of the Veneti, and had all the elders of the tribe executed. The rest he sold into slavery. (It has been estimated that Caesar sent up to a million slaves to Rome from his wars in Gaul, a traffic from which he benefited financially).

Meanwhile Sabinus was in lower Normandy, facing a force assembled by Viridovix, the leader of the Unelli. Sabinus had camped on a hilltop near Le Petit Celland, which is close to Avranches, with his three legions. But he seems to have been reluctant to engage with the Gauls, for reasons that are not entirely clear. For weeks the Unelli attempted to provoke a battle, but Sabinus stayed his hand, even when the Gauls were taunting his men from just outside the perimeter of his camp. The Gauls retired to their camp at night, and eventually Sabinus sent out a *"very clever"* Gallic ally, who pretended to be a deserter and who told the Unelli that not only were the Romans weak and afraid to confront them, but that they planned to leave the following night to go to Caesar's aid.

The Unelli decided to force a battle before Sabinus could leave, and in the morning they headed up the gentle slope of about a mile to the Roman camp, carrying bundles of faggots and brushwood to fill in the ditch outside the bank and stockade that formed the defences of the camp. When they reached the camp, they were naturally tired and disorganised, so as soon as they arrived Sabinus opened two of the gates and his soldiers charged into the Unelli, routing them with a single sortie. The Romans pursued the survivors fleeing from the scene and cut them all down.

After these battles, the Gauls of Armorica were largely pacified, although a further rebellion followed in 54 BC, and in 52 BC they sent troops to support the revolt of Vercingetorix which ended at Alesia. This was the battle that finally broke the resistance of the Gauls. In Caesar's Gallic Wars he describes the forces arrayed against him at this decisive engagement. The largest tribes, such as the Héduens and their client tribes contributed 35,000; a similar number were provided by the Arvernes and their allies; the Séquanes, Sénons, Bituriges, Santons, Rutènes and Carnutes eacb contributed 12,000 men; the Bellovaques 10,000; the Pictons, Turons, Parisii, Helvètes, Ambiens, Médiomatrices, Petrocorii, Nerviens, Morins and Nitiobroges each contributed 5,000; a similar number from the Alerques Cénomaines; 4,000 from the Atrebates; 3,000 from the Véliocasses, Lexovii, Aulerques and Eburovices; and 1,000 from the Rauraques and the Boïens.

The Armorican tribes of the Coriosolites, Redones, Ambibarii, Calètes, Osismes, Lémovices and Unellis supplied 20,000 fighters in total (an average of 2,850 per tribe). This tells us that all of these tribes were relatively small, and that they were regarded as a group acting en bloc. Moreover, the absence of any contribution from the Veneti confirms that the whole tribe, or at least its men of fighting age, had indeed been sold into slavery in 56 BC.

So at the scene of the battle, a Gaulish force of more than 180,000, led by Vercingetorix, defended an oppidum on a hilltop. They were confronted by a Roman army of about 50,000, but instead of attacking the Gaulish positions, Caesar ordered his army to construct a containing system of defences all around the town. At one point, some of the Gaulish cavalry were able to escape and went to summon a relief force, so Caesar then had to build a second defensive encirclement outside the first one, to protect his positions from attack from the rear. After a relief force of about 100,000 appeared, combined attacks from the Gauls in the town and the relief force outside failed to break the Roman positions, and, with the town and his army starving, Vercingetorix was forced to surrender. He himself was taken to Rome and paraded before the public; and after five years in prison he was executed.

5.3   What Did Roman Rule Mean in Practice?

It is tempting to think of the relationship of the Channel Islands with the Roman Empire, following the conquest of Gaul, as a bit like the relationship today of the Channel Islands with the European Union – i.e. outside the club, but with a trading relationship with the Empire. But we simply do not know what influence the Romans had in the Islands.

This is by no means a problem confined to the Channel Islands. Our knowledge of the relationship of the Romans with Brittany is equally opaque. Not a single piece of parchment survives to describe the operation of Roman rule in that region; *"The Gallo-Roman epigraphy of the area is therefore relatively poor; some 30 inscribed milestones, and about 60 public or private inscriptions, discovered chiefly in eastern parts, such as Nantes, Rennes or Corseul"* are all that survive.[1]

Nor do we know to what extent, if any, the Romans put in place a constitutional structure to regulate the Channel Islands, but it is generally assumed that there was no Roman system of government at all. François Eudes de Mézeray, the Historiographer to the King of France (1610 – 1683), says that Gaul was divided into provinces under Octavian (who became Augustus, the Roman Emperor from 27 BC to AD 14), and that Normandy was sub-divided into presidencies. Charles Noblot ('Geographie Universelle - Historique et Chronologique, Ancienne et Moderne', 1725) says that the ten presidencies *"together with the inhabitants of the islands lying near them, were known in Celtic Gaul by the name of the League of the Eleven Cities and this appears to have been in the time of the Romans."* This suggests that there was a system of government in the Normandy of Roman times, which included the Channel Islands, but the evidence is very slight, and given the time lapse before the above texts were written, they cannot be regarded as authoritative on this point.

According to Noblot, the 'Eleven Cities' were the Velocassi, who were settled near Rouen; the Biducassi, in the Pays de Caux; The Eburans, who lived around Evreux; the Alesians, from the town called Pont l'Arche; the Sessuens, from Seez or Sais; the Bayocassi, from Bayeux; the Abricates, from near Avranches; the Lexobicos and Uneliens, between Cherbourg and

---

1 Pierre-Roland Giot, Philippe Guigon and Bernard Merdrignac, 'The British Settlement of Brittany' (2003).

Coutances; and the Ambilexiens, who lived near Ambie, between Avranches and Coutances; plus the Channel Islands.

As we shall see in 5.6 and Chapter 6, it is likely that the Channel Islands played a part in the 'Saxon Shore' defences of the Empire against Germanic raiders, and, as part of that, the Romans clearly directed the construction of a fort in Alderney in the late 4th century (the Nunnery at Longis Bay). So Roman engineers must have visited and worked on Alderney, but this does not constitute evidence of a system of government.

However, an absence of Roman administrators was not untypical of the Roman provinces generally. After conquering a country or region, the Romans did not leave a vast army of soldiers and administrators behind to govern it, and in Gaul the legions were largely removed or disbanded by 49 BC, only seven years after the events described above. The only legion that is recorded as being based in modern France in the period up to AD 250 was the Legio VIII Augusta, based at Strasbourg, but smaller units were later deployed at some of the forts of the Saxon Shore. This was hardly an army of occupation.

Britain was more troublesome to the Empire, with frequent insurrections from the tribes of the north and west. Once conquered in AD 43, it was policed by four legions – perhaps 22,000 men. There is little evidence of southern European DNA in the British population today, so the 'Romans' did not leave a significant genetic legacy. However, there is archaeological evidence from cemeteries at Wasperton (Warwickshire) and Lankhills (Winchester) that some of the 'Romans' were from central or southern Europe.[2] The Legio II Augusta was based at Caerleon in Wales, the Legio VI Victrix was based at York, the Legion IX Hispana was also based at York and the Legio XX Valeria Victrix was based at Chester. Even though other units participated in the various wars against the Picts, a resident of the south-east of England might not have seen Roman soldiers from one month to the next.

So the administration of Roman provinces was left almost entirely to the notables of their cities, supported as necessary by a small number of Roman officials. The whole of northern and central Gaul formed part of the Roman province of Lugdunensis, of which the capital was Lyon, so any Roman control over the Channel Islands would have been remote. More locally, it appears that Carhaix (Vorgium to the Romans) was the main centre of Roman activity in Brittany.

Therefore Roman rule can only have operated with the acquiescence,

2 Härke, 'Anglo-Saxon Immigration and Ethnogenesis', (2011)

indeed the positive support, of a large number of people in the subject territories. And we can only assume that they accepted the obligation to pay Roman taxes because they saw benefits in the relationship, of which probably the most important was peace – an end to the petty feuds that had dogged the history of the Celtic tribes. Of course the relatively high standard of living of the Romans must also have been seductive, and the indigenous populations were no doubt impressed by Roman technology and engineering (especially plumbing).

Whoever was in charge of the administration of Brittany and Normandy, they must have been aware of the Channel Islands, because of the pre-existing trade relationships. Later on, at the end of the 3rd century, a troop from the Roman army was based at Alet, but even before then the Islands would have been visible to anyone who cared to look out to sea from the coast of Normandy. However, the populations were almost certainly too small to be of interest as a source of tribute or slaves, and the Roman fleets in the English Channel were fully occupied ferrying supplies to their legions (in the early days) or defending the eastern end from Saxon pirates and the western end from Irish pirates (later on). Policing the Channel Islands would not have been top of their priority lists unless the Channel Islands had become a base for pirates, and we can only assume from the absence of evidence of direct Roman intervention in the Islands that this did not happen. So, apart from a possible reconnaissance mission to Guernsey, on which I have speculated earlier (see 4.6), it appears unlikely that any significant Roman forces ever set foot in the Islands.

However, whatever level of independence the Channel Islands may have had, the influence of Latin must have been felt in the Islands, once this became the official language of the principal trading partners of the Islands. We can assume that the Islands had previously spoken Continental Celtic, but the peoples of the adjacent coasts of France and Britain increasingly spoke Latin dialects, which in Gaul became Gallo-Roman. In towns with a Roman presence, like Cherbourg (Coriallo) and Coutances (Constantia), and among the provincial administration generally, better quality Latin would have been heard, and we know that the administrators of Roman provinces kept plentiful records written in Latin, which, frustratingly, have not survived.

This is not to say that Continental Celtic, or Gaulish as the version spoken in Gaul is termed, immediately disappeared, because we know that it continued to be spoken, especially by the ordinary people. At the end of the 2nd century AD, Saint Irenaeus was forced to preach in Gaulish to be understood by his congregation in Lyon, the capital of the province of

Lugdunensis. If this was the situation in the provincial capital, how much Latin would have been understood in more remote towns? It is not known when Gaulish died out, but in some rural areas it may still have been spoken in the 5th century (see 4.5).

The Channel Islands, being a relatively remote archipelago that, nevertheless, had a lot of contact with its neighbours, may have been bilingual, as they have been for much of their history. However, within the Islands there is no evidence of Roman style place names (eg names ending in '-ac', '-ia', '-is' etc), although that is not surprising since there were no oppida. Beyond the influence which Latin has inevitably had on Gallo-Roman and Norman French (Grouville, Longueville, Torteval etc), it is hard to distinguish any Latin substratum in the local toponymy.

5.4   The Implications for Trade

The conquest of Transalpine Gaul opened up new trade routes for Italian products, and Italian wine, in particular, found a ready market. The Romans were simply amazed at the demand for this, and the prices it could be sold for. Diodorus Siculus (who worked between 60 and 30 BC) wrote: *"Many Italian merchants, with their love of quick profit, look on the Gallic passion for wine as their treasure trove. They transport the wine by boat on the navigable rivers and by wagon through the plains and receive in return an incredibly large price: for one amphora of wine they receive a slave – a servant in exchange for a drink."*

So we know that the rivers were used for transport, and we also know that there was, in particular, a trade route down the Garonne River to Bordeaux, where wine could be loaded onto ships and sent up the French coast. Some of the wine evidently reached Hengistbury via Guernsey (as shown by the trail of amphorae), but we do not know whether the wine was shipped around Finisterre or shipped to the south coast of Brittany, unloaded and taken by road or river to Alet, and then shipped from Alet to Guernsey and onwards to Hengistbury. Amphorae of the 1st century BC are found all over Brittany (at more than 70 sites), but the only finds from the sea have been some amphorae trawled up by fishing boats south of Belle Île (one of them was full of wine, so these were not empties being returned!).[3] This is an ambiguous location, because the vessel(s) concerned could have been travelling towards Finisterre or towards Southern Brittany. But

3 Jacques Andre, 'Notes d'Archaéologie Sousmarine, Annales de Bretagne, 1961'.

the absence of any finds of amphorae off the western coast of Finisterre suggests that the wine took the overland route to Alet.

In Armorica, the largest concentrations of Dressel 1 amphorae have been found at Carhaix and Angers, and the next largest concentrations have been found at Carnac, Vannes, Plouer-sur-Rance and Alet, with a similar concentration at Quimper. Smaller quantities have been found all around the coast, particularly in the area near Douarnenez. But there is no evidence of any special concentration at Brest, and no finds at all at Le Yaudet.[4]   To me, the 'trail of empty bottles' suggests several conclusions:

- Angers (and not Nantes) was the major city on the western Loire.
- Carhaix, where seven roads met, was the regional capital of Brittany. It was probably supplied with wine by ships arriving at Quimper.
- Wine heading for Britain probably travelled overland from Carnac or Vannes to the River Rance at Plouer, and then down to Alet.

This is not to say that ships did not sail around Finisterre into the English Channel, because we know from several classical sources that they did (eg Julius Caesar in 'De Bello Gallico', and Strabo, Book IV, 5.3: *"There are only four passages which are habitually used in crossing from the mainland to the island, those which begin at the mouths of the rivers — the Rhenus (the Rhine) the Sequana, (the Seine) the Liger (the Loire) and the Garumna (the Garonne)"*. But before Europeans learned about the rudder, in the mid-first century AD, the journey around Finisterre would have been particularly daunting, and must have been avoided whenever possible.

For the Roman wine merchants, the development of an Atlantic trade route in wine was a two-edged sword, because it resulted in the expansion of shipping further down the Atlantic seaboard. Ships that could reach Bordeaux from Vannes could just as easily reach Spain, and goods from the Iberian Peninsula and North Africa started to enter the supply chain to Britain. By the 1st century BC, amphorae of wine from Catalonia were reaching Hengistbury. And the ships carrying the wine also carried olive oil, fruit products, garum and other foodstuffs from the length of the Atlantic coast of Europe.

With the defeat of the tribes of the northern coast of Gaul, the situation of western Britain changed dramatically. The Romans now had supplies of tin from Brittany as well as Spain, and the independent British Celtic tribes were seen as a continuing threat to the Empire. Substantial trade

---

4 Fabienne Olmer, 'Amphores en Gaul aux IIe et Ier siècles avant notre ère, Aspects épigraphiques, quantatifs et economiques', 2008.

across the western Channel ceased, possibly on the direct orders of Caesar himself, and wine imports at Hengistbury dried up. The Romans seem to have redirected cross-Channel trade to the more malleable Belgic tribes in the south-east of England, as observed by Barry Cunliffe ('Armorica and Britain' 1997): *"By, (56 BC) Alet had emerged as a significant port in northern Brittany and, though Hengistbury was still in use, Poole Harbour now seems to have become the favoured port of entry for central southern Britain. The volume of trade to the Solent was, however, insignificant compared with the intensity of development which now linked the Roman ports of the northern French coast to the estuaries of Essex".*

In the period immediately after the conquest of Gaul, the Romans considered the British Gallic tribes to be hostile, and a principal reason given by Caesar for his two incursions across the Channel in 55 and 54 BC, was to punish the British for their support for rebellious mainland Gauls. However, these invasions did not achieve much, and no British territory was gained by the Romans as a result of their actions.

The first incursion took Caesar into Kent, but no further, and the second, the following year saw him cross the Thames, possibly at Westminster, to confront the British leader Cassivellaunus at his stronghold, possibly at Wheathampsted. The confrontation was inconclusive, and terms were negotiated through the efforts of Commius, the leader of the Atribates, whom Caesar had sent ahead to negotiate a submission. Caesar took hostages and withdrew to Gaul, leaving not a single Roman soldier in Britain.

Caesar never got near the territory of the Durotriges in Dorset, still less the Dumnonii in Cornwall, but in any case the Romans now had the power to shut British exports out of the Continental market. The freeze on trade across the western end of the Channel lasted the best part of a century, until Rome conquered Britain in AD 43, and the traffic moved to the ports of the Belgic tribes around the Thames Estuary, who paid tribute to the Romans.

Caesar himself became distracted by a power struggle with Pompey and a faction of the Roman Senate, which resulted in the dissolution of his army in Gaul and his recall to Rome from his base in Cisalpine Gaul in 49 BC. In response he 'crossed the Rubicon', the river which divided his provinces from the Roman homelands, with one legion. The resulting civil war saw the defeat and murder of Pompey and Caesar's installation as a de facto dictator (although he rejected that title). And his pre-occupation with eliminating his political enemies prevented him from pursuing his territorial ambitions further, so Britain remained independent for the best part of a century. Caesar had, however, made some dangerous enemies along the way, and former officers of Pompey's army murdered him in 44 BC.

For almost a century, the Roman Empire co-existed with an independent Britain, and the tribes of Britain paid tribute to the Romans on a scale that made it seem uneconomic to the Romans to invade. Strabo explained the position in his day: *"At present, however, some of the chieftains there, after procuring the friendship of Caesar Augustus by sending embassies and by paying court to him, have not only dedicated offerings in the Capitol, but have also managed to make the whole of the island virtually Roman property. Further, they submit so easily to heavy duties, both on the exports from there to Celtica and on the imports from Celtica (these latter are ivory chains and necklaces, and amber-gems and glass vessels and other petty wares of that sort), that there is no need of garrisoning the island; for one legion, at the least, and some cavalry would be required in order to carry off tribute from them, and the expense of the army would offset the tribute-money; in fact, the duties must necessarily be lessened if tribute is imposed, and, at the same time, dangers be encountered, if force is applied."*

However, material gain is not the only motive for conquest, and Britain was a tempting target for a campaign motivated by personal vanity. Caesar's reign was followed after a period of civil war by that of another great leader, Octavian, who founded the Roman Empire proper. But Octavian (who became known as Caesar Augustus) was followed by a series of Emperors who were at best inconsequential, and at worst mad (including Caligula and Nero). Among them was one who was to have a major impact on the history of Britain.

5.5   The Romans in Britain

Claudius became Emperor in AD 41, with a reputation as a buffoon, which had protected him from the worst of the political intrigues in Rome. Like many of his predecessors as Emperor, he decided that he needed an early military triumph to consolidate his position, and he decided that the prime target was Britain. So in 43 AD a Roman fleet set off from Boulogne, ostensibly to install an exiled king of the Atribates, Verica, as a puppet ruler (although Verica is not mentioned again).

For the history of this period, we look primarily to Tacitus, but unfortunately his account of the invasion and its aftermath are missing, so we have only second-hand reports written about 160 years later. But it is believed that Claudius' force consisted of four legions, with cavalry and auxiliaries, and perhaps numbered about 40,000. The only legion that can be identified with certainty was the Legio II Augusta, commanded by a future Emperor, Vespasian, but fortunately this is the unit most relevant to the Channel Islands.

After an unopposed landing, Claudius defeated two British 'kings', Caratacus and Togodumnos. He clearly went looking for a battle, because he needed to report a military victory to the public in Rome, but it seems he had to march to the territory of the Catuvellauni (Hertfordshire) to find it. As Bede puts it *"Before Claudius no Roman, either before or since Julius Caesar, had dared to land on the island; yet, within a few days, without battle or bloodshed, he received the surrender of the greater part of the island."*

The IInd legion was then sent along the south coast to subdue the tribes there. A minor battle ensued at Maiden Castle near Dorchester, the largest

Iron Age fort in Britain, where some of the Durotriges evidently put up a resistance, because 38 skeletons have been found there. But the Durotriges were one of the tribes most familiar with the Roman world, through their trading links with the Continent, and they seem to have been merchants rather than warriors. Armed with slings and pebbles from Chesil beach at Weymouth, they would have been no match for the IInd Legion. (No doubt they also had swords and spears, but the Romans would have removed these, so we do not have the evidence). Hengistbury gave up without a fight, despite also being protected by impressive earth ramparts.

Vespasian continued along the coast, meeting and overcoming some resistance at hill forts on the way, and when he got to Exeter he built a base for his legion there. Shortly after the invasion, the Romans built a defensive structure called the Fosse Way (probably an embankment and ditch), which connected Exeter and Lincoln. This marked the limit of the area under Roman rule at the time, and was defended at various points by 'castra', now evident in the names of towns ending in '-cester', such as Ilchester, Cirencester and Leicester.

It is apparent that the Romans had quickly absorbed the area occupied by the Belgic tribes of the south-east and the more Romanised Celtic tribes of the borderlands, such as the Durotriges, thus entrenching the underlying cultural divide which is still fairly visible in the political map of Britain today. The names of the tribes to the south and east of this line are rarely mentioned after the Roman invasion, but the subsequent history of the areas to the north and west is one of alternating periods of submission and revolt.

However, even the tribes of the south-east were provoked to revolt not long after the invasion by some oppressive and unintelligent Roman behaviour. The Iceni were a Belgic tribe in what is now Norfolk, and their king was an ally of the Romans. Unfortunately, however, he did not have a son, so he left his kingdom to the Roman Emperor Nero and his two daughters jointly. The concept of female rulers was alien to the macho and militaristic Roman army, and some very foolish tax collectors scorned his will, flogged his wife Boudicca and raped his daughters.

In AD 61, Boudicca led her people in revolt, at a moment when the Roman commander Gaius Suetonius Paulinus was campaigning against the Druids in Anglesey. Her forces destroyed Colchester and the Roman IX Hispana Legion. They then marched on London and burnt that, slaughtering anyone who could not escape, before moving on to destroy St Albans (at which point they had razed the three largest towns in Roman Britain). Paulinus returned from North Wales with his XIV Gemina Legion and parts of the XX Valeria Victrix Legion, making a total of about 10,000 men, including auxiliaries. The II Augusta Legion failed to join him from Exeter.

Being heavily outnumbered, Paulinus picked his ground carefully, near Watling Street in the Midlands, and fought in a narrow valley where he could not be outflanked and with a wood behind him to protect the rear of his position. His skilful command resulted in a defeat for the British, who suffered heavy casualties.

The Romans had very nearly lost the whole province, through the barbarous behaviour of a few individuals, and, because they learned the lesson, they never again had to fight the tribes of the south-east. The position in the rest of the country was very different.

The high-water mark of Roman control was achieved in AD 84, when Gnaeus Julius Agricola defeated the Caledonians in Scotland, but his territorial gains proved untenable and the Picts drove the Romans back to the Solway – Tyne line. The Emperor Hadrian visited Britain after he took the throne in 117, and, finding the north of the country in revolt, ordered the construction of a defensive wall which was completed in about 128. Fourteen years later, a further push northwards resulted in the construction of the Antonine Wall on the Forth – Clyde line, but this expansion could not be sustained and the Romans subsequently retreated to Hadrian's Wall.

The constant struggle along the northern frontier may have made the headlines of this period for the military historian, but it had a beneficial effect in the south of Britain. Four standing legions was a significant proportion of the whole Roman army (which Octavian had reduced to twenty five legions, but which grew again to thirty legions by AD 200), and indeed the Roman army in Britain outnumbered the population of Roman London for much of the period. So Britain absorbed a significant share of the Empire's military budget, despite being only one of its forty regions, and the British economy was sustained by a continual inflow of funds to pay the troops. In effect, between AD 43 and c.200, Britain received large subsidies from Rome, out of which some British merchants became rich. But unfortunately from a Channel Islands perspective, the great bulk of this trade was passing through the ports of south-east England, especially London.

Roman military campaigns in Britain continued until the early 3rd century, but eventually the drain on the resources of Rome and more pressing claims for military intervention elsewhere, exhausted Rome's appetite for conquest in its most northerly province. From the second half of the 3rd century, the Romans were merely fire fighting in Britain, responding to the raids of pirates or the uprisings of usurpers for whom Britain, with its large standing army, was a magnet.

The first attempted coup backed by British legions had occurred earlier, when Clodius Albinus came close to gaining the Imperial throne in 197, before he narrowly lost a decisive battle at Lyon. And as we shall see, others followed. A pattern emerged that whenever the legions were withdrawn from Britain to support a campaign on the Continent, the northern tribes would seize the opportunity to revolt, requiring the Romans to mount a campaign to recover northern Britain once the civil war on the Continent was concluded.

However, in general, this was a relatively peaceful period in southern England and northern Gaul, during which populations grew and became wealthier. The population of Brittany may have doubled between 50 BC and AD 250 (to perhaps 600,000), and the population of Britain grew prosperous on the back of Roman subsidies. But for the subject populations, the benefits of Roman rule carried a price in terms of taxation.

5.6   The Channel Islands in the Roman World

One of Octavian's first acts was to conduct a census throughout the Roman world in 27 BC (a further census of Syria and Judaea undertaken by Quirenius in AD 6/7 was of course referred to in St Luke's Gospel). Since one of the primary purposes of a census was to establish a basis for taxation, this may have caused a flight of money. Nine hoards of mainly Coriosolite coins, with some Unelli and Durotriges coins, have been found in Jersey. The Marquanderie hoard found in 1935 comprised some 12,000 coins, and the Le Catillon hoard found in 1957 amounted to more than 2,500 coins. The latest find, announced in June 2012, comprises perhaps 70,000 coins, the largest single hoard of Iron Age coins found in Europe, but at the time of writing little detail is available on this. Archaeologists are carefully separating the coins, which were brought to the surface in a block of clay weighing three quarters of a ton. If the number of coins in the find matches the estimates, this would bring the total number of coins found in Jersey to around 90,000. To put this in perspective, the total number of Iron Age coins found in the whole of the rest of Britain is about 50,000.

No such hoards have been found in Guernsey, but in Chapter 1, when discussing the clothing worn by Celts in circa 100 BC, we noted that the graves of a number of Celtic warriors have been found on the island, for example at Kings Road in St Peter Port. These burials are similar to the inhumations of that period found in Gaul, and it is not clear whether this is evidence of the adoption by Guernsey residents of the funerary customs of mainland Gaul, or whether the warriors were Gallic émigrés. On the whole, I favour the latter interpretation, because it is hard to imagine that Guernsey could have sustained a warrior class.

The response of the Romans to any attempt to move either money or refugees offshore seems not to have been more direct intervention in the Channel Islands, but rather an attempt to deny them access to the Empire. In AD 10, Alet was entirely destroyed by fire. This may have been part of a more general protectionist stance by the Empire, since the Romans had suffered a severe setback to their ambitions in Germany the previous year, when three legions had been annihilated in Teutoburg Forest. It seems that this caused Octavian to conclude that the Empire was over-extended and that it should consolidate and seal its borders.

After the Roman conquest of England, trade resumed through St Peter Port, which seems to have been particularly active in the period AD 50 – 300 based on the mass of archaeological evidence found in the town. Towards the end of this period, Saxon and Irish pirates threatened the sea routes across the Channel, and the Romans had to fortify key ports on both coasts. There is evidence of Roman fortification on Guernsey, and it is my belief that there is more waiting to be discovered on the hills above St Peter Port, perhaps to the north of Les Cotils.

The sites of the Roman fortifications along both sides of the Channel help to identify where the significant ports of the period were: on the British side it is no surprise to find Richborough, Dover, Pevensey and Portchester among those listed in the Notitia Dignitatum,[5] and there were, in addition, Roman forts at Clausentum and on the Isle of Wight. On the French side, in the Tractus Armoricani et Nervicani, we can identify from the Notitia Dignitatum the ports of Rouen, Coutances, Avranches, Alet and Brest among others, and there were in addition known Roman forts at Cherbourg (Coriallo), Guernsey and Alderney.

5 The Notitia Dignitatum describes the administrative organisation of the Eastern and Western Roman Empires, and is considered accurate for the Western Empire as of about 420

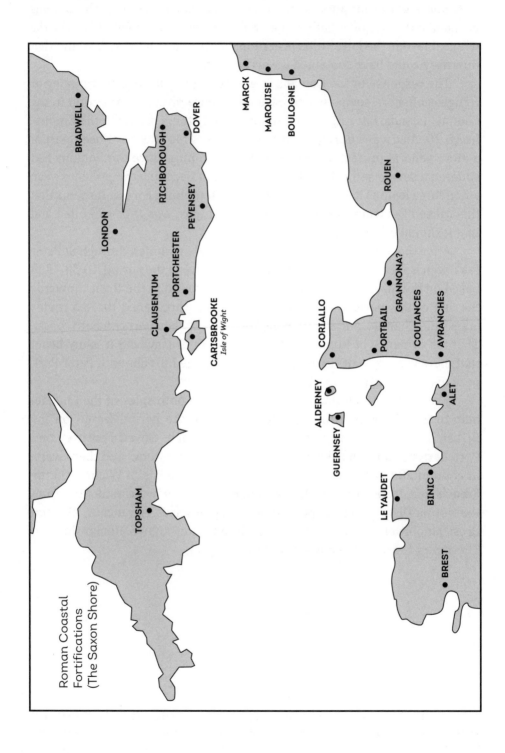

Roman Coastal
Fortifications
(The Saxon Shore)

BRADWELL

RICHBOROUGH

DOVER

MARCK

MARQUISE

BOULOGNE

ROUEN

LONDON

PEVENSEY

PORTCHESTER

CLAUSENTUM

GRANNONA?

CARISBROOKE
Isle of Wight

CORIALLO

PORTBAIL

COUTANCES

AVRANCHES

ALDERNEY

ALET

GUERNSEY

TOPSHAM

LE YAUDET

BINIC

BREST

It requires some effort to imagine the geography of St Peter Port when sea levels were 6 – 8 metres lower than the current level, but in effect the high tide level must have been a couple of metres above the present low tide level. This would have meant that at high tide, the sea was lapping at the foundations of the present harbour walls, and the Roman era quayside is now buried deep below the present waterfront. At low tide, the harbour would have drained to a line between Castle Cornet and the White Rock, a navigation mark now buried beneath the north arm of the harbour walls. There was nothing like the present Castle on the islet of Cornet, but there may have been buildings and even fortifications on or around it. These would have been destroyed in the construction of the present Castle from the 13th century onwards and the construction of the southern arm of the present harbour, which commenced in 1853.

The islet was connected to the waterfront by a spit of land, or at least a promontory of rocks, which would probably have been above water at all states of tide. At the end of this promontory of rocks, on its northern side, there was a small shingle beach, now called Cow Bay. This beach was probably hidden from the waterfront by the promontory leading out to the islet, and it seems to have been useful as a temporary storage place for goods unloaded from the ships beached on the sand of the harbour. There may have been storage buildings on the foreshore.

We know that there were two large stone-built storage houses near the harbour, in the area now called La Plaiderie (the Court House, first referred to in writing in documents dating from the 12th century), which contained wine, garum and pots from Armorica. Evidence of Roman occupation is uncovered on practically every building site in central St Peter Port – eg at 18/20 The Pollet, at Les Canichers, at the Royal Hotel site and in particular at the Bonded Store site under the present Market buildings. Large quantities of pottery from eastern Gaul have been found at the latter, dating from the 1st to the 3rd centuries AD. Some of the pots can even be traced to their makers, who operated in Lezoux, central Gaul, from 160 – 190 AD, because they stamped their names on the bottom. The finds include amphorae from France, Italy and Spain, and pottery from France, Germany, Spain and Britain, demonstrating the international scope of the trade passing through the town.

Nearby a smelting furnace and slag have been found, evidencing metal production, and at the Plaiderie site there was equipment for counterfeiting Roman coins of the first half of the 3rd century! So the local traders seem to have been fairly enterprising. Examination of the material recovered tells us that St Peter Port was much more than a Roman trading post. A large area of the town itself was occupied from the early 2nd century to the 4th century AD, and the town also at least one suburb – it was within a short walk of the Celtic village at Kings Road. There must be much more evidence under the largely 18th century buildings of St Peter Port, and under its harbour walls, but what we have already found is evidence of extensive, and intensive, occupation.

At a village at Les Tranquesous, in St Saviours to the west of the island, terra nigra pottery from Rennes has been found alongside other Gallic pottery, evidencing a trade in ceramics passing through the island. As at Kings Road, the site shows evidence of Celtic round houses, and also enclosures, possibly for animals. It has therefore been identified as a farmstead.

Uniquely outside the Mediterranean, there are the remains of several Roman-era ships in the mouth of the present harbour of St Peter Port, which at the time would have been a drying beach. And substantial quantities of Roman material, including pottery similar to that found in the Bonded Store site, have been found on Cow Bay. (Incidentally 'cau' in Catalan means hidden or cache, which suggests a Continental Celtic origin for the name. 'Hidden' is a good description of the bay, and would certainly make more sense than 'cow'). This material shows that there was harbour-side activity in that area, and possibly on the site of Castle Cornet itself.

One of these ships has been nicknamed 'Asterix', after the cartoon character. She was 82 feet (25 metres) in length, and similar to the ships of the Veneti described by Caesar. Her main cargo was pitch, from the Les Landes region of southwest France, but she also carried amphorae from Spain and Algeria (probably containers for wine and olive oil), and pottery containers from the Saintonge region of France (north of Bordeaux). Pottery flagons from Saintonge were often used to transport Bordeaux wines, so the wine trade through Guernsey had clearly diversified from the original market in Italian wine to include Spanish and French products. From coins found in the wreck, we can deduce that the ship sank between 280 and 286 AD, burnt to the waterline by a fire.

Unusually, because the ship carried a cargo of pitch, which melted in the fire, a number of perishable articles that would not normally have survived to posterity were preserved. So we know that the crew's diet included, in addition to various animals: oysters, ormers (abalone), scallops, crabs, winkles, cockles and limpets. They had fruit and walnuts, and a large amount of grain – in short the ingredients for an excellent 'fruits de mer', possibly followed by cheese and fruit, together with a selection of wines.

It is obvious that the shipping passing through Guernsey was now voyaging far down the western coast of Europe and possibly into the Mediterranean, and the importation into Europe of the rudder as a means of steering was probably the catalyst to this expansion. While commerce with the tribes of Armorica had resumed, the absorption of England into the Roman Empire substantially increased the trading opportunities for Guernsey and its merchants. The export of metals may not have been the business it had once been, but the island had become an emporium for a wide variety of products, and ships were venturing further than they had customarily done before.

Stone ballast of Jersey and Guernsey origin, dating from the 1st century AD, has been found at Fishbourne, near Chichester, where there was an important Roman villa belonging to the kings of the Atribates, and this strongly suggests that ships from the Channel Islands visited Chichester Harbour. The purpose of the voyages to Fishbourne must have been to replenish the wine cellars and pantries of the royal household. Archaeology at Alet suggests there was an increase in trading activity in the period 275 to 320, followed by a falling away afterwards.[6] By then Hengistbury had been replaced by Hamworthy in Poole Harbour and Clausentum (at Bitterne), as the northern ends of the western Channel trade routes, and Alet had been fortified, presumably against the Saxons.

Jersey has not produced the same amount of Roman material as Guernsey, although a burial site and some Roman construction have been found at Grouville. The reason for this is almost certainly that the ports of Jersey were not as accessible as St Peter Port, so most of the trade passed through Guernsey. However, outside of St Peter Port there is little evidence of Roman settlement in either island. For example, we know of no Roman villas in the Channel Islands. But from the remains of Roman tiles found in the walls of the present day Castel Church, in the centre of Guernsey, it is believed that the Romans may have built a fort on the site ('Castel' obviously means castle). There is certainly a well-preserved Roman fort, dating from about 320 AD, at Longis Bay in Alderney, so there must have been a Roman presence on that island towards the end of the Roman era, probably to protect it from Saxon pirates.

When the Empire finally collapsed, Bede reflected on the almost 400 years of Roman rule in Britain, the construction of cities, forts, bridges and paved roads across the country, and said that *"they also held nominal jurisdiction over the more remote parts of Britain and the islands beyond it."* That seems to me to perfectly summarise the relationship of the Channel

6 L. Langouet, 'La Cité d'Alet'

Islands with Rome, but obliquely, the Roman Empire left one huge legacy in the Channel Islands – its religion.

5.7   Christianity

The year of Jesus' birth has been variously estimated at any point between 7 BC and AD 2, with perhaps a central estimate of around 2 BC. According to St Luke he was about 30 years of age when he started his ministry, and he was crucified during the prefecture of Pontius Pilate, AD 26 – 36. A central estimate for the year of his crucifixion is AD 33.

Roman involvement in the region to the east of the Mediterranean dates from 63 BC, but in 6 BC Judea became part of a province of the Roman Empire and so Jesus grew up in the Roman world. After his crucifixion, his disciples and a growing mass of followers spread his teachings to other parts of the Roman Empire in the Near East, including Syria, Jordan and Egypt. In particular St Paul (c. AD 5 – 67), who was born in Tarsus in what is now southern Turkey, made three missionary journeys in the region, before travelling to Rome, and when he got there he found there was already a Christian community. It was at Antioch (in modern Turkey, but then part of Syria) that the followers of Jesus were first called 'Christians', possibly as a pejorative term. Antioch was a major city of Hellenistic Greece, and the third most important city in the Roman Empire, so St Paul devoted much of his mission to teaching there.

Initially, Christianity was considered to be part of the Jewish faith, but, by the end of the first century AD, it was being recognised as a separate religion. By that time, the spread of Christianity was supported by organised churches, with bishops (eg Clement of Rome), presbyters and deacons, and the new religion rapidly gained followers throughout the Roman Empire. But we know more about the spread of this religion from the history of the persecutions that attended its expansion than from the church itself. For example, between 109 and 111, Pliny the Younger was sent to the province of Bythinia in Anatolia (eastern Turkey), and enquired about the charges against, and punishment of, Christians. And in the mid 2nd century there was a persecution in Lyon, which shows that Christianity was well rooted in the heart of Roman Gaul by that time.

Bede tells us that Lucius, a British king, wrote to the Roman emperor Marcus Antoninus Verus in 156, asking to be made a Christian by his direction, which wish was granted. But the earliest archaeological evidence of Christianity in Britain is a 2nd century 'word square' (found in what is now Manchester), which forms an anagram of 'Pater Noster'. The first clear written reference to Christianity in Britain is a passage by Tertullian (c. 200), referring to *"all the limits of the Spains, and the diverse nations of the Gauls, and the haunts of the Britons, inaccessible to the Romans but subjected to Christ."* And the first British martyrs, among them St Alban, were executed during the persecutions of Diocletian, Emperor from 284 to 305.

In terms of churches and church artefacts, the 3rd or 4th century provide us with the remains of buildings which may have been wooden churches in Lincoln and Silchester (Hampshire), and, more certainly, baptismal fonts found at Richborough (Kent) and Icklingham (Suffolk). These finds, together with the evidence of the early church in Lyon, suggest that Christianity reached Britain along the Roman trade routes to Boulogne in northern Gaul and across the Channel to south-eastern England.

As we have seen, Christians were subject to occasional persecutions in the first three centuries AD. But in 313, Constantine the Great, together with his co Emperor in the East, promulgated the Edict of Milan, which ordered a policy of religious tolerance throughout the Empire. Constantine, whose mother Helena was a Christian, was himself not yet a Christian at the time, and was only baptised (as an Arian Christian) shortly before his death in 337. But the momentum was now with the faith, and Christianity was made the official religion of the Roman Empire by the Emperor Theodosius in 391.

According to Gregory of Tours, the Roman church sent seven bishops to Gaul in 250, including Gatianus who founded the church at Tours, and when the bishops of the Latin world assembled at Arles in 314, a dozen bishops of towns in (mainly southern) France appended their signatures No representative of Tours attended the Council of Arles, and Gregory of Tours does not mention it, so the seed planted by Gatianus appears not to have taken hold. Martin of Tours, a follower of Hilary of Poitiers, established his monastery at Ligugé Abbey in 361, the first in Gaul, and evangelised the countryside round about. He became Bishop of Tours in 371, and in about 372 he founded the monastery at Marmoutier, on the opposite bank of the Loire. Three thousand, six hundred and sixty churches are dedicated to St Martin in France alone, far more than for any other saint, which makes it difficult to know where exactly he preached, but it is clear that his teachings reached Normandy, with dedications at Maromme (near Rouen), Cruelly (near Caen), Harfleur etc. They also reached Brittany as far west as Finisterre (near Morlaix), and it would be a reasonable assumption that they reached the Channel Islands by the early 5th century.

Another prominent early Christian evangelist in Gaul was John Cassian (d.435), who founded a monastery with separate halls for men and women, near Marseilles early in the 5th century. John Cassian's teachings inspired St Benedict (St Benoit), who drew up the monastic rule which became the code for all Benedictine monks.

5.8   The Roman Names of the Channel Islands

Much effort has been expended on trying to discover the names of the Channel Islands in the Roman era, for which the evidence is very patchy. Caesar does not refer to them at all. We do, of course, have some history for the name of Britain, although even that is surprisingly recent. Herodotus does not use the word 'Britannia', or anything like it, and it appears that Ireland (Ierne) was better known to the ancients of the Mediterranean.

The ancient name of Britain was 'Albion', possibly meaning 'white', perhaps a reference to the white cliffs of Dover. However, Pytheas (from Marseilles) is reported to have referred to Britain in his account of his voyage to (and possible circumnavigation of) Britain in about 350 BC. His account of the voyage does not survive, except in references in other works (which frequently cast aspersions on Pytheas' credibility), but the commentaries tell us that he described his destination as 'Brettaniai'. This is the earliest known reference to the name.

The work 'De Mundo', attributed in the Middle Ages to Aristotle but possibly written up to 200 years after his death (and therefore c. 350 -150 BC), shows that the ancient Greeks knew the names of Britain and Ireland, and that there were a large number of islands around them: *"Beyond the Pillars of Hercules [the Straits of Gibraltar] the ocean flows round the earth; in this ocean, however, there are two islands, and these are very large, called Bretannic, Albion and Ierne, which are larger than those before mentioned, and lie beyond the Kelti;....moreover, not a few small islands, around the Bretannic Isles and Iberia, encircle as with a diadem this earth, which we have already said to be an island".* But they apparently did not know the names of any of the smaller islands.

One potential source for the names of the individual Channel Islands is the Antonine Itinerary, dating from the end of the 3rd century AD. This was prepared for the Roman Emperor Marcus Aurelius Antoninus, and it is a description of the main routes throughout the Empire. In one part, it lists a number of 'islands' to be found around the Empire, and there is a section within this on the islands to be found in 'the sea which separates Britain from Gaul'. There are many difficulties of interpretation of this text, which reads as follows:

"MARI OCEANO QUOD GALLIAS ET BRITANNIAS INTERLUIT

Insula: Orcades No. 3 Insula Clota in Hivernia, Vecta, Riduna, Sarmia, Cae-
sarea, Barsa, Lisia, Andium, Sicdelis, Uxantis, Sina, Vindibilis, Siata, Arica"

This is the fragile evidence on which it has been believed for centuries that the Roman names of Jersey, Guernsey and Alderney were Caesarea, Sarnia and Riduna respectively. The first point to note is that only two of the 'islands' in the list can be identified with absolute certainty, and that some of the names may not be islands at all. The two that are well attested are Vecta (i.e. Vectis - the Isle of Wight) and Uxantis (Ushant).

'Insula Orcades No.3' is said to mean 'three Orkney Islands'. The Orkneys are hardly 'islands in the sea between Britain and Gaul'! And which three? There are about 40 of them. 'Insula Clota' may be the River Clyde, or possibly the Isle of Arran. Clota may be in Hivernia, or Clota and Hivernia may be two separate places. Hivernia is presumed to be Ireland.

The Scilly Isles have been suggested for Sicdelis, but the problem here is that we have contemporary sources for the name of those islands as 'Scillonia Insula' or 'Silia Insula', neither of which are very like 'Sicdelis'. Moreover, 'Sicdelis' sounds plural, and we know that at the time there was only one island of Scilly – as reflected in the Latin word 'insula'. We also know that it had previously been called 'Ennor', which equally does not resemble 'Sicdelis'. In my opinion, the Sept Îles are more convincing candidates, especially as there appear to be only six of them.

'Sarmia' was almost certainly Sark, rather than Guernsey. The identification of Riduna as Alderney gains support from accounts of events in the mid 6th century, and the documented history of that period also supports the view that Andium (possibly 'largest'?) was Jersey, and that Lisia was Guernsey. So these identifications are relatively secure.

The first Vita Samsonis, probably of the 7th century, describes a visit by St Sampson to 'Lesia' and 'Augie' to raise a fighting force. The 12th century 'Life of St Sampson' by Baudri de Bourgueil, archbishop of Dôl, also refers to Lisia, and in the 14th century Chronique Briocense, which reproduces the work of Baudri, the text is amplified to identify the location of the island *("In Lisia insula* in partibus Neustrie situata") *("In the island of Lisia* situated in part of Normandy") (in some manuscripts, the name is spelt 'Lesia' or

'Lesiam').[7] Combined with the fact that local legend tells us that St Sampson visited Guernsey (which was allegedly still pagan), these texts suggest that Guernsey was Lisia.

A possible explanation of the name 'Lisia' is the Welsh word 'llys', meaning hall or palace, but there is very little evidence of Brythonic influence in Channel Islands place names, and it is hard to see what relevance 'hall' or 'palace' would have had, so personally I discount this. A rather more exotic interpretation is that Lisia is a corrupt form of Elysium, or the Elysian Fields, a place of the afterlife in Greek mythology. As we have seen, according to Homer, this was located at the western edge of the Earth, by the river Oceanus, and it was a place where the gods and heroes went to live after death. See Chapter 5 for a discussion of the possibilities.

With these identifications in place, the list in the Antonine Itinerary looks very much like a list of the islands in the order in which they would be encountered on a voyage from the Isle of Wight around Finisterre to the Bay of Biscay:

Vecta	The Isle of Wight
Riduna	Alderney
Sarmia	Sark
Caesarea	?
Barsa	?
Lisia	Guernsey
Andium	Jersey
Sicdelis	The Sept Îles
Uxantis	Ushant
Sina	Île de Sein

Vindibilis, Siata and Arica would then be islands in the Bay of Biscay, which need not concern us (Vindibilis is often assumed to be Belle Île).

The problem, therefore, is identifying Caesarea and Barsa. And the principal difficulty here is that there was only one island, the 'super Herm', between Sarmia and Lisia (see the map at 4.5). At a stretch the Ecrehous could have been included in the itinerary, but they were not really on the course from Vectis to Uxantis (being to the north-east of Jersey), and I do not find that identification persuasive. It is even possible that there was another island, now entirely submerged, at the Schôle Bank, but this would have been very small.

7 Para 21 of the Chronique Briocense and Vita Sancti Samsonis II, 25

Suggestions for 'Barsa' have been the Île de Batz (formerly known as the Île de Bas), or the Île-de-Bréhat. But these identifications would not fit the apparent travel order of the Itinerary. It seems to me that Barsa may have been the enlarged Herm, which would have been mainly low-lying, and I am then left struggling to locate Caesarea, obviously a place with Roman connections. Across all of the islands around Britain, the one that has produced by far the most archaeological evidence of Roman occupation is Guernsey, and specifically St Peter Port, where there was quite clearly a Roman town of some significance. It is therefore likely that Caesarea was associated with Guernsey, and, given that Lisia seems to have been the name of the island, it seems that Caesarea may have been the name of the town. It would at first sight appear odd to find a town on a list of islands, but there are several other anomalies in the list so this possibility seems plausible.

The doubts about this identification include not only the fact that St Peter Port is a town, rather than an island, but also the difficulty of fitting it into the list in the travel order of the Itinerary. This may be explained by the fact that most navigators approaching St Peter Port from the north would have rounded the southern end of the 'super-Herm' and headed back up the channel between Herm and Guernsey, rather than taking the direct route south through the narrow channel between Herm and Guernsey, which was rocky and shallow. So leaving Sark to port, the ship would have sailed a U shaped course around the south of Herm, to arrive in St Peter Port heading north, with Herm then on its starboard side and Guernsey to port.

Corroboration for some of the Roman names can be found in Pliny the Elder's Naturalis Historia, published in AD 77 – 79. The Chapter on Britain,[8] lists a number of islands said to be found around the British Isles, including some which lie *"between Hibernia and Britannia"*, one of which is named as Vectis (the Isle of Wight). Since this island clearly does not lie between Britain and Ireland, it suggests that some of the other places named on the list may also be found elsewhere.

Other islands on the list include Ricina, Limnus, Andros, Mona and Monapia. Mona and Monapia are almost certainly Anglesey and the Isle of Man. But Ricina, Limnus and Andros look like Riduna, Lisia and Andium, so Pliny appears to have mixed up some very different island groups. He also says that 'further down' are Samnis and Axanthos. Axanthos is probably Ushant and Samnis is perhaps the Île de Sein. Despite the strenuous efforts that have been made by writers down the ages to identify all of these as islands in the Irish Sea, I take Pliny's list as support for the identification of

8 Book 4, Ch.30

Riduna, Lisia and Andium as the names of the three largest Channel Islands.

There has also been conjecture about the name of the Channel Islands as a whole, and in recent years it has been broadcast far and wide that their name was the Lenur Islands, on the basis of the evidence of the Peutinger Table. As we have seen, the Peutinger Table is a 13th century copy of an earlier map, probably based on data from around AD 300, showing the main roads throughout the Empire.

It shows an island, between Britain and the Continent, which is ascribed the name "i.Lenur". The letter 'i ' could be an abbreviation for 'insula' (island) or 'insulae' (islands). And on the basis of this evidence, some writers have concluded that 'i. Lenur' is the Channel Islands. It is equally possible that 'i. Lenur' is the (single) island of Ennor, ie the ancestor of the Scilly Isles, before the sea flooded the central plain to make the present archipelago, but there are no other records of 'Lenur' to assist us. I am heartened that Richard Coates ('The Ancient and Modern Names of the Channel Islands, a linguistic history' 1991) shares my scepticism that the name has anything to do with the Channel Islands, but, despite the lack of evidence, the myth is becoming the reality.

So to summarise, I can now complete the Antonine Itinerary from the Solent to Finisterre, with a certain amount of conjecture, as follows:

The Isle of Wight	Vecta or Vectis
Alderney	Riduna
Sark	Sarmia
St Peter Port	Caesarea
'Super Herm'	Barsa
Guernsey	Lisia
Jersey	Andium
Sept Îles	Sicdelis
Ushant	Uxantis

The Scilly Isles were the Scillonia Insula, and I believe that they may have been referred to as the Insula Lenur on the Peutinger Table, after the older name of the island.

Chapter 6:
Decline and Fall (300 – 500)

6.1   The Crisis 250 – 300

In many senses the decline of the Roman Empire had begun long before the Crisis of 250 to 300, and indeed the decline of the Western Empire had already started when Claudius invaded Britain. But in north-west Europe, the Empire stumbled along, with occasional hiccups, albeit without major catastrophes, until about 250. Given the abysmal characters of some of its Emperors, this is a testament to the fundamental qualities of the Empire.

However, between about 250 and 300, there was a crisis in the Western Empire, with one convolution following another. Although the events of this period affected Britain less than the Continent, the whole region was unstable. The combined effect of these events may have been to reduce the population of Gaul to Iron Age levels, or even lower in the worst affected areas, and Britain is likely to have experienced a similar depopulation to a lesser extent. The crisis was the result of a collapse of social order within the Empire, as much as the external threats from barbarians seeking to plunder its wealth.

In 259, a Continental civil war resulted in the establishment of a separate Gallic empire, under Postumus, who was murdered in 268. Britain formed part of this empire, which survived until 273 when Aurelian put down the secessionists. However, order in Britain was not re-established for long, because there was a further revolt in the late 270s, which was put down by Probus.

In 275 to 280 a Frankish army penetrated 300 to 450 miles into Gaul, pillaging and destroying some fifty towns, possibly in alliance with disaffected Gaulish outlaws called the Bagaudae, whose uprisings happened periodically from the end of the 2nd century to the middle of the 5th century. It is traditional to regard the Bagaudae as dispossessed bandits, but they may have seen themselves as freedom fighters. At least some of them appear to have had knowledge of Roman fighting techniques, and they may therefore have been ex-legionaries.

In response, many cities in Gaul were dramatically reduced in size, and fortified against further attack. Rennes had previously covered 225 acres; it now covered just 22. Vannes had previously covered 100 acres; this was reduced to 13. Corseul, which had covered 250 acres, was replaced by a fortified castrum of 30 acres, and a nearby 'castellum' (on the site of La Tour Solidor), both at Alet.[9] The fortification of Alet took place in the period 270 – 280, roughly the period of the Frankish incursion, and a unit of the Roman army was thereafter stationed in the town.

In late 285 the Romans appointed a Belgic soldier called Carausius, a man of humble origins, to clear the seas at the eastern end of the Channel of Saxon pirates. Carausius had had some success in suppressing the Bagaudae, and seemed to be well qualified to command the Classis Britannica, the fleet based at Dover, Richborough and Boulogne. (The Classis Armorica protected the western end of the Channel). The ships used were galleys, as demonstrated by the discovery of part of a bulkhead from one of them on a beach at Tardinghen in the Pas-de-Calais. They were probably the fast, forty-oared scout ships called 'pictae', which were painted sea-green as camouflage, so they would have been used as interceptors rather than as a fleet designed to maintain long patrolling voyages.

However, Carausius was soon accused of being in league with the Saxons (it was said that he waited until the Saxons had completed their raids before capturing their booty, which he retained), and he was condemned to death. He escaped by fleeing to Britain, where he proclaimed himself Emperor, and it seems to me significant that a member of the Belgic Menapii tribe was accepted as a leader by the tribes of England. Two and a half centuries after the Roman invasion of Britain, there clearly remained strong connections between the Belgae and the people of England, probably including a common language. That the influence of Carausius extended beyond the south-east, to the borders of what I call Belgic England, is evidenced by an inscription of his name on a milestone near Carlisle. His 'empire' also included a part of north-eastern Gaul, and his coins were for a time issued at Rouen.

The Romans also responded to the threat of the Saxon pirates by building a system of fortifications on both sides of the Channel, called the Saxon Shore. The fort at Longis Bay in Alderney may possibly have been part of this chain of defences, which is mentioned in the Notitia Dignitatum of c.420. The nine British forts mentioned (using their modern names)

9 Pierre-Roland Giot, Philippe Guigon and Bernard Merdrignac, 'The British Settlement of Brittany' (2003)

are Brancaster, Norfolk; Burgh Castle, Norfolk; Bradwell-on-Sea, Essex; Reculver, Kent; Richborough, Kent; Dover Castle, Kent; Lympne, Kent; Pevensey Castle, East Sussex; and Portchester Castle in Hampshire. Some other forts which are not mentioned in the Notitia were also clearly part of the same system of defences – such as Carisbrooke Castle on the Isle of Wight and Clausentum at Bitterne, near Southampton.

There was a similar system of forts on the French coast, examples being those at Rouen, Cherbourg, Coutances, Avranches, Alet, Brest and Nantes, but apart from the castle at Brest, these were not built on the same scale as the forts in south-east England.   They were generally little more than defensive towers, whereas the British sites enclose significant areas of land. Some of these also seem to have been quite a distance inland (eg Rouen and Coutances), and some commentators have wondered whether the French 'Saxon Shore' actually meant 'the shore occupied by the Saxons'. But this is a minority view, and it is generally thought that the it was 'the coast fortified against the Saxons'.

After he lost Boulogne to a Roman force led by Constantius I, Carausius was murdered in 293. Constantius was a 'Caesar' (ie second in command and appointed successor) to the Western Roman 'Augustus' (ie Emperor) Maximian. Carausius was succeeded by his treasurer, Allectus, and coins minted by both are found in Belgic Gaul as well as Britain; so it appears that Allectus' influence in Gaul survived the loss of Boulogne.

In 296 Constantius, reinvaded Britain to suppress the breakaway state, in a fleet that sailed in two waves. One was commanded by Constantius and sailed from Boulogne, the other left from the Seine under the command of Asclepiodotus. Asclepiodotus landed In the Solent area and headed inland where he surprised and defeated Allectus.   Constantius sailed up the Thames and took London, which he then rebuilt, along with York and St Albans.

Roman activity in Guernsey appears to have diminished after about 300, and the circumstantial evidence suggests that piracy played a part. St Peter Port itself may have been attacked, and, indeed, pirates may have been the cause of the fire that destroyed the 'Asterix' in 280 – 286. Since Alet had just been fortified, the evidence suggests that there was an unresolved problem with piracy in this period.

6.2   The Division of the Empire, and Withdrawal from Britain and Gaul.

The Roman Empire reached its maximum extent under the Emperor Trajan (96 – 117), when it covered the area from Spain in the west to Iraq in the east.   With the primitive communication systems available, the administration and military resources of the Empire had become very over-stretched, and indeed the manpower resources of what was at heart a city-state, were simply inadequate to the task of maintaining control.   The rights of Roman citizenship, and various sub-categories of Romanisation, had been extended to select nobles in the conquered territories, but this was an inadequate response to the problem.   In 212 the Roman Emperor Caracalla issued an edict that all free men in the Roman Empire should be given Roman citizenship, and all free women in the Empire should have the same rights as Roman women.   This may have expanded the pool of potential Roman officials, but the communication problems remained.

The Emperor Diocletian created two separate administrations for the Eastern and Western halves of the Empire in 285, when he appointed Maximian a co-emperor to rule in the west.   Each Emperor (called an 'Augustus') had a second-in-command and appointed successor, called a 'Caesar'. Maximian was based at Mediolanum (Milan) and his Caesar was Constantius I. Diocletian ruled in the east from Nicomedia (now Izmit in Turkey), and his Caesar was Galerius. None of the principal players trusted each other very much, so Constantius sent his oldest son Constantine to the court of Diocletian, as a sort of hostage.

Diocletian retained responsibility for the overall constitutional structure, and he saw to it that Britain's government was reorganised in line with the wider arrangements. By 312 – 314, the country had been divided into four provinces, and the civil government had been separated from the military command.

Constantius had re-invaded Britain in 296 to depose the usurper Allectus, and he returned in 305 to launch another campaign against the Picts. Aware that the position of his son, Constantine, was precarious at the court of the Eastern Emperor, he sent a request to Diocletian that Constantine should be allowed to join him in Britain. Constantine obtained Diocletian's consent over dinner, when Diocletian was drunk, and fled from the court very early the following morning before Diocletian could change his mind. He then made his way via Boulogne to join his father in Scotland.

Whatever course the campaign in Scotland may have taken (and we have no details), Constantius had returned to York by the end of the year, evidently suffering from ill health. His son was at his bedside when Constantius died in 306. Galerius promptly appointed one of his relatives to succeed Constantius, but the late Western Emperor had declared that he regarded Constantine as his successor, and the Roman army in Britain duly proclaimed him as such (ie a full Augustus).

At some point, under the influence of his mother, Constantine adopted the trappings of Christianity. (It appears that he was only actually baptised shortly before his death, so some have regarded this as a political manoeuvre more than a conversion). The Roman Emperors had always been staunchly pagan, and, as we have seen, the Christians in the Empire had been subjected to occasional persecutions, particularly in 303. But in the Edict of Milan in 313, Constantine and his eastern co-Emperor Licinius pronounced a policy of religious tolerance, which particularly benefited the Christians.

However, in 320, Licinius revoked the religious freedoms promised in the Edict of Milan, provoking renewed civil war in the Balkans. The conflict was overtly religious, with each side fighting for its faith, and the Christian forces of Constantine were fired with religious zeal. Constantine was eventually successful and Licinius surrendered to him in Nicomedia in 324. Initially Constantine was merciful (responding to the pleas of his sister, Licinius' wife) and merely exiled Licinius: but the following year he accused him of plotting a revolt and had him hanged.

So Constantine reunited the Roman Empire under his sole command, and in 330 he established his capital at Byzantium, which was subsequently renamed after him. While the choice of Byzantium may appear strange to readers with a western perspective, the city was actually close to the geographic centre of the Empire, which stretched from Spain in the west to Mesopotamia in the east; and it was also equidistant from the Empire's most contested borders, in what are now Iraq and Germany.

With Constantinople established as the centre of power, Rome's standing declined, and the western part of the Empire came under increasing attacks from the north and east. The Roman body politic was riven with internal power struggles, which did not make the task of defending its borders any easier, and Pictish and Scottish (ie Irish) raiders began to plague Britain from the 340s onwards. The cost of defence, for example the maintenance of Hadrian's Wall, fell heavily on the ordinary people of Britain; and the economy began to collapse under the weight of taxation.

The divisions at the heart of Rome were illustrated by the revolt in 353 of a usurper called Magnentius, who was a commander of the Imperial Guard, against an unpopular Emperor Constans, one of the three sons of Constantine who had survived him. Magnentius attracted the support of the Roman provinces in Britain, Gaul, Hispania and Africa, and the suppression of his regime required the intervention of the Byzantine Emperor Constantius II.

In Jersey, a coin hoard dating from the period 290 – 354, has been found at Le Quennevais. This horde may be further evidence of early tax evasion, because history records that Constantius appointed one Florentius as Praetorian Prefect of Gaul in 357, and that when the revenues from the poll tax and land tax failed to reach the budgeted target, he took measures to impose special levies. Fortunately for the people of Gaul, the commander of the Roman forces in the west, Julian, opposed these additional charges and the Emperor Constantius overruled Florentius. But someone may have decided that this was a problem that was likely to recur and that he should take appropriate precautions!

In Britain the raids of the Picts and Scots intensified from the 360s, such that by then Roman-style civilisation was disintegrating. Villas were no longer being built or repaired, and the pottery and metalworking industries went into a steep decline. By the end of the century, iron nails were no longer being produced and in many parts of the country there were no working potteries. The countryside and suburbs declined first, leaving the city centres as the last bastions of civilisation. The centres survived, although considerably reduced in size, for another half century.

The attacks of the Picts and Scots reached their peak in the 367, when the Count of the Saxon Shore was killed. This prompted a response from Rome, and in 368, Count Theodosius arrived in England with four Germanic legions to restore order. This development presaged to some extent the 5th century British kings' employment of Saxon mercenaries against the Picts and Scots, and one can only wonder how many of the soldiers of Count Theodosius' army retired in Britain and raised Germanic families, long before the arrival of the Saxon hordes. However, those who remained on active service were not to remain in Britain for long.

In 383 Magnus Maximus, a Spaniard in command of the legions in Britain, gained a decisive victory over the Picts and Scots, and his army decided that he would make a better candidate for Emperor than the incumbent Gratian. Maximus took his legions to the Continent, leaving Britain substantially undefended, and they never returned. He defeated Gratian, who was murdered by one of his own officers, and thereafter ruled an 'Empire' comprising Gaul, Britain, Iberia and Africa, from his capital at Trier in Gaul. But a subsequent attempt to seize Italy was repulsed, and he himself was defeated by forces assembled by the Eastern Roman Emperor in 388, after which he was executed.

According to Breton legend, Maximus' legions from Britain were dispersed in Gaul to assist in the defence of the Empire. About 60 towns and communes in France and Germany bear names that testify to the presence of British military units – examples include Bretteville (Normandy), Bretenoux (the Lot), Bretoneux (Picardy), Breteuil (Picardy) and Brittenheim (the Rhineland). But particularly significant numbers of British troops seem to have been stationed in what is now Brittany, along the northern coast, and at Brest and Vannes. Whether these units arrived all at once or in a series of deployments we do not know, but it has been suggested that British pottery found at Alet and Pont Croix may indicate the route taken by some of the troops to get to their new quarters.

In Gaul, the Saxons remained a menace, but now other peoples from further east came pouring over the Danube and the Rhine. The first of the new wave were the Huns, who were nomads from east of the Volga River. They reached Europe in about 370, with an attack on the Alans, a Sarmation tribe, parts of which had settled in the Balkans. This precipitated a chain reaction of migrations, which was eventually to see some of the Alans settled in Brittany, and which developed into the 'Völkerwanderung' of the period AD 400 - 800.

The next to emerge were the Visigoths from Dacia, who asked the Romans for permission to settle on the south bank of the Danube in 376 to escape from the Huns. The Romans agreed to this because they thought that the Goths would be a useful source of mercenaries for the Roman army. However, the Romans then failed to provide the food and land that they had promised, and the Goths were driven to revolt. They crushed the army of the Eastern Roman Empire, and killed the Emperor Valens, at the battle of Adrianople in 378. This defeat signalled the end of Roman military dominance across the whole Continent of Europe, and the populations of Britain and Gaul would have realised that they could no longer look to the legions to guarantee their security.

A peace treaty was then concluded between the Visigoths and Romans, but after a period of mounting friction and provocation, the Goths invaded Italy and sacked Rome in 410. By that time, the Western Empire was governed from Ravenna, but Rome still remained the largest city in Italy, indeed probably the known world, so these events shook the Western Empire to its foundations. Subsequently the Visigoths moved into south-west Gaul and Spain, where we will next encounter them in their confrontations with the Franks.[10]

As the period of Roman rule in Britain came to a close, the economy went into a steep decline. In most of Britain, the depression was only indirectly caused by the raids of barbarians, but along the coasts the predations of the Picts and Scots must have caused significant local damage. Bede tells us that single legions were twice sent to Britain to expunge the raiders, but that the Belgic British had become weak and impotent: *"The Romans, however, now informed the Britons that they could no longer undertake such troublesome expeditions for their defence, and urged them to take up arms for their own part and cultivate the will to fight, pointing out that it was solely their lack of spirit which gave their enemies an advantage over them."* If they had not realised it before, the peoples of the Roman provinces now knew that they could not rely on the legions for their safety, and efforts were made to put city walls into a better state of repair, even in towns far from the coasts. Life in some British cities remained busy, as evidenced by the well-worn late 4th century streets of Bath, and by repairs to the city walls of Cirencester, but finds of coins are increasingly rare for the later years of the century.

Similar raids were experienced in the Channel Islands. The Plaiderie site in St Peter Port was destroyed by fire and rapid demolition at the end of the 4th century (leaving quantities of valuable goods in the ruins), which I take to be evidence of pirate activity. But trade across the Channel still continued, as evidenced by the late 4th century wreck of a ship carrying British lead, on the Sept Îles. The lead was presumably to be used for plumbing, so some infrastructure was clearly still being built, at least in Gaul, and the mining industry of the East Riding may still have remained in production. (The use of lead for plumbing unfortunately resulted in a large number of deaths through saturnism).

The ingots of lead from the wreck site are marked with inscriptions in Latin and symbols of the Iceni and Brigantes tribes.[11] No trace of the ship or its equipment survives, but it seems very likely that the ship was making for Le Yaudet, from a port of embarkation in or near the territory of the Iceni in what is now Norfolk. Whatever course it may have taken down the English Channel, the ship would have passed within a few miles of Guernsey, and

10 Note: There were two separate tribes called 'goths', the Visigoths (the western Goths) and the Ostrogoths (the eastern Goths). The Ostrogoths, originally from the area south of the Baltic Sea, built up a large empire between the Baltic and the Black Sea in the 3rd century, but were forced to submit to the Huns in 370. As a result, many Ostrogoth refugees settled in the Balkans, and some started to appear in Western European history in the 5th century.

11 In a strange twist of fate, some of the lead, which is now devoid of radioactivity after so long in the sea, is being used by scientists trying to identify Dark Matter. So the ship did not perish entirely in vain.

it is likely that Guernsey was its last port of call before disaster struck. As with any voyage up or down the Channel, the captain would have needed to wait in port for the favourable tide.

As the Western Empire collapsed, the Eastern Roman Empire remained substantially intact, despite the battering it had received from the Visigoths in 378. In 395, the Empire had been formally divided once more, and nominal Western Emperors were appointed. These may have had the title, but they were in practice little more than figureheads for a regime increasingly run by military commanders.

The forces attacking the Western Empire were of course pagans, but even within an increasingly Christian Roman Empire, there were considerable religious tensions. In particular, the church in Rome was much vexed by Arianism, which was a doctrine attributed to Arius, a preacher from Alexandria in Egypt (who lived circa 250 – 336). This held that Christ had not always existed but rather had been created by, and was subordinate to, the Father. This view was declared heretical by the Trinitarians of the Roman church, but Arianism attracted some prominent supporters (including the Emperors Constantius II and Valens). In the west, Arianism was dominant among the Christian Germanic tribes, and was only really suppressed after Clovis converted to the Nicene Creed in 496.

Another example of a schism in the church arose towards the end of the 4th century, when Britain became enthralled with the teachings of Pelagius, a Celtic monk born in about 354, probably in the British Isles. His doctrine held that there was no such thing as 'original sin' and that men were all perfectly capable of performing good works without any divine intervention – a view again condemned as heretical by the Roman church.

The Empire was crumbling, and in 401 Roman troops were again withdrawn from Britain to fight against the Visigoths. Roman coinage ceased arriving after 402, so the central authorities were not paying any forces left in Britain after that year. The discontent of the British led to a succession of short-lived governors, culminating in Flavius Claudius Constantinus in c.408. Bizarrely, he decided on a war of conquest and set off for the Continent with what was left of the Roman army in Britain. Neither he nor the army ever returned, and when, in 410, Honorarius told the British towns to look to their own defences, nearly four centuries of Roman rule had come to an end.

The La Plaiderie site in St Peter Port ceased to be used at the end of the 4th century, and the latest surviving trace of the Romans in the Channel Islands consists of two bronze Nummus coins, found in Guernsey recently. This type of coin, which dates from 395 to 403, is the last minted in Rome that is commonly found in Britain, so the find strongly suggests that the Roman influence in the Channel Islands died out at the same time as their involvement in the history of Britain, and indeed of Brittany.

6.3   Britain after the Romans

There are two views on the period from 410 to 600, which was the period when the Saxons settled in England.   The traditional view is based on the writings of early Welsh authors, who describe a forcible conquest of England, perpetrated by cruel barbarian invaders and resisted by heroic 'Romano-British' forces which were eventually forced into submission or driven into exile in Brittany.

The second hypothesis is that of a largely peaceful migration of peoples from north Germany and Denmark who settled initially in marginal land in a depopulated East Anglia, and who gradually over a period of centuries became the dominant power within England. This theory obtains support from the archaeological evidence of the period and from the genetic evidence of today.[12]

Perhaps fortunately, this book does not need to delve too deeply into this controversy, but my own view falls somewhere between the two extremes. The archaeological evidence does not present us with mass graves of slain warriors, but rather community cemeteries (such as that at Wasperton in Warwickshire) in which some people in c.500 were buried with the traditions of the indigenous British and some were buried with Anglo-Saxon grave goods. Moreover, there is archaeological evidence of a 'population retreat' in the east of England, where the reduction of land under cultivation suggests that the population may have declined by as much as a half in the 5th century. Bede tells us of the aftermath of the Roman regime in Britain, when even the pastors had *"given themselves up to drunkenness, hatred, quarrels and violence". "Suddenly a terrible plague struck this corrupt people, and in a short while destroyed so large a number that the living could not bury the dead."* So the depopulation may have been due more to disease, the collapse of Roman society, and the resulting liberation of the serfs, than to the actions of the Anglo-Saxons.[13]   And the genetic evidence we saw in Chapter 1 suggests strongly that the Anglo-Saxons were never numerically a majority of the population, except possibly, in eastern England, so the

12 For an exposition of this theory, see Robin Fleming's 'Britain after Rome', 2010.
13 See Chris Wickham, 'Framing the Early Middle Ages', 2005.

migration was not a mass displacement of the indigenous peoples.

However the immigration of perhaps 200,000 people over 150 years cannot have been accomplished without friction, even if the indigenous population of 3 – 4 million considerably outnumbered the migrant community, and clashes between the indigenous people and the 'incomers' must have occurred. The men of the period certainly got into fights, as evidenced by their mortal remains, and perhaps half of the Anglo-Saxon graves of adult males contain weapons, usually a spear and sometimes a spear and a shield. The spear is ambiguous, since it could have been interred to enable the deceased to go hunting in the afterlife, but the shield can only have been for his defence.

The evidence of the early authors cannot be ignored, but equally we know that the histories of the period have to be read with care. They often contain semi-mythical genealogies, designed to prove that the great men of the day were descended from heroes of the past, or even gods. Moreover, some episodes seem to have been 'borrowed' from other histories, and clearly the later authors were recording oral traditions that were centuries old. Even Gildas was writing a century after the first Anglo-Saxon settlements.

I have already expressed my view that the first Saxons settled in a region of Britain which was culturally 'Belgic', and therefore distantly of German origin. If this is correct, the people among whom the Saxons were settling may have had more in common with the Saxons than they did with the western Celtic tribes of Britain. However, the Belgae of England were 'Romanised' and Christian, in stark contrast to the Saxons, and the two nations were therefore quite distinct. So my starting point is that there were three nations sharing England in the Early Middle Ages: the Brythonic Celtic speakers in the west and north, the Belgic speaking Belgo-Romans in the centre, and the Anglo-Saxons in the east. I will explore the linguistic evidence of the outcome of the cultural competition between these three nations in Chapter 9.

There is a tendency to lump the first two of these groups together, as 'the Romano-British', but there was nothing particularly Roman about the Celtic west and I find this term unhelpful. The regions which most strongly resisted the encroachment of the Saxons were precisely the regions which had most strongly resisted the Romans, so they were the least Latinised parts of the British Isles. The vast majority of the migrants from the West Country and Wales who settled in Brittany spoke Brythonic, not Latin. Only the religious community and the elite in Wales had a command of Latin, and in the 5th century, Latin would have been much more widely spoken or at least understood in London than in Wales or Cornwall.

It was in fact the most Roman regions of Britain that appear to have most readily absorbed the Saxons, and this may have been due in part to a long tradition of recruitment of Germanic soldiers into the Roman army. It may equally be due to a degree of kinship between the Saxons and the Belgic inhabitants of the east – which perhaps found a parallel in the alliances between the Saxons and the Franks in Gaul.

The main war zones in Britain remained the northern border of England and to a lesser extent the borders of England with Wales (west of Offa's Dyke) and with Cornwall. These had been the classic zones of confrontation since the Roman conquest of England, and attacks by Picts on England had continued right up to the end of the Roman era.

Turning now to the conditions of life in the Britain of the day, it is very clear that the first Saxon settlers were arriving in a country which had been devastated by years of economic collapse and Pictish raids. Nennius, who will be properly introduced shortly, tells us that: *"The Britons were once very populous, and exercised extensive dominion from sea to sea."* Clearly they were no longer so numerous, and there is archaeological evidence of a significant decline in the population, particularly of eastern England, during the 5th century. This left a vacuum in agriculturally marginal areas of the country, and much of Britain must have been a wasteland. Robin Fleming ('Britain after Rome' 2010) writes: *"By 420 Britain's villas had been abandoned. Its towns were mostly empty, its organised industries dead, its connections with the larger Roman world severed: and all with hardly an Angle or a Saxon in sight."*

Into the eastern part of the country, Saxon peasants started to migrate from about the 420s, driven by poverty and overpopulation in their homelands. Part of the migrant community may have been warriors, or at least pirates who had decided to settle rather than raid. But we know that the majority of their dead were buried without military paraphernalia. Their skeletons reveal that the men lead lives of hard toil, and the women spent a lot of time crouching, doing domestic work, just like their British contemporaries. While many of the men had suffered wounds, these people appear to have been farmers more than warriors. Nor do their graves exhibit the kind of wealth that would be associated with an aristocracy, so there is no reason to suppose that the first immigrants arrived as a ruling elite.

We do have written sources for this period, but they are all non-contemporaneous and extremely partial. They cannot be ignored, but equally they must not be taken as gospel. We have three main sources for the events of the 5th and 6th centuries.

- The first is the 'De Excidio et Conquestu Britanniae' by Gildas, a British monk who lived c. 500 to 570. This is largely a polemic against the rulers of Britain and the sins of the population.
- The second is the 'Historia ecclesiastica gentis Anglorum' written by Bede, an Anglo-Saxon monk from Northumbria who lived c.672 to 735.
- And the third is the Historia Brittonum, a compilation of texts that is attributed to a Welsh monk called Nennius who lived in the 9th century.

The value of Gildas' work is limited by the fact that he was not so much interested in history as in prophesying the ills that would befall the British for their impiety (it has been aptly described as a 'whine'), but it is the most contemporary record for the period we are considering, even if it was written a century after the first migrations. Neither of the other two histories is a contemporary account, but it is thought that Bede had access to earlier records in the excellent library of his monastery in Jarrow, which do not survive. The Historia Brittonum, supposedly put together in the 9th century, is clearly and explicitly a compilation of material from earlier times. Indeed Nennius tells us that *"I have made a heap of all that I could find"*, but it is not possible to date the underlying material with any accuracy. So none of these texts are entirely reliable.

Gildas was a monk who was born in Scotland around the year 500, and who died on the island of Houat in Brittany in 570. Two biographies of his life exist which were written many years after his death, and which do not accord in every detail. But the general gist is that he was educated in Wales and was a companion of St Sampson. He became a monk and went to Ireland where he founded monasteries and churches, and from there he may have crossed to north Britain. He may also have made a pilgrimage to Rome, but he then chose a life of solitude on the wild and bleak Breton island of Houat. The Bretons induced him to found a monastery at Rhuys, the peninsula to the east of the entrance to the Morbihan, and it was there that he wrote his 'De Excidio'.

Gildas tells us of the *"groans of the Britons"*, a final appeal to the Roman general Aetius for military assistance made in the mid-440s. But this was the era of Attila the Hun, and the Roman Empire had other concerns on its mind; Aetius (who knew Attila personally) was in no position to support the British.

Gildas then says that a British king, who he refers to only as *"that proud usurper"*, foolishly invited the Saxons to Britain as mercenaries, and that the first three long ships were soon followed by others. The Saxons complained that they were not being given adequate supplies by their British hosts, and threatened to pillage the country, threats which they soon carried out. *"So that all the columns were levelled with the ground by the frequent strokes of the battering-ram, all the husbandmen routed, together with their bishops, priests, and people, whilst the sword gleamed, and the flames crackled around them on every side."*

This story is strongly reminiscent of the history of the Visigoths being invited to settle on the south bank of the Danube in 376, by the Emperor Valens, and then being denied the supplies that the Romans had promised them. This eventually resulted in the Roman defeat at the Battle of Adrianople in 378, when Valens was killed. Is it possible that the two histories had become confused in British folklore?

Some of the British were then, according to Gildas, driven into the mountains, some overseas, and some became slaves to the invaders.

"But in the meanwhile, an opportunity happening, when these most cruel robbers were returned home, the poor remnants of our nation (to whom flocked from divers places round about our miserable countrymen as fast as bees to their hives, for fear of an ensuing storm), being strengthened by God, calling upon him with all their hearts, as the poet says,--

"With their unnumbered vows they burden heaven, that they might not be brought to utter destruction, took arms under the conduct of Ambrosius Aurelianus, a modest man, who of all the Roman nation was then alone in the confusion of this troubled period by chance left alive. His parents, who for their merit were adorned with the purple, had been slain in these same broils, and now his progeny in these our days, although shamefully degenerated from the worthiness of their ancestors, provoke to battle their cruel conquerors, and by the goodness of our Lord obtain the victory."

So we must assume that this is what the Saxon encroachment looked like from the Celtic fringe of Britain, or at least from the Rhuys peninsula in southern Brittany. We learn that conflicts arose between the Saxons and the British, which resulted in a battle, which the British won under the command of Ambrosius Aurelianus.

Nennius laments that the British had thrown out the Roman authorities, and created the circumstances of their own insecurity: " *Thrice were the Roman deputies put to death by the Britons, and yet these, when harassed by the incursions of the barbarous nations, viz. Of the Scots and Picts, earnestly solicited the aid of the Romans. To give effect to their entreaties, ambassadors were sent, who made their entrance with impressions of deep sorrow, having their heads covered with dust, and carrying rich presents to expiate the murder of the deputies. They were favourably received by the consuls, and swore submission to the Roman yoke with whatever severity it might be imposed.*

The Romans, therefore, came with a powerful army to the assistance of the Britons; and having appointed over them a ruler, and settled the government, returned to Rome: and this took place alternately during the space of three hundred and forty-eight years. The Britons, however, from the oppression of the empire, again massacred the Roman deputies, and again petitioned for succour. Once more the Romans undertook the government of the Britons, and assisted them in repelling their neighbours; and, after having exhausted the country of its gold, silver, brass, honey, and costly vestments, and having besides received rich gifts, they returned in great triumph to Rome.

After the above-said war between the Britons and Romans, the assassination of their rulers, and the victory of Maximus, who slew Gratian, and the termination of the Roman power in Britain, they were in alarm forty years".

Nennius then says that in about 446, the British king Guorthigern (Latinised as Vortigern), no longer able to call upon the forces of Rome to assist in the defence of his kingdom, solicited the help of Saxon mercenaries led by two warlords called Hengist and Horsa. ('Hengist' and 'Horsa' mean 'stallion' and 'horse' in Anglo-Saxon, so this story is considered by some to be apocryphal). These reinforcements were apparently invited to settle in the Isle of Thanet, in Kent. But the Saxons soon realised how weak the Britons had become, and conceived a wider scheme of conquest. Nennius then continues:

"Vortigern then reigned in Britain. In his time, the natives had cause of dread, not only from the inroads of the Scots and Picts, but also from the Romans, and their apprehensions of Ambrosius.

In the meantime, three vessels, exiled from Germany, arrived in Britain. They were commanded by Horsa and Hengist, brothers, and sons of Wihtgils..... Vortigern received them as friends, and delivered up to them the island which is in their language called Thanet, and, by the Britons, Ruym. Gratianus Aequantius at that time reigned in Rome. The Saxons were received by Vortigern four hundred and forty-seven years after the passion of Christ, and, according to the tradition of our ancestors, from the period of their first arrival in Britain, to the first year of the reign of king Edmund, five hundred and forty-two years; and to that in which we now write, which is the fifth of his reign, five hundred and forty-seven years.

111

At that time St. Germanus, distinguished for his numerous virtues, came to preach in Britain: by his ministry many were saved; but many likewise died unconverted.....

After the Saxons had continued some time in the island of Thanet, Vortigern promised to supply them with clothing and provision, on condition they would engage to fight against the enemies of his country. But the barbarians having greatly increased in number, the Britons became incapable of fulfilling their engagement; and when the Saxons, according to the promise they had received, claimed a supply of provisions and clothing, the Britons replied, "Your number is increased; your assistance is now unnecessary; you may, therefore, return home, for we can no longer support you;" and hereupon they began to devise means of breaking the peace between them.

But Hengist, in whom united craft and penetration, perceiving he had to act with an ignorant king, and a fluctuating people, incapable of opposing much resistance, replied to Vortigern, "We are, indeed, few in number; but, if you will give us leave, we will send to our country for an additional number of forces, with whom we will fight for you and your subjects." Vortigern assenting to this proposal, messengers were despatched to Scythia, where selecting a number of warlike troops, they returned with sixteen vessels, bringing with them the beautiful daughter of Hengist. And now the Saxon chief prepared an entertainment, to which he invited the king, his officers, and Ceretic, his interpreter, having previously enjoined his daughter to serve them so profusely with wine and ale, that they might soon become intoxicated. This plan succeeded; and Vortigern, at the instigation of the devil, and enamoured with the beauty of the damsel, demanded her, through the medium of his interpreter, of the father, promising to give for her whatever he should ask. Then Hengist, who had already consulted with the elders who attended him of the Oghgul race, demanded for his daughter the province, called in English Centland, in British, Ceint, (Kent). This cession was made without the knowledge of the king, Guoyrancgonus who then reigned in Kent, and who experienced no inconsiderable share of grief, from seeing his kingdom thus clandestinely, fraudulently, and imprudently resigned to foreigners. Thus the maid was delivered up to the king, who slept with her, and loved her exceedingly.

Hengist, after this, said to Vortigern, "I will be to you both a father and an adviser; despise not my counsels, and you shall have no reason to fear being conquered by any man or any nation whatever; for the people of my country are strong, warlike, and robust: if you approve, I will send for my son and his brother, both valiant men who at my invitation will fight against the Scots, and you can give them the countries in the north, near the wall called 'Gual'.

The incautious sovereign having assented to this, Octa and Ebusa arrived with forty ships. In these they sailed round the country of the Picts, laid waste the Orkneys, and took possession of many regions, even to the Pictish confines.

In the meantime, Vortigern, as if desirous of adding to the evils he had already occasioned, married his own daughter, by whom he had a son. When this was made known to St. Germanus, he came, with all the British clergy, to reprove him.....*

Vortigern then retreated to Wales, where, on the slopes of Mount Snowden, he had a premonition concerning the future of his kingdom (the story includes the first reference to Merlin). He took refuge in various places in Wales, and perhaps further afield (see below). Meanwhile his son Vortimer (Guorthimer in Brythonic) took up the standard against the Saxons:

" At length Vortimer, the son of Vortigern, valiantly fought against Hengist, Horsa, and his people; drove them to the isle of Thanet, and thrice enclosed them with it, and beset them on the western side. The Saxons now despatched deputies to Germany to solicit large reinforcements, and an additional number of ships: having obtained these, they fought against the kings and princes of Britain, and sometimes extended their boundaries by victory, and sometimes were conquered and driven back.

Four times did Vortimer valorously encounter the enemy; the first has been mentioned, the second was upon the river Darent, the third at the Ford, in their language called Epsford, though in ours Set thirgabail, there Horsa fell, and Catigern, the son of Vortigern; the fourth battle he fought, was near the stone on the shore of the Gallic sea, where the Saxons being defeated, fled to their ships.

After a short interval Vortimer died; before his decease, anxious for the future prosperity of his country, he charged his friends to inter his body at the entrance of the Saxon port, viz. Upon the rock where the Saxons first landed; "for though," said he, "they may inhabit other parts of Britain, yet if you follow my commands, they will never remain in this island." They imprudently disobeyed this last injunction, and neglected to bury him where he had appointed.

After this the barbarians became firmly incorporated, and were assisted by foreign pagans; for Vortigern was their friend, on account of the daughter of Hengist, whom he so much loved, that no one durst fight against him. In the meantime they soothed the imprudent king, and whilst practicing every appearance of fondness were plotting with his enemies. And let him that reads understand, that the Saxons were victorious, and ruled Britain, not from their superior prowess, but on account of the great sins of the Britons:

God so permitting it.

For what wise man will resist the wholesome counsel of God? The Almighty is the King of kings, and the Lord of lords, ruling and judging every one, according to his own pleasure.

After the death of Vortimer, Hengist being strengthened by new accessions, collected his ships, and calling his leaders together, consulted by what stratagem they might overcome Vortigern and his army; with insidious intention they sent messengers to the king, with offers of peace and perpetual friendship; unsuspicious of treachery, the monarch, after advising with his elders, accepted the proposals.

Hengist, under pretence of ratifying the treaty, prepared an entertainment, to which he invited the king, the nobles, and military officers, in number about three hundred; speciously concealing his wicked intention, he ordered three hundred Saxons to conceal each a knife under his feet, and to mix with the Britons; "and when", said he, "they are sufficiently inebriated, cry out, "Nimed eure Saxes", then let each draw his knife, and kill his man; but spare the king on account of his marriage with my daughter, for it is better that he should be ransomed than killed."

The king with his company, appeared at the feast; and mixing with the Saxons, who, whilst they spoke peace with their tongues, cherished treachery in their hearts, each man was placed next his enemy.

After they had eaten and drunk, and were much intoxicated, Hengist suddenly vociferated, "Nimed eure Saxes!" and instantly his adherents drew their knives, and rushing upon the Britons, each slew him that sat next to him, and there was slain three hundred of the nobles of Vortigern. The king being a captive, purchased his redemption, by delivering up the three provinces of East, South, and Middle Sex, besides other districts at the option of his betrayers.

The story of a massacre at a feast recalls the treacherous slaughter of the Western Roman commander Odoacre and his senior officers, by the Ostrogoth Theodoric, at a feast in Ravenna in 493 (which we will come to at 6.8), the event that marks the end of the Western Roman Empire. Again, one cannot help wondering if the Roman history has been 'borrowed' by the British.

St. Germanus admonished Vortigern to turn to the true God, and abstain from all unlawful intercourse with his daughter; but the unhappy wretch fled for refuge to the province Guorthegirnaim, so called from his own name, where he concealed himself with his wives: but St. Germanus followed him with all the British clergy, and upon a rock prayed for his sins during forty days and forty nights.

The blessed man was unanimously chosen commander against the Saxons. And then, not by the clang of trumpets, but by praying, singing hallelujah, and by the cries of the army to God, the enemies were routed, and driven even to the sea.

Again Vortigern ignominiously flew from St. Germanus to the kingdom of the Dimetae, where, on the river Towy, he built a castle, which he named Cair Guothergirn. The saint, as usual, followed him there, and with his clergy fasted and prayed to the Lord three days, and as many nights. On the third night, at the third hour, fire fell suddenly from heaven, and totally burned the castle. Vortigern, the daughter of Hengist, his other wives, and all the inhabitants, both men and women, miserably perished: such was the end of this unhappy king, as we find written in the life of St. Germanus.

Others assure us, that being hated by all the people of Britain, for having received the Saxons, and being publicly charged by St. Germanus and the clergy in the sight of God, he betook himself to flight; and, that deserted and a wanderer, he sought a place of refuge, till broken hearted, he made an ignominious end.

Some accounts state, that the earth opened and swallowed him up, on the night his castle was burned; as no remains were discovered the following morning, either of him, or of those who were burned with him.

He had three sons: the eldest was Vortimer, who, as we have seen, fought four times against the Saxons, and put them to flight; the second Categern, who was slain in the same battle with Horsa; the third was Pascent, who reigned in the two provinces Builth and Guorthegirnaim, after the death of his father. These were granted him by Ambrosius, who was the great king among the kings of Britain. The fourth was Faustus, born of an incestuous marriage with his daughter, who was brought up and educated by St. Germanus. He built a large monastery on the banks of the river Renis, called after his name, and which remains to the present period."

It is believed that Faustus was the Abbé Faustus de Lérins, who went on to become the Bishop of Riez in 462. Faustus, a devotee of Pelagianism, is known to have been British, but no biography of his life survives. The Lérins are islands near Hyères in the south of France, which experienced an early monastic colonisation. Saint Honorat established a monastery on the principal island in 375, and a branch of this monastery was established on the Île du Levant at the beginning of the 5th century.

6.4 Guorthigern's Exile

There are literally dozens of manuscript copies of parts or the whole of the Historia Brittonum, and spellings vary from one to another. The oldest appears to date from the 10th or 11th century, but some date from the 12th. The most authoritative analysis of these is contained in J.A. Giles 'History of the Britons', published in 1838, and Giles prefers the spelling 'Guorthigern' to the more commonly used Latin version, 'Vortigern', for the name of the British king.

This section focuses of the part of the narrative when, having had the existence of a watercourse beneath the foundations of a castle he was trying to build revealed to him by a boy called Ambrose, Guorthigern decides to leave Wales. The Latin text as set out by Giles is as follows:

"Et arcem dedit rex illi, cum omnibus regnis occidentalis plagae Brittanniae; et ipse cum magis suis ad sinistralem plagam pervenit, et usque ad regionem, quae vocatur **Guunessi***, aufugit, et urbem ibi, quae vocatur suo nomine Cair Guorthigern, aedificavit."*

Giles translates this as: *"Then the king assigned him (Ambrose) that city, with all the western provinces of Britain; and departing with his wise men to the sinistral district, he arrived in the region named* **Guerneri***, where he built a city, which, according to his name, was called Cair Guorthigern."*

The location of Guunessi or Guerneri has not hitherto been identified, but some commentators have placed it in Gwynedd in North Wales or in the north of England. Various spellings of this place are recorded in the manuscripts, such as:

Guenesi	The Cottonian Manuscript
Guennesi	Corpus Christi College, Cambridge
Gueneri	The Vatican Library
Genness	The Vatican Library

Commentators have naturally focused on 'the sinistral district' as a description of the location of Guunessi, and clearly this means a western region. This has been assumed to mean a western region of Britain - hence the suggestion that it might refer to Gwynedd, or Nant Gwrtheyrn in northwest Wales. But these theories ignore the point that Nennius has just told us that Guorthigern had given away all the western provinces of Britain.

What we do know is that, in the 5th century, lots of people fled from Britain, and indeed specifically from Wales, in the face of the Saxon advances. And we know that they migrated to Armorica, now called Brittany. One of them may even have been Guorthigern's son Faustus. If *"the sinistral district"* was western Gaul, Guunessi could very possibly be Guernsey.

It is significant that the name of 'Guerneri' or 'Guunessi' is recorded in the Nennius manuscripts in two forms, which I can loosely categorise as the 'ri' ending and the 'ey' ending. The attested history of the name of Guernsey shows that it was consistently recorded in the 'ri' or 'roi' form until about 1100, and thereafter consistently in the 'ey' form. Examples are:[14]

Greneroy	1027-35	Restitution and donation by Robert the Magnificent
Greneroy	c.1040	Donation by William the Conqueror
Greneroi	c.1052	Document of Hugues, Bishop of Avranches
Guerneroi	c.1090	Charter of Néel II
Ghernesei	1168	Instrument ecclesiae Baiocensis
Gerneseie	1213	Wendover Chronicle
Gernesoy	1274	Letter of Prior of Mont St Michel

Wace (c.1105 to c.1175) calls the island Guernesi. Although originally from Jersey, he had been educated at Caen, so he probably knew some of the history of the Channel Islands in the period up to 1100 from both the Norman and the local sides. The oldest surviving manuscript of the Historia Brittonum dates from about 1100, so it is not surprising to find that most versions of the name in Nennius take the 'ey' form.

The 'ri' or 'roi' endings mean king or kingdom and derive from Celtic or Latin, and the 'sey' or 'si' endings mean island, and derive from Saxon or Norman, so we can see very precisely that a change took effect at the end of the 11th century. And we can guess why. When William the Conqueror died in 1087, he left the Duchy of Normandy to his oldest surviving son Robert, and the Kingdom of England to his younger surviving son, William Rufus. It might have been considered awkward for the Duchy of Normandy to contain within it a 'kingdom' of Guernsey, so it appears that, a few years after the inheritance, a policy decision was taken in Caen to change the name of Guerneroi to Guernsey, which in any case brought it into line with Jersey ('the island of Geirr' – a Norse personal name – according to Coates).

What this suggests, of course, is that the surviving manuscripts of

14 For a full discussion of the history of the name, see Richard Coates, 'The Ancient and Modern Names of the Channel Islands'

Nennius' Historia were transcribed in Normandy, for the education and benefit of the new rulers of England. And that in transcribing the text, the clerks made diplomatic amendments to the original, to make it acceptable to their masters. The fact that both the 'ri' and 'ey' variants are attested in historical documents relating to Guernsey, and are both found in the manuscripts of the Historia Brittonum, lends considerable weight to the argument that we are talking about one and the same place. To find one version of the name which is a near-identical match in both sources would be strong enough. To find both is surely more than a coincidence.

Indeed, this construction would explain the present name of the island of Guernsey, which is otherwise something of a mystery. It is clear that the Roman name for the island was something else, probably Lisia, and no one has produced a convincing theory to explain why, by the end of the first millennium, it had changed to substantially its modern form. The 'ey' element is easy, because it means island in the Norse and German languages – as in Anglesey, Bardsey, Brownsea, Mersea, Ronaldsay etc. But the earlier 'ri' variant is perplexing.

There are various theories on the meaning of 'Guern', the most commonly expressed of which is that it comes from the Old Norse word 'graenn', meaning 'green'. One problem with this is that the 's' in the middle of 'Guernsey' is possessive, and 'green's island' does not make sense. But the counter-argument is that this 's' did not figure in the name until the end of the 11th century, before which the name ended in 'ri' or 'roi', meaning kingdom. So, on that analysis, 'Greneroi' meant 'green kingdom', which seems almost as improbable as 'green's island', if only because it would be a mixture of Old Norse and Celtic.

A more plausible explanation is that 'Guern' is a personal name, or a contraction of a personal name, and Coates considers the possibility that it represents the Scandinavian name 'Grani'. However, having discussed the subject exhaustively, he concludes: *"It appears, on balance that Kendrick's hypothesis of Scandinavian origin is true only in a general way; the name consists of a word in the genitive plus ey "island".*" In summary, he found the name of the island problematic.

But if an English king was exiled in Guernsey, such a momentous event in the life of a small island might well have caused its name to be changed from Lisia in honour of the royal connection. And it is easy to see how 'Guorthigerneroi' could be shortened to 'Guerneroi' over a period of a few hundred years.

However one issue needs to be addressed: as we have seen (at 5.8), Guernsey appears to be the island that was referred to as 'Lisia' in Baudri de changed, why did Baudri use the old name, 700 years after Guorthigern's death? There are various possible explanations, varying from 'old habits die hard', to the fact that the 'Vita Sancti Samsonis' was written in Latin, so the use of the Latin name of the island should not be surprising. But I think that the simplest is that the 12th century 'Life' was based on earlier texts, including a 'Life of St Sampson' written fairly soon after the saint's death, and it preserved the ancient version of the name. We know for a fact that Guernsey was not called 'Lisia' in the 12th century (still less the 14th century), so in referring to 'Lisia' (if indeed he meant Guernsey), Archbishop Baudri was consciously using an archaic name.   Baudri clearly had older source material, perhaps dating from the 5th century, and used the old name, either out of ignorance or for literary effect.

It may also have been the case that early Breton authors were reluctant to honour the name of Guorthigern, especially in works celebrating the life of a Celtic saint who was driven abroad by the Saxons. But later on, the Bretons were inclined to take a more charitable view of Guorthigern. There is one other source on his life, the 'Vita Sancta Gurthierni', written by Juthael, a *'faithful layman'*, in the 12th century. This recounts various miracles performed by the now saintly Guorthigern, to justify his beatification.

And in respect of his exile, the Vita has this to say:

"Then they [Guorthigern and his mother] departed from that place, and from the banks of the river which is called Tamar, where they dwelt for a long time. Then came the angel of the Lord to him, saying: "Look toward the sea each day, a boat will come to you and you will enter it". By this [boat] they sailed, and brought the boat to land at a certain island and were there for a period of time. After this, an angel came to him and said "Go forth to the other promised place, which is called Anaurot".

Indeed, Saint Gurthiern came to designate this place as his own, remaining there continuously to the end of his days, performing signs and wonders both before and after [his death].

The angel of the Lord committed to him that whole region of Brittany in order that the whole domain of Saint Gurthiern, served Anaurot, because that city was chosen by God; and the angel promised victory in battle to all the rulers who observed this pact with Saint Gurthiern……

Concerning the acquisition of the remains of Saint Gurthiern, and other Saints, in the time of Abbot Benedict and Guigon the son of Huelin of the house of Hennebont, which were discovered on the island of Groe by Oedrio the monk.

Gurthiern's remains are here, who was king of the English. Who, if you will, held the kingdom of his father, but nevertheless, esteemed the contemplative life over the active, and in this regard, left his father and came in a small boat to the island called Groe, from which determination came many miracles...."

It is hard to recognize the Guorthigern of Nennius in this description, but the assertion that he was king of the English confirms that the Vita is talking about one and the same person. What we can glean from the Vita is that Guorthigern is said to have taken refuge on an (initially unidentified) island; that he then went to Anaurot (which has not been identified – possibly Alderney?); and that his relics ended up on the island called Groe (which is traditionally translated as the Île de Groix). The author then changes the story slightly and says that Groe was the island Guorthigern first went to.

I believe that this 'biography' generally supports the hypothesis that Guunessi was Guernsey, by stating that Guorthigern was exiled on an island, and that he had possession of Brittany. The place of exile was clearly not north Wales, in the view of the author of the Vita. Alneroi is an attested name for Alderney, which is very close to Anaurot, so it is possible that Guorthigern moved from Guernsey to Alderney, or indeed back and forth between the two.

In terms of archaeology, a late Roman era castle is known to have been situated at the Castel Church site in Guernsey, and another Roman fort still survives at Longis Common in Alderney, so there would have been ready-made castles for Guorthigern to use on both islands. But obviously that does not prove that he used them.

So, to summarise, the case for the proposition is that:

- The toponymic argument is persuasive, especially since both the 'ri' and 'ey' versions of Guernsey's early name can be matched to Nennius manuscripts;
- 'Greneroi' was probably somebody's kingdom, and no other plausible king has been suggested. Similarly no explanation has previously been advanced for the erstwhile 'royal' name of Alderney, 'Alneroi'.
- No other explanation for Guernsey's name is convincing.
- No other candidate for the location of 'Guunessi' is convincing
- The pattern of Celtic emigration from Britain to Armorica in the middle of the 5th century is an established fact (and Guorthigern's son Faustus is believed to have migrated to Gaul).
- The account in the Vita clearly associates Guorthigern with Brittany and with islands.

The evidence is very strong, if not conclusive, and, in my opinion, the probability that Guorthigern was exiled in Guernsey, and possibly later in Alderney, is above 90%.

6.5   The Bretons

The decline of the Western Roman Empire left Gaul a patchwork of city-states and provinces, under the control of a variety of powers. In the south-east, the Germanic Burgundians controlled the Rhône valley, and to their west the Visigoths ruled what is now the Languedoc and Spain. But north of the Loire, the decline of the Roman Empire left a weak Gallo-Roman regime in charge of a shrinking area based around the Seine valley, with its capital at Soissons. This area extended in the west to the Avranchin, and may have included the Channel Islands.

Apart from this province, all that remained of the Western Empire, outside Italy and Cisalpine Gaul, was a strip of the North African coast, west of modern Libya, and the eastern coast of the Adriatic Sea.

As we have seen, from around the middle of the 4th century, there was a military migration from Britain to Gaul, particularly into the northern coast of Brittany, the Côtes d'Armor. This concentration may have been the result of strategic planning by the Roman commanders, or it may have arisen because the two main ports of entry on the north Brittany coast were Alet and Le Yaudet. But in any case it is obvious that the people on either side of the western English Channel (which the Bretons still call the Mor Breizh – the British Sea) had been in close contact since time immemorial. As a result, the communes of Léon, Tréguier, St Brieuc and St Malo received a significant influx of migrants, and the area eventually became known as Dumnonée (after the Celtic tribe in Devon).

It appears that Brittany was exceedingly poor at the end of the 4th century, because there is an almost complete absence of finds of ornamental objects from this period (eg brooches, bracelets and buckles) in cemeteries west of modern Normandy. It may also have been partially depopulated by the ravages of the Saxons and the Bagaudae, so it is possible that the Britons were migrating into a largely unoccupied wasteland.

However, this was not the only part of Gaul to gain military reinforcement by British units in the Roman army. They were stationed along the north coast of Armorica, in locations from the mouth of the Aulne to the mouth of the Canche. In later Breton tradition, this military migration was associated with the removal of the Roman legions from Britain in 383, and it is known that these legions never returned. Of course, the soldiers in the British legions were not all Britons, but to the extent that they were recruited in Britain it is likely that they came from the north of England, where three of the legions were based. And it is likely that they were recruited from the Belgo-Roman population, and not the Celts of Strathclyde (who were as often as not the opponents of the legions).

This suggests that the late 4th century military migration to Brittany was very different to the 6th century migration of Brythonic speakers from Wales and Cornwall. Beyond the obvious fact that Roman soldiers must have spoken some Latin, it is likely that the mother tongue of these men was Belgic.

The Romans abandoned Brittany at very much the same time as they left Britain. We do not know exactly what Roman forces were left in Britain after Maximus took his army to Gaul, but the Notitia Dignitatum refers to units of the Legio II Augusta and the Legio VI Victrix stationed on the Wall or in York. It is likely that the old Legions had been broken down into smaller units, and these may have been redeployed elsewhere, or they may simply have dissolved when the units found they were no longer being paid. At any rate, the last Roman forces in Britain had disappeared by 408 at latest, and the last Roman legion left Brittany in c. 411. It is probably no coincidence that a British commander called Luomadus, with about 1,000 men, took Blois from the Saxons in 410 – it appears possible that his force came from Brittany, and that they then remained in Blois.

Even after the legions departed, the area which is now England appears to have regarded itself as at least allied to the dwindling Roman Empire, and in the middle of the 5th century it appears that the Belgo-Romans were sufficiently satisfied with domestic security that they could answer an appeal for assistance from the Roman Emperor. In 468 the Emperor Anthemius asked for British help to contain the expansion of the Visigoths in Gaul, and a British 'king' Riothamus (a title, meaning 'high king') took a force of 12,000 men to Berry. But before he could meet up with the Roman army he was supposed to be reinforcing, the Visigoths under their King Euric confronted this force at Bourg-de-Déols. The British were overwhelmed after a long battle, and a great many of them were killed. Some of the survivors fled into Burgundy and others may have settled elsewhere in Gaul, possibly including Bourges.

Before the battle, the British forces seem to have been a nuisance to the local population, because the Bishop of Clermont felt obliged to write to Riothamus:

"To his friend Riothamus

I will write once more in my usual strain, mingling compliment with grievance. Not that I at all desire to follow up the first words of greeting with disagreeable subjects, but things seem to be always happening which a man of my order and in my position can neither mention without unpleasantness, nor pass over without neglect of duty. Yet I do my best to remember the burdensome and delicate sense of honour that makes you so ready to blush for others' faults. The bearer of this is an obscure and humble person, so harmless, insignificant, and helpless that he seems to invite his own discomfiture; his grievance is that the Bretons are secretly enticing his slaves away. Whether his indictment is a true one, I cannot say; but if you can only confront the parties and decide the matter on its merits, I think the unfortunate man may be able to make good his charge, if indeed a stranger from the country unarmed, abject and impecunious to boot, has ever a chance of a fair or kindly hearing against adversaries with all the advantages he lacks, arms, astuteness, turbulences, and the aggressive spirit of men backed by numerous friends. Farewell."

The less charitable will think that the conduct complained of illustrates the age-old anarchy of groups of British youths on tour, but I prefer to think that it demonstrates the libertarian instincts of the mid-5th century British soldiery! What this episode most clearly shows, however, is that the British were not engaged in a mortal combat with the Anglo-Saxons in 468, and indeed that the country was free from Pictish raiders at that time, because otherwise a force of 12,000 soldiers could not have been spared for an expedition in France.

6.6   The Franks

The vacuum created by the slow collapse of Roman authority in northern Gaul invited expansion by the Visigoths in Aquitaine, who took control of the whole of south-west France up to the Loire, and the Burgundians in the Rhone Valley, who completed the isolation of the Roman province from Cisalpine Gaul.   But also, to the north-east of the Roman province, the territorial ambitions of the Franks were stirring. The Franks were a Germanic tribe, or rather several related tribes, who had been Roman allies since the time of Carausius. The 'Salian Franks' ('salty Franks') lived by the coast and the 'Ripuarian Franks' (riverbank Franks) by the Rhine. In the mid 4th century, they were settled some distance away from Roman Gaul, in what are now the Dutch and Belgian provinces of Noord-Brabant, Antwerp and Vlaams-Brabant.

But because the Romans employed significant numbers of Franks as mercenaries, they also effectively held territory in Gaul. The Notitia Dignitatum records that there was a garrison of Frankish mercenaries at Le Mans by the end of the 420s. Similarly there was a British enclave at Blois, also to the south-west of the Roman territory, which had been taken from the Saxons by a British commander called Luomadus in 410. These garrisons were on the front line of the Roman defences against the Visigoths, who had established themselves north of the Loire, but they were also defences against the Saxons who had established themselves in Orleans and on several islands in the Loire river itself.

In 444, the Salian Franks crossed the immense Forêt Charbonnière, which guarded the eastern boundary of Roman Gaul, and seized the cities of Tournai, Cambrai and Amiens, which they made their capital. Three years later, they sent an army across the Somme to mount an assault on the Roman capital at Soissons, 60 miles north east of Paris, but they were repulsed with ease. Clearly they did not yet have the strength to overthrow the Romans, but in making peace with them, the Roman commander Aetius confirmed their entitlement to the three cities they had previously taken. The Franks were now established in two areas, one to the north-east and the other to the south-west of the Seine Valley.

In 449, folklore has it that the throne of the Salian Franks passed to Merovech, a semi-legendary king, who was to give his name to the first dynasty of French kings – the Merovingians. As usual for this period, we know very little about Merovech. But in 451 he joined a coalition of forces (including the Visigoths, Burgundians and Alans), under the command of the Roman Aetius, to fight against Attila the Hun at the battle of Châlons. It is said that 300,000 men were killed at this battle (including the king of the Visigoths), but the Romans and their allies secured a victory that ended Attila's ambitions in Gaul. It is also said that there were Franks fighting for both sides, Attila having subjugated a number of Germanic tribes, possibly including the Ripuarian Franks. Defeated in Gaul, Attila then raided northern Italy, causing much damage but failing to take Rome The threat from the Huns was finally ended by a coalition of Germanic tribes at the Battle of Nedao in 454.

Nothing more is recorded of Merovech by near-contemporary historians. The first Merovingian king who is recorded in any detail is Merovech's son, Childeric I, who was born in c. 436 and who succeeded his father in c. 458. According to Gregory of Tours, his life was *"one long debauch"*, and he made enemies by seducing the daughters of his subjects.

This resulted in him having to flee for his life in the late 450s, whereupon the Franks appointed the Roman Aegidius (successor to Aetius) to rule over them, while Childeric took refuge with King Bisinus and his wife Basina in Thuringia. However, the Franks did not find life under Roman rule to their liking, and Childeric was recalled to the throne after eight years. He was soon joined by Basina, who deserted her husband.

So in the mid-460s, the Romans and their fœderati, the Franks and the British, were defending northern Gaul against the Saxons from the north and the Visigoths from the south. In 463, a Saxon raid up the Loire captured Angers, but Childeric expelled them the following year. Childeric then pursued the Saxons to the islands in the Loire which they occupied, and destroyed their bases in 465. The leader of the Saxons is named by Gregory of Tours as Odoacre, possibly, but not certainly, the leader of the Herules who went on to depose the last Roman Emperor in 476.

In 468, as we have already seen, a British force was destroyed by the Visigoths near Bourges, but the Visigoths were then in turn defeated by a coalition of Roman and Frankish armies under the command of Count Paul, the Comes of the Tractus Armoricanus (the military zone extending from the Somme to the Loire). Although Count Paul was killed fighting the Saxons the following year, this battle seems to have marked a turning point because in 470 Childeric took Orleans, Loches and Amboise, extending his control of the north bank of the Loire, where the Visigoths retained only Tours. And it also marked a turning point in Frankish international relations, because Childeric apparently now decided on a policy of 'divide and rule'. He entered into a pact with the Saxons, under which it seems the Saxons abandoned their ambitions in the Loire Valley, presumably in return for security of tenure in their communes along the north coast, around Bayeux and Boulogne.

Thereafter, the Saxons only appear in battles in France as allies of the Franks, or acting for one Frankish faction against another, and their territorial ambitions appear to have been diverted to England. It was this alliance, I believe, which sparked off the wars between the British and the Saxons, particularly after the arrival of a Saxon warlord called Ælle, with his three sons, in Sussex in 477.

One consequence of the treaty between the Franks and the Saxons was that a number of Alan horsemen formerly under Saxon command were resettled in Brittany, which explains the frequent occurrence of the name 'Alain' in Brittany today. It may also explain the later reputation of Brittany as a source of good cavalry. But the key point is that Childeric was able to direct the deployment of the Alans to the Côtes d'Armor, and therefore presumably exercised some degree of control in northern Brittany, despite the nominal authority of the Roman governors.

When Childeric died in 481, the Romano-Frankish alliance held nearly all of the territory north of the Loire, except for the British enclave at Blois and their territory in the western peninsula, including Nantes. The city of Tours was in Visigoth hands. The Notitia Dignitatum tells us that there had been Frankish laeti in Rennes earlier in the century, so the area of the peninsula occupied by the Bretons probably covered the territory broadly to the west of the present N137 motorway.

Childeric was succeeded as King of Tournai by his son Clovis I, in 481, when Clovis was just 15. Over the course of his life, and in a manner that would have been applauded by any Ottoman Emperor, Clovis systematically eliminated any threat to his lineage or authority from amongst his siblings and relatives. His main biographer, Gregory of Tours tells us that, towards the end of his career he remarked to his courtiers: *"How sad it is that I live among strangers like some solitary pilgrim, and that I have none of my own relations left to help me when disaster threatens."* Gregory comments that *"He said this not because he grieved for their deaths, but because in his cunning way he hoped to find some relative still in the land of the living who he could kill".*

Having disposed of his relatives in Le Mans, Clovis focused on the Romans, who had been under the command of Aegidius' son Syragius since 464. In 486, in conjunction with Ragnachar, the Frankish king of Cambrai (who Clovis later slew with his own hand), he defeated Syragius, and thereby became master of the Roman province in northern Gaul. Syragius fled into the land of the Visigoths and sought refuge at Toulouse, but after Clovis threatened the Visigoths, they handed Syragius back. He was imprisoned and secretly murdered.

Clovis then turned his attention to Burgundy, which he sought to acquire by marrying a princess called Clotild, a daughter of a deceased Burgundian king Chilperic. Clotild was a Christian, who lobbied hard to convert her husband (her arguments including the memorable line *"What have Mars and Mercury ever done for anyone?"*). And she eventually succeeded after Clovis won the battle of Tolbiac against the Alamanni in 496. At a moment of crisis in the battle, Clovis felt that his spontaneous prayer for divine intervention was answered and was so impressed that he decided to convert. He was baptised in Reims shortly afterwards into the Roman faith (at a time when most Germanic Christians were Arians), which meant that he acquired the support of the Roman Catholic Church, and eventually of Rome itself.

He went on later to defeat and subjugate the Visigoths in 507. But the focus of this book is on Guernsey, and specifically here on the fate of Brittany, which had a significant bearing on the course of events in the Channel Islands, so we need to return to 486. Back then, the Franks had two competitors in Armorica, the Visigoths in Tours and the Bretons in Blois and the Brittany peninsula. Clovis obviously calculated that it would be easier to deal with the Bretons first, but the presence of the Visigoths in Tours, on the north bank of the Loire, was an irritant. He managed to take the city for a brief period from 494 to 496, but the Visigoths then expelled Volutien, the Bishop that Clovis had installed. He retook it briefly in 498, but the Visigoths were only finally expelled in 507.

Brittany was ruled by a number of local 'kings' and had never formed a single autonomous territory. As we have seen, Childeric appears to have had some authority in the region, and Clovis no doubt believed that his defeat of the Romans had given him dominion over this area by right of conquest. But the Bretons were noted for their independent spirit, and probably had de facto control of the peninsula. The Bretons and Franks had been allies in the wars against the Saxons and Visigoths, but an old alliance had not stopped Clovis from defeating and killing Syragius. And although the Bretons were noted for their valour, they were not very numerous and Clovis would have been confident that he could reduce them to submission.

Procopius tells us that the Franks wanted to subdue the 'Arborykhes', *"who had become Roman soldiers"* because their *"territory was adjacent to their own, and they had changed the government under which they had lived for a long time".* This suggests that the Bretons had effectively declared independence from Roman Gaul. As a first step, Clovis drove the Bretons out of Blois in 490. He then set his sights on the remaining Breton territory; but most specifically he focused on Nantes, the gateway to the sea.

There followed a confrontation between the Franks and the Bretons over Nantes and the rest of Brittany, but unfortunately this is the least well-documented part of Clovis' life, and our most reliable source, Gregory of Tours, has nothing to say on the subject at all. But since Gregory was a loyal subject of the Franks, he can hardly be expected to be impartial in his accounts, and he would not have wanted to record the details of a Frankish defeat.

Procopius, writing in Constantinople, tells us that *"the Franks began to pillage their lands, then, very bellicose, marched against them with all their people. But the Arborykhes proved their merit and their loyalty to the Romans and showed in this war that they were very brave. The Germans not having won by force, considered it advisable to make friends with them and get closely connected."* Further detail is provided by the Abbott Dubos,[15] who tells us that Nantes was put under siege for two months by a Saxon called Chillon, acting for Clovis. Dubos dates the siege to a time a little before Clovis' conversion to Christianity, so before 496 (some consider that the baptism took place in December 499, but I do not agree with those, like Fleuriot, who say that it took place after, and as a condition of, the treaty with the Bretons). This is instructive, because we see for the first time that Saxons were now in the employment of the Franks as mercenaries fighting the Bretons, a development which continued into the next century. We also happen to know who was commanding the Breton forces at Nantes, because Eusèbe, count of Nantes had died in 490, and was succeeded by his brother Budic. They were both sons of the late Audren, a Breton 'king' who we will consider in more detail in Chapter 7.

But then Clovis suddenly stopped dead and signed a peace treaty with the Bretons, sometime between 496 and 499. Gregory of Tours is completely silent on the subject, and no trace of the treaty survives. The bare facts suggest strongly that Clovis encountered a massive and unexpected resistance, resulting in a heavy defeat and a mauling for his army. And as we will see in Chapter 8, it is possible that he was checked by Arthur. A by-product of the treaty was that the Bretons were reinforced by some of the remaining Romans in Armorica, who had evidently hung on in enclaves since 486. Procopius tells us that *"Other Roman soldiers were also garrisoned on the Gallic extremities to be watched over. As they had no way of returning to Rome, and did not want to surrender to their enemies who were Arian, they gave themselves up to the Arborykhes and to the Germans, with their military standards and the lands they had guarded before for the Romans".*

No one is quite sure where these lands were, but it appears likely that the 'Gallic extremities' were along the coast, and it is plausible that they were the remaining elements of the Tractus Armoricanus. There is also some uncertainty over the exact terms of the territorial settlement that resulted from this treaty, beyond the broad principle that the Bretons retained the lands formerly occupied by the Osismes and the Veneti. Some have speculated that the Bretons gained the lands of the Coriosolites, but I doubt that their victory over Clovis gave them that much bargaining power. However it does seem that the Bretons retained Nantes. Some early authorities (Pères Le Cointe and Ruinart) state that Clovis acquired Nantes

15 'Histoire critique de l'établissement de la Monarchie française', book III, chapter 24

in 511 (which seems unlikely, since that was the year of his death)[16] , but Gregory of Tours says that Nantes did not come under Frankish rule until 560, in the reign of Clotaire I, a date which seems more credible.

The distribution of Breton place names suggests that Clovis ended up in control of the lands formerly occupied by the Coriosolites, the Redones and the Namnetae (other than Nantes), and we do know that the Franks sacked Mont St Michel (which was a castle rather than a monastery at that time). If the ancient tribal boundaries were respected, Clovis then had control of the north coast of Armorica as far west as St Brieuc, and he also held Rennes, which is a disposition certainly consistent with subsequent events. But the later expansion of Brittany (in the 9th century) resulted in many Breton place names in formerly Coriosolite territory, so it is now difficult to discern where the boundaries lay at the end of the 5th century.

Quite why Clovis called a halt to his advance at this line is a subject we will return to later, but it is possible that he felt that he had more pressing concerns with the Alamanni. He fought a battle against them at Tolbiac in 496, and depending on the date of his treaty with the Bretons, this was either immediately after his campaign in the west or immediately before it. If the Battle of Tolbiac took place after the treaty, he may have been in a hurry to leave Brittany, having heard news of an invasion by the Alamanni. However, his apparently generous treatment of the Bretons was in marked contrast to his behaviour elsewhere in Gaul, especially in that the Bretons were not required to pay tribute to Clovis (according to Procopius), confirming their status as allies rather than subjects of the Franks.

From the perspective of the Channel Islands, the result of these events was that the Islands were now surrounded on the east and south coasts of the Bay of St Malo by territory under Frankish rule. The Bretons remained in control of the west side of the Bay, but had probably lost their territory east of St Brieuc. In practice this meant that virtually all of the commercial relationships of the Channel Islands with Gaul were now with Frankish controlled towns, and this must have had an effect on the language spoken in the Islands.

There is today a small minority of people in Brittany and lower Normandy (about 10,000) who speak Gallo, a Gallo-Romance language, which is vaguely similar to Dgernesiais and Jerriais, the French dialects spoken today in the Channel Islands, but without the Norman influence. Originally the centre of the population that spoke this language was Le

16 Nicolas Travers, 'Histoire civile, politique et religieuse de la ville et du comté de Nantes'

Mans, so we can assume that Gallo-Roman was the language spoken by the Franks. Increasingly, from 500 onwards, the Islands would have been exposed to this language, and I believe they had adopted it within a few centuries. The origins of the local languages therefore, in my view, predate the Normans.

While the Islands would have had increasing contacts with the Bretons, who became Brythonic speakers with the immigrations of the 6th century, I do not believe that Brythonic had any influence over the languages spoken in the Islands. There is certainly almost no evidence of early Brythonic influence in Channel Islands place names. The cultural influence of the Bretons in the Channel Islands was largely confined to matters of religion, and developed from the mid-6th century onwards.

After defeating the Visigoths, Clovis was appointed a Roman Consul by the Emperor Anastasius in 508, which would have legitimised his entitlement to the former Roman province, probably including the Channel Islands. But we do not know to what extent, he exercised his dominion over them. We learn of a Comes Insularum (Count of the Islands) in the 6th century, so it appears that some kind of administrative regime was put in place, and, as we shall see, at that time the Frankish kings obviously considered themselves entitled to make dispositions concerning the Islands. So we must conclude that after c.500, the Islands had become a very small part of a very extensive Frankish kingdom.

By the end of his life, Clovis ruled essentially the whole of modern France, except for Burgundy (under the control of the Burgundians), the Mediterranean coast (under Visigoth rule with Ostrogoth support) and Brittany. And the Frankish empire extended north east to include modern Belgium, and into the lands east of the Rhine, including parts of Frisia and the Ruhr Valley in modern Germany. But on his death in 511, Clovis divided this kingdom between his four sons and thus precipitated a period of civil war, which was perpetuated with brief interludes until the end of the Merovingian dynasty, in 751. After the 'partage' of the empire, the Channel Islands formed part of the kingdom of Neustria, of which the capital was Paris, under King Childebert I.

6.7   The Saxons

As we saw in Chapter 5, Saxon pirates had been raiding the coasts of Britain since the 2nd century, resulting in the creation of the Saxon Shore defences in the late 3rd century. They had then started to settle in the east of the country from the 420s (or if the early authors are to be believed, from c.446 -449).

They had similarly raided the coasts of Gaul, and from c.370 there were two sections of the Saxon Shore defences along the northern coast of France. The western part of these defences was called the Tractus Armoricanus. However, at much the same time, other Saxons were being settled as fœderati along the northern coast of Gaul. A cemetery at Vron in Picardy contains remains of people assumed to be Saxons, dating from the 4th and 5th centuries, and colonies are known to have been established in places like Boulogne and Bayeux. There are several places in France with Saxon names (ie with typical –thun (-ton), –ing, or –ham endings) in Normandy, and especially near Boulogne. Examples are Alincthun, Verlincthun, Pelingthun, Cottun, Ouistreham ('oyster village') and Etreham, but some of these may date from later periods of settlement. The Saxons at Ponthieu preserved elements of their native culture until the first half of the 6th century.

Like the later Vikings, some Saxons took to making raids up the river Loire, and in 463 they actually held the town of Angers for a year. After they had been driven out of the Loire by Clovis, it seems that he agreed to allow them to remain in their northern enclaves provided they desisted from their territorial ambitions on the Loire. There was a Saxon presence at Frénouville, Hérouvillette, Giberville and St Martin-de-Fontenay in Normandy. And by the end of the century they were allies of Clovis against the Bretons. Saxons from Gaul who still harboured territorial ambitions may now have turned their attention to Britain, because further waves of Saxons were arriving in Essex and Sussex at this time.

The first Anglo-Saxon settlements in England were the southern colonies in Kent and Sussex, and the eastern colonies in Essex and the former territory of the Iceni in Norfolk and Suffolk. But around 480, Angles started to settle north of the Wash in the areas north and south of the Humber River. The Lincolnshire villages of Winteringham and Winterton, on the banks of the Humber, were named after one of the first Angle kings, Winta. These people called themselves the Lindisware. And a separate tribe of Angles called the Spaldingas were settled in what is now called the South Holland district of Lincolnshire, on the western shore of the Wash. These Angles were politically distinct from the Angles north of the Humber, who formed the kingdom of Deira. The extent of the Anglo-Saxon penetration into England in the mid-5th century may be evidenced by the Anglo-Saxon cemetery of that period at Kettering, about 20 miles north-east of Watling Street.

At around this time, all the Anglo-Saxon tribes south of the Humber seem to have coalesced under the leadership of Ælle, King of the South Saxons, because Bede tells us that he was the first 'high king' of the Saxons, the 'bretwalda'. Significantly, the second was Caelin, King of the West Saxons who died c.593, so there was a gap of about 60 years between the first two high kings. The Saxons of the 5th and 6th centuries have left us no written records, but the Anglo-Saxon Chronicle, written in c.890, records three events relating to Ælle. In approximately 477 he came to England with 3 sons, and fought with the British, slaying many of them. He is again recorded as fighting against the British in 485, and in 491 Ælle and Cissa, one of his sons, besieged Pevensey Castle in West Sussex and slew every person in the Castle. After that, there is no further record of him and no record of his death.

So Ælle certainly embarked on a war of expansion against the indigenous population, and we know from Nennius and other sources that this first 'Anglo-Saxon war' ended when the native British won a battle at Mount Badon ('Mons Badonicus') at the end of the century. Nennius records 12 battles of this period in which he says the British were led by Arthur, of which Mount Badon was one, but as we shall see I am not convinced that all of these battles took place in Britain. Some have speculated that Ælle may have been the Saxon leader at Mount Badon,[17] while others reject this idea.[18] But a date of 493 for the battle, as recorded by Bede, would be entirely consistent with the elimination of Ælle at this time.

To understand the events of this period, and to locate some of the battles that were recorded by Nennius, we need to assess the political situation. From Ælle's perspective, his 'empire' in the south was divided from the other Anglo-Saxon enclaves by Belgo-Roman London, at the end of a broad peninsula of land from the west, and the tribes in East Anglia were divided from the tribes in Lincolnshire by the marshes around the Wash, notwithstanding that the Spaldingas had found some habitable areas on the higher ground. The Anglo-Saxons were probably not yet strong enough to take London, but a surge of new immigration into the Anglo-Saxon colonies in the east and south-east was putting pressure on their land resources, and stimulating expansionary ambitions in the east Midlands and Lincolnshire.

Lincoln itself was the Roman city of Lind Colun, and like all other Roman cities in Britain it had fallen into decay by the early 5th century. A mass of 4th century British belt buckles found there testify to its former importance, and an absence of early Anglo-Saxon cemeteries around the city suggest

17 James Bradbury - The Routledge Companion to Medieval Warfare, (2004)
18 Philip Warner – British Battlefields; The Midlands, (1972)

that it remained a Belgo-Roman settlement for some time after the Angles had settled in the surrounding countryside. But by c.480, the Angles had a small cemetery on the east side of what is now Middle Street, and the city was clearly falling under Angle control. So the focus of Ælle's attentions would have been to consolidate the Anglo-Saxon dominion over the county, and to expand the territory of the colonies eastwards in order to establish a secure land bridge through Cambridgeshire and Northamptonshire, connecting Lincolnshire with Norfolk and Suffolk.

It is in these areas that we are most likely to find the sites of the battles between the British and the Anglo-Saxons of the late 5th century. We will see (in 7.1) that, according to Nennius, four of the battles fought by Arthur were fought on the 'River Dubglas' in *"regione Linnuis"* and a fifth was fought on the River Glein. These were his first battles, and, as in his other battles, Arthur is reported to have been victorious in all of them. 'Linnuis' may well be the area now called Lindsey, the area around Lincoln, and there is a river Glen in Lincolnshire, in the land settled by the Spaldingas. My assessment of the Arthurian legends follows in the next chapter, but if he or any other British leader did win some battles in Lincolnshire early in the war, it would appear from the archaeological record that he did not succeed in holding back the tide of Anglo-Saxon colonisation, which continued to consolidate its hold on the eastern counties.

With regards to Mount Badon, this is the battle for which we have by far the most historical evidence, although the connection with the shadowy Arthur remains tenuous. Gildas dates the battle to 44 years and one month after the arrival of the first Saxons, but this only suggests a date at the end of the 5th century or the beginning of the 6th. The Venerable Bede says it took place in 493, but the Annales Cambriae say 516 (which is certainly too late). For reasons that will become apparent later, I support the date provided by Bede, the most reliable of our historical sources.

Gildas described the battle as a siege (*'obsessio'*), which suggests it was fought at a castle, and 'Mons' clearly means it was on a hill. We are told the battle lasted three days (according to the Annales Cambriae) but this is no real help, beyond suggesting that the site was readily defensible. More usefully, it seems that the British leader may have been Ambrosius Aurelianus, a Roman, and while it is not impossible that a Roman leader would have been commanding an army in the Celtic west, I think it is more likely that the battle was fought in Belgic British territory, notwithstanding that the 'Romans' may well have had support from Celtic British allies.

As to the location, various suggestions have been put forward: Badbury near Swindon, Badbury Rings in Dorset, Solsbury Hill near Bath, or Bardon

Hill in Leicestershire all have their supporters.[19]   However, all of these, with the exception of Bardon Hill, seem to me too far to the west, and therefore remote from the probable zone of conflict. Advocates of Bardon Hill point out that there is a nearby field called Battle Flat, but the problems with this identification are (a) that there is no evidence of fortification of the hill and (b) Battle Flat appears to have been the site of a skirmish in the English Civil War of the 17th century.

I suggest that the site of the battle may have been Arbury Hill, near Badby in Northamptonshire. The hill, which is 738 ft high, is surmounted by the vestiges of Iron Age earthworks consisting of a square single embankment and ditch, with sides about 200 metres in length. It is situated just to the west of Watling Street, which may well have been a British line of defence against the Anglo-Saxons, possibly in conjunction with the upper reaches of the River Trent. (Incidentally, central and southern Northamptonshire were historically within the territory of the Belgic Catuvellauni).

Arbury Hill was called Badden Byrig in a charter of 944, by which King Edmund I gave lands to Bishop Aelfric of Hereford. 'Byrig' is an Old English word meaning 'fortified place', an ancestor of the word 'bury', sometimes used to describe ancient earthworks. For example Aylesbury was originally Aegelesbyrig and Canterbury was originally Cant-wara-byrig, the burgh of the men of Kent. But 'byrig' also appears to be related to the Celtic word 'berg', meaning mountain and it is not hard to see how an earlier name of 'Badden Berg' (literally Mount Badon) could have been recorded as Badden Byrig in 944. The word 'bury' also appears in the names of various places in the valley of the Oise, northern France, and in Belgium, eg Bury in Tournai and Bury at Margency in the Oise Valley.

One factor which I regard as supportive of this identification is that the earthworks at Arbury Hill have been virtually erased, to the point that its identification as a hillfort was disputed by a Royal Commission in 1981, which thought that the earthworks were medieval or a natural feature. However these interpretations are inconsistent with the fact that the site was referred to in the charter of 944. Archaeologist Alexander Kidd lists the site as "undated hillfort?" (www.le.ac.uk/ulas/publications/documents/19nh!stmill_000.pdf)) and Alison Deegan and Glenn Foard write *"The hillforts at Arbury Hill, Castle Yard, Hunsbury and Crow Hill are each situated in elevated positions overlooking the Nene Valley".[20]* An important consideration is that, wherever Mount Badon was located, within about 50

---

19 For a full discussion of the main theories, see Mike Ashley, 'A Brief History of King Arthur' (2005).

20 'Mapping Ancient Landscapes in Northamptonshire', (2008), p.94.

years of the battle, the site was in the possession of the Anglo-Saxons. It is hardly likely that they would have preserved a monument to their greatest defeat, and there is every reason to suppose that they would have razed it to the ground.

Incidentally, it is also curious that there appear to have been at least two high hills in central England called Bardon/Badden. There is also a Barden Village, Barden Fell and Barden Moor in the Craven District of North Yorkshire, and a Barden near Skipton in the West Riding. This suggests to me that this word had a specific meaning that is now lost, especially as Badon is a region in Wallonia, Belgium. Of course, the word 'baden' meant bath in Latin, which explains many Baden place names (such as Baden-Baden in south-west Germany, Baden in the Morbihan, Brittany and Baden in Switzerland), but the word in this context does not appear to come from the Latin. Various suggestions for the origin of the English names have been put forward, from 'bear's den' to the Anglo-Saxon 'beow denu' ('valley of barley'), but these seem unconvincing to me. 'Badan' in Gaelic means grove or thicket, which would seem to me a more hopeful starting point.

At any rate, wherever the battle took place, conflict between the Britons and the Saxons seems to have come to a temporary end, around the year 500, and thereafter there appears to have been peace for a generation. Ælle and his sons disappeared from the record, and, according to Bede, no other Saxon chief was acknowledged as 'bretwalda' until Caelin in the second half of the 6th century. All the evidence points to a crushing defeat, which left the Anglo-Saxons temporarily impotent to pursue their territorial ambitions. We will consider the legendary aspects of the events of this period in more detail in Chapter 7, but for the time being I have endeavoured to confine this analysis to the historical evidence.

6.8   The End of the Western Empire

The Empire was formally split into two in 395, and from then on, although Western Emperors were appointed, they were mere figureheads for military regimes under the control of generals. Rome had been sacked by the Visigoths in 410, who went on a three-day rampage through the city, and the authority of the Romans throughout the Empire had been greatly diminished as a result. Over the next half century, its decline gathered pace, but as Edward Gibbon wrote in 'The Decline and Fall of the Roman Empire', this is not something that should surprise us:

"The decline of Rome was the natural and inevitable effect of immoderate greatness. Prosperity ripened the principle of decay; the cause of the destruction multiplied with the extent of conquest; and, as soon as time or accident had removed the artificial supports, the stupendous fabric yielded to the pressure of its own weight. The story of the ruin is simple and obvious: and instead of inquiring why the Roman Empire was destroyed we should rather be surprised that it had subsisted for so long."

A succession of weak Emperors brought only dishonour and contempt onto Rome, while the Eastern Emperors were constantly manipulating and interfering in Roman politics. The indignity of the sacking of the city by the Visigoths in 410 was exacerbated 45 years later. The Vandals were another eastern German tribe who in 429 migrated to Africa and conquered the Roman provinces there. From Africa they launched invasions of Malta, Sicily and the Balearic Islands, and they then invaded Italy from the south, sacking Rome in 455.

But international trade continued through the period of political disintegration, and it is possible that the former provinces still considered themselves 'Roman', even after the departure of the legions. In particular, the Celtic trade routes along the Atlantic coast appear to have survived, because Mediterranean pottery of the period from 450 to 550 has been found in the west of England.[21]

The Eastern Empire was itself attacked, particularly by the Huns who crossed the Danube and ravaged the Balkans from 443, but it survived in one form or another for a thousand more years until the fall of Constantinople in 1453. The Huns were repelled from the gates of Constantinople probably around 445, and were then bought off at great expense, to induce them to leave the area.

After the chaos of the first three quarters of the 5th century, a general called Odoacre (a leader of the Germanic Herules, who were Roman fœderati) deposed the Western Roman Emperor Romulus in 476, and sent the imperial regalia to the Eastern Roman Emperor. This is possibly the same Odoacre who the Franks encountered leading Saxons on the Loire in 465, but we cannot be certain of this. Being a barbarian, Odoacre was not able to take the imperial throne himself, but the Eastern Emperor was forced to recognise his de facto authority, at least temporarily. He is sometimes referred to as a 'king' of the Romans, but no contemporary use of that title is recorded. On the other hand, he was not the Germanic invader

---

21 J W Hayes, 'Late Roman Pottery', 1972.

that some claim, but rather a member of the Roman military establishment, despite being a barbarian married to a Visigoth. He even tried to maintain the fiction of a continuing Western Empire, ruling initially in the name of the nominal Emperor Nepos, from 476 and then after the death of Nepos in 480, in the name of the Emperor in the East.

The Eastern Roman Emperor Zeno eventually decided to depose him, and approved an invasion of Italy by Ostrogoths, who were by then Roman fœderati, led by Theodoric. This resulted in a treaty between the Ostrogoths and the Romans, which the Ostrogoths treacherously breached in 493. Odoacre and his senior officers were massacred at a 'celebratory feast' in Ravenna, and at the same time the Ostrogoth army killed the Roman soldiers in the city. Theodoric was then appointed a Roman Consul by Zeno, but the Western Empire was in reality finished.

Chapter 7:
The Arthurian Legends

7.1   Did Arthur Exist?

No discussion of this period of history would be complete without a reference to the Arthurian legends, which are persistent in the cultures of Britain, Ireland and Brittany and therefore certainly have their origins in the Insular Celtic tradition. Arthur is supposed to have been a British leader of the late 5th and early 6th centuries, who fought against the Saxons. Because of the extreme paucity of evidence for his life, some historians have dismissed the Arthurian legends as being of no historical value, and those who accept that he was a historical figure do so mainly on the 'no smoke without fire' principle.

Various semi-historical or legendary characters have been suggested for the identity of Arthur, but none of these identifications are persuasive. An example is an Arturius of Dalriada who was killed in a battle in the region of Camloden, possibly a fort on Hadrian's Wall, in about 590. However, this date does not agree with the supposed date of the Battle of Camlann, and most commentators reject this 'northern Arthur' theory.

Arthur is not mentioned by Gildas, the only near contemporary writer on the 5th century. But Caradoc (in his 'Vita Gildae') tells us that Arthur killed Hueil, Gildas' brother, who was leading raids on northern Britain from Scotland (presumably from Strathclyde, unless Hueil was a Pict). Following this slaying, Arthur had to beg for Gildas' pardon. So it has been suggested that the rather sour Gildas was deliberately ignoring Arthur as a result of a family feud. But I think there is a simpler explanation for why Arthur was fighting a Celtic British warrior leading raids from Strathclyde, and indeed why he was, according to the legends, mortally wounded fighting a later battle at Camlann (assumed to be in Cornwall): he was a Belgo-Roman. This would explain why Arthur is barely mentioned in the annals of the contemporary Welsh scribes.

Arthur's name is likely to come from the Latin surname 'Arturius' (and probably not from the Latin name of the star Arcturus, though this would not affect my argument), which strongly suggests he was from a Roman family. According to legend, his grandfather was Constantus or Constantine, clearly a Roman name, and his father was Uther Pendragon. If 'Uther Pendragon' is the Welsh 'Yther Pendragwn', it means 'Terrible Head Dragon', which is a title, not a name.

The earliest written source which refers to Arthur is the Historia Brittonum, attributed to Nennius, who wrote of Arthur's rise to prominence after the death of Vortigern: *"Then it was, that the magnanimous Arthur, with all the kings and military force of Britain, fought against the Saxons. And though there were many more noble than himself, yet he was twelve times chosen their commander, and was as often conqueror."*

It is notable that the Historia describes Arthur as a *dux bellorum*, a war leader, but not a king, and tells us that there were *"many more noble than himself"*. This suggests that Constantus or Constantine was not a king, as Geoffrey of Monmouth claims. But Constantine must have been quite a common name among the Belgo-Roman aristocracy of the 5th century, having been the name of the Emperor and former commander of the British army, Constantine the Great (272 – 337). That most illustrious Constantine was succeeded by his son Constans (323 – 350), who was murdered by troops acting for the usurper Magnentius.

The legends tell us that Arthur's grandfather, Constantine was succeeded by his son Constans, who was murdered by Picts acting on the instructions of Vortigern – and I think we can see where this story has come from. Perhaps more usefully, Geoffrey of Monmouth also tells us that Constantine was a younger brother of King Audren in Brittany, and that Arthur's mother Igraine was the wife of Uther's enemy King Gorlois. Since Gorlois surely means Gaulois, both stories point to a Gallo-Roman ancestry – through Arthur's grandfather or his mother (or both).

The point to consider here is that if Constantine was born in Armorica in the early 5th century, it is very unlikely that he was a Breton in the sense of a Brythonic-speaking emigrant from Wales or Cornwall. We know of very few Breton émigrés of such an early period – St Corentin of Quimper (c. 375 - 460) is the earliest of the seven founding saints of Brittany (by a distance), and he was born in the province (ie he was a Roman). St Brieuc, born in c. 409, became a priest in c. 447 and then migrated to Brittany, and the others were all 6th century imports. So, born in the period 410 – 430, Constantine and Audren would almost certainly have been Gallo-Romans.

Gildas (c.500 – 570) refers to a Constantine who was clearly a contemporary of his, and who he describes as *"the tyrannical whelp of the unclean lioness of Damnonia"*. From the dates, this cannot have been

Arthur's grandfather, and indeed Geoffrey of Monmouth makes him Arthur's successor, after the Battle of Camlann. The word 'Damnonia' is usually taken to be a misspelling of Dumnonia, but the Damnonii were a people of southern Scotland mentioned by Ptolemy, so it is possible that Arthur's successor came from Strathclyde. This Constantine is said to have been distantly related to Arthur. Either way, this reference does not confirm or eliminate the possibility that Arthur had Brythonic-speaking relatives, but if he was a leader of the forces of a Belgo-Roman/Celtic alliance, it may be supposed that he was at least familiar with the Brythonic language.

Further corroboration that Arthur existed comes from the Annales Cambriae (the 'Annals of Wales'), written at latest in the 10th century, which mention Arthur twice, and also Medraut (Mordred) and Myrddin (Merlin). Arthur is said to have *"carried the cross for three days"* at the Battle of Badon Hill (dated in the Annales as 516), and to have fought Mordred at the Battle of Camlann (c.537), where he may have been mortally wounded. Merlin is said to have 'gone mad' at the Battle of Arfderydd in c. 573. (If this is the Merlin of the legends, and if the chronology suggested in this book is correct, Merlin was considerably younger than Arthur).

A Welsh poem, the Y Goddodin, may contain the earliest reference to Arthur, in describing a warrior called Gwawrddur. It says that *"he was no Arthur".* The origins of this poem go back to anywhere between the 7th and 11th centuries, so the reference could date, at earliest, to c.600. Otherwise the earliest Welsh reference dates from the early 12th century, and the comparative silence of the Welsh sources on such an illustrious figure has long been a puzzle. To me, this is a clear indication that the hero was not Welsh, except by later adoption in tradition, when his name was Celticised to Arthur.

A fundamental question, assuming that Arthur was an historical figure, is whether he campaigned in Brittany as well as in Britain. The Arthurian legends are certainly very strong in Brittany, but that might of course be because the Bretons took the stories with them when they migrated to Armorica. Nennius names 12 battles which Arthur is said to have fought, and most British historians assume that all 12 took place in Britain.

"The first battle in which he was engaged, was at the mouth of the river Gleni.[22] The second, third, fourth, and fifth, were on another river, by the Britons called Duglas,[23] in the region Linuis.[24] The sixth, on the river Bassas.

22 *Glein in some manuscripts*

23 *Dubglas*

24 *Linnuis*

The seventh in the wood Celidon, which the Britons call Cat Coit Celidon. The eighth was near Gurnion[25] castle, where Arthur bore the image of the Holy Virgin, mother of God, upon his shoulders, and through the power of our Lord Jesus Christ, and the holy Mary, put the Saxons to flight, and pursued them the whole day with great slaughter. The ninth was at the City of the Legion, which is called Cair Lion. The tenth was on the banks of the river Trat Treuroit.[26] The eleventh was on the mountain Breguoin,[27] which we call Cat Bregion. The twelfth was a most severe contest, when Arthur penetrated to the hill of Badon. In this engagement, nine hundred and forty fell by his hand alone, no one but the Lord affording him assistance. In all these engagements the Britons were successful. For no strength can avail against the will of the Almighty"

One writer, Ronald Millar ('Will The Real King Arthur Please Stand Up?' 1978) has identified potential sites in Brittany for all of the battles, but this suggestion is too far-fetched. We know from Gildas that Mount Badon, at least, was in Britain. But nevertheless, some of the battles may have been fought in France. A monk in Brittany, writing a life of St Goeznovius, 'Legenda Sancti Goeznova', in 1019, said: *"In due course the usurper, Vortigern, to strengthen the defence of Britain, which he held unrighteously, summoned warriors from the land of Saxony and made them his allies. Since they were pagans and possessed by Satan, lusting to shed human blood, they brought much evil upon the Britons.*

Presently their pride was limited for a while through the great Arthur, king of the Britons. They were largely expelled from the island and reduced to subjection. But when this same Arthur, after many glorious victories which he won in Britain and in Gaul, was summoned at last from human activity, the way was open for the Saxons to again enter the island and there was great oppression of the Britons, destruction of churches and persecution of saints. This persecution went on through the times of many kings, Saxons and Britons fighting back and forth."

So by the early 11th century there was a tradition firmly established in France that some of Arthur's battles had been fought in France. Is this plausible? There can be little doubt that close relations were maintained between the British and the Armoricans, and on both sides of the Channel the Celtic and Roman communities were being pressed hard by the Saxons and Franks respectively. So it is not at all absurd to think that Arthur might

25 *Guinnion*
26 *Tribruit*
27 *Agnet*

have been moved to go to the aid of the Bretons against the Franks, especially if the Bretons had earlier furnished assistance to him against the Saxons. However, the timeline of the Breton wars against the Franks suggests that he could not have gone there before 493, the date of the Battle of Mons Badonis according to Bede, and that suggests that the battles described by Nennius may not be set out in chronological order.

There are of course numerous places in Brittany that are associated with Arthur by toponymy or local tradition. British commentators generally dismiss the Breton folklore, and the result is a kind of 'tug-of-war', contested between the British and Bretons, in which both claim a share, or even the totality, of the Arthurian legends. Exactly the same phenomenon is seen in the near contemporary legends of Tristan and Isolde, which British commentators claim to be set in Cornwall, and which French commentators are equally convinced took place in Brittany.

Since both sets of legends were written, in the main, by Norman French authors and written in Old French, textual analysis inevitably tends to support the French point of view, but of course the British argue that the Norman-French authors were merely reducing to writing the earlier British oral traditions. Some at least of the stories are very hard to locate in Britain, and I do not believe that all of them can have their origins in British folklore. Just as one example, there is a story in the Béroul version of 'Tristran et Issault' of a visit by Queen Issault (Isolde to the British) to the monastery of St Sampson, accompanied by Dinas of Dinan and others. Dinan is about 15 miles from Sampson's monastery at Dôl in Brittany, founded in the mid-6th century. And the poem also refers to people who only existed, if they existed at all, in Brittany (such as 'Salemon'), and to places that are clearly on the southern side of the Channel (eg the 'Costentin', which is clearly the Côtentin peninsula in Normandy). So I think it is pretty clear which monastery founded by St Sampson Béroul was referring to. But despite this clear identification, British commentators persistently locate this place as a monastery in the civil parish of St Sampson in Cornwall, formerly known as Golant, where the church was dedicated to St Sampson in 1509. There is no record of any monastery in Golant, although there were several nearby. It is of course possible that Béroul was recording (and perhaps distorting) an old Cornish legend, but we really cannot say that the story as written supports the notion that these events took place in Cornwall.

But equally, if the legends reflect real events that took place around the year 500, we should note that this period predates the main influx of Welsh and Cornish immigrants into Brittany. Almost by definition, this did not start until after Arthur's death. The Brittany of Arthurian legends was therefore probably more Gallo-Roman than Breton, and it is noticeable, for example, that there are no place names in the Arthurian legends beginning with the characteristic Breton prefixes of Ker-, Pol- or Poul-.

If any historical facts are to be determined from the legends at all, we have to strip away this nationalist colouring. But at the end of the day, determining what is or is not historical in the Arthurian legends is rather like trying to discern a history by watching hours of television soap operas. Occasionally a character will speak of places that really exist, or historical figures, but we would have to wade through hours of footage to try to reconstruct any history from the material. And unfortunately an element of distortion was introduced into the stories at the outset, for political motives. To make due allowance for this, we need to understand the background to the recording of the stories.

7.2   The Recording of the Legends

Most of the legends of the 'Arthurian' period come to us through Norman French writers of the 13th century, in particular Geoffrey of Monmouth and Chrétien de Troyes, and as a result suffer from serious distortion. The distortion is partly a consequence of infelicitous transmission, but also partly the result of political spin.

The Norman authors were describing conflicts between the Gallo-Romans and the Franks, and between the Belgo-Romans (possibly with Celtic allies) and the Saxons, in which their ancestors had played no part. And despite the fact that the Normans had developed alliances with the Bretons from the 10th century onwards, it is evident from the material in the Arthurian legends that, to the authors of the legends, the staunchly independent Brittany was a foreign country (Brittany remained independent of France until 1532).

Moreover, the recording of the legends had an underlying political purpose. The Normans had invaded and conquered England in 1066, and were trying to establish their political legitimacy by appealing to the Belgic/Celtic British traditions in England over the heads of the Anglo-Saxons who had ruled England for 500 years. The Arthurian legends were written down for the entertainment of the reader, certainly, and it is quite probable that both author and reader recognised that much of the material was fiction. But the higher purpose was to establish the Normans as the custodians of an earlier tradition of chivalry and honour, which the vile Saxons had displaced. The Normans therefore claimed to be the rightful heirs of Arthur.

Indeed, beyond that, the Normans claimed religious legitimacy for their regime, and the stories concerning the Quest for the Holy Grail were intended to demonstrate that the purest exponents of their code of chivalry had attained a seal of approval from Christ himself, expressed by admission to the select band who had celebrated Mass by drinking from the sacred chalice.

The stories therefore paint Arthur and his associates as super-heroes, who espoused a code of chivalry to which the Normans were heirs, and who fought against the evil Saxons. Even if there had been no connections to northern France, it is arguable that the Normans would have had to invent some, but conveniently it appears that Arthur may have been active in Brittany, so all the Normans had to do in order to purloin this history was to elide the distinctions between Brittany and Normandy, and between the Franks and the Saxons.

7.3   The Conflict Between the Bretons and the Franks

It is not the purpose of this book to rehearse the Arthurian legends, about which an enormous amount is already in print. Rather I will examine the possible Arthurian aspects of the troubled relationship between the Bretons and the Franks, in order to explore the implications for the Channel Islands and, as a side issue, to show that the Breton history may validate both the existence of Arthur and the basic timeline of his life.

The conflict between the Bretons and the Franks at the end of the 5th century does in fact appear in the Arthurian legends, as a relatively small and unremarked side story. (To me this is like one of those historical nuggets that we might have found by trawling through hours of soap operas). The essence of the Arthurian legends relating to this topic can be summarised as follows:

- There were two kings of Brittany, called Ban and Bors.
- Ban ruled over Benoic and Bors ruled over Gannes.
- Their mortal enemy was Claudas, who ruled over the 'Land Laid Waste', of Bourges and the surrounding district of Berry.
- Claudas had broken faith with King Aramont (or Hoël) of Brittany, and had allied himself with 'the King of Gaul'. In consequence Aramont and Uther Pendragon (Arthur's father) had attacked Bourges and the district around it (Berry), and laid waste the land – hence

its name.

- After the death of Uther Pendragon, and at a time when Arthur was distracted by his wars with the Saxons, Claudas invaded Benoic and Gannes and killed Ban and Bors.
- In return for assistance earlier provided by Ban and Bors to Arthur, in his struggles against the Saxons, Arthur came to Hoël's assistance and fought a battle at Trèbes with Claudas, as a result of which Claudas 'fled to Rome'.

There is quite a lot of helpful additional colour around these stories, for example that at the city of Gannes, the gate facing Brittany was called the Breton Gate, but we will refer to this material as and when necessary. But how does this narrative fit with the known history? Firstly, we know that there had been a British force of 12,000 men in Berry in 468, when Riothamus had answered the Emperor's call for assistance against the Visigoths. That force had been defeated after a long and hard-fought battle, but some remnants may have remained in Gaul, perhaps around Bourges. We also know that there had been a British garrison at Blois since 410, and it is possible that men from Blois took part in the battle of 468. After the battle at Bourges, the Romans and Franks had defeated the Visigoths and the Franks had seized most of the north bank of the Loire. Presumably these are the events that underlie the story of the 'land laid waste' at Bourges.

Clovis succeeded to the Frankish throne in 481, and in 486 defeated the Romans. He then expelled the Bretons from Blois in 490, put Nantes under siege and invaded Brittany. I think we can identify Clovis as Claudas (his name to the Franks was Chlodovech, and in Latin Chlodovechus, so it is not surprising to find a 'd' in the legendary version of the name). I think we can also see that he 'broke faith' with his former allies, the Bretons, both in expelling the Bretons from Blois and in besieging Nantes. The King of Brittany may very well have been Hoël, and although we have no record of who Ban and Bors were, clearly a number of Bretons would have been killed in the conflict. Claudas is then said to have 'fled to Rome', whereas we understand that in fact Clovis went off to fight the Alamanni at Tolbiac. But this is not an essential detail, and his destination would not have been clear to the Bretons.

I therefore think that the first elements of the Arthurian legendary version of the story are founded in fact, and that encourages me to think that the final element, the intervention of Arthur, may also be historical. I am encouraged in this view by the circumstantial evidence, and I think we need to focus on the missing pieces of history – the story told by Gregory of

Tours' silence on the subject. We know that Clovis employed Saxon allies under Chillon to lay siege to Nantes, and that Clovis made unsuccessful forays into Brittany, but we have little detail on this campaign (see Chapter 6). Then, in c. 496 - 499, Clovis suddenly decided to conclude a treaty with the Bretons, which gave them autonomy in the ancient lands of the Osismes and the Veneti and which imposed no obligation to pay tribute to Clovis upon them. This has never been satisfactorily explained.

Clovis was not the compromising kind: we know that he was brutal, territorially ambitious, driven and relentless. His personal emblem was the bee – perhaps a reflection of his industry, but certainly also a symbol of his sting. However, we also know that he compromised when he had to – for example he later abandoned his campaigns against the Burgundians in the Rhône Valley and the Goths on the Mediterranean coast in the face of strong opposition. Were the Bretons such strong opponents? Although the Bretons were notable fighters, on the face of it, I suggest that Clovis should have been able to subdue the sparsely populated Brittany peninsula, even if the Bretons had been able to count on the support of the Alans and Romans living among them.

There seems to be a piece of the story missing, and according to the legends that piece was Arthur, presumably with British reinforcements. The legends tell us a number of things about the British involvement in Brittany, none of which are patently absurd. They tell us that Arthur's father had fought at Bourges, which may or may not have been the case. They tell us that Arthur came to the aid of the King of Brittany in repayment of support given to him by the Bretons in his battles with the Saxons. And it is perfectly plausible that Gallo-Roman or Breton troops did fight with the British against the Saxons.

One obvious way to corroborate the story would be to relate the battle at Trèbes to one of the battles in Nennius' list. 'Treb' meant 'village' in Breton, so that does not help to identify a precise location. Alternatively, there is a Trévé near Loudéac, in the centre of the post-496 border between the Bretons and the Franks. In 1274, the name of the village was recorded as Treves. And of course Trêve in modern French means 'truce', so perhaps Trèbes was not a battlefield at all, but rather the place where a truce was signed – or perhaps both.

According to Nennius, Arthur's 10th battle was fought on the banks of the river Tribruit (or Trat Treuroit). Could this be the Battle of Trèbes of the Arthurian legends? There is no river Tribruit in Brittany today, but there is a river Trieux, (formerly the Trifrouit) in the Trégor peninsula, with an ancient castle and town now called Guingamp, located on a bend above the river. This area is close to Châtelaudren and to Binic. (And note that Arthur's 8th battle was fought near 'Gurnion Castle'). The comparison is tempting, but not conclusive.

The key point is that if Arthur intervened in the Breton war, it is clear that he must have been free of the Saxon threat in England, and if this did happen, that has implications for the timeline of events in Britain, because we know that the treaty between the Bretons and the Franks was concluded in c. 496 – 499. Which means that the Battle of Mount Badon must have taken place before then. There is therefore no reason, on the basis of the events in Brittany, to dispute Bede's assertion that the British victory over the Angles and Saxons took place in 493.

This in turn suggests that Arthur cannot have been born long after 470. He was allegedly 15 when he inherited his position from his father, so that suggests that his father died in or before 485, which ties in with the legend that the confrontation at Bourges in 468 took place in Uther Pendragon's time. Certainly Arthur could not have been Riothamus, as some have suggested. And a date of Arthur's birth in the late 460s also ties in with the range of suggested dates of Arthur's death at the Battle of Camlann in 537 – 542.

However, linking the legends with historical figures in Breton history is nearly impossible, for the simple reason that so little is known of the Breton kings. Legend has it that the first of their leaders was Conan Meriadoc (allegedly 350 – 421) but his existence is unproven. He is believed to have been followed by Gradlon and then Salomon I (who allegedly died in 446).

But Audren, the supposed son of Salomon I, we know quite a lot about from Breton tradition and archaeology, and we can use this information to test the historicity of the Arthurian legends. We understand that in about 447, Audren (or Aldrien) built a motte (a raised earthwork castle) on the banks of the Leff River, at what is now Châtelaudren, defending the northern route into Brittany. According to one view he died in 464 and was succeeded by Erich, who died in 478, but according to the Chronique de St Brieuc, Audren was succeeded by Budic and then Hoël.

Audrien left a significant toponymic footprint in Brittany. In addition to Châtelaudren, there is a Ville Audrain at St-Jacut-du-Méné, and, in the style of the Breton language, a Keraudrain (at La Grée, near Ruffiac) and a Keraudren (near Brest). So there is no doubt that he is an historical figure. 'Aldroen' appears in Geoffrey of Monmouth's work too, where he is described as a king of Brittany two generations before Arthur, who sent his brother Constantine to Britain in response to a request from Archbishop Guethelin for assistance in driving out some Picts. According to the legends that Constantine was Arthur's grandfather, and if 'Aldroen' was born in the early 410s, or 420s (consistent with his having built Châtelaudren in 447) and he was two generations older than Arthur, that would be consistent with a date of birth for his grand-nephew, Arthur in about 470. And it would make Arthur a contemporary of Hoël, so thus far the legends, traditions and the very little history we have are at least consistent.

There is no trace of Bors in Breton place names, and the only possible trace of Ban is the area known as Bannalec near Concarneau in southern Brittany, for which the traditional toponymy is unconvincing, but where an attribution to Ban is equally uncertain.

7.4   The Rest of the French Legends

The French legends tell of various battles in which Arthur was allegedly involved in France, besides the struggle at Trèbes, but nearly all of these can be dismissed as folklore memories of other events. For example, Arthur is supposed to have fought against the Romans at Soissons, when it was clearly Clovis and the Franks who fought against Syragius at Soissons. Similarly Arthur is supposed to have fought at Paris, but there is no realistic possibility that this happened.

In Brittany, the legends tell us that he fought several battles at Carhaix (where Arthur 'had a court') and at 'Anablayse', in support of Leodegan, Guinevere's father, against a Saxon force led by Rions. It is of course possible that Saxon mercenaries may have attacked Brest and its hinterland, and Carhaix certainly exists, having been an important Roman town to the east of Brest. Moreover the Saxon Chillon did attack Nantes – could Rions be Chillon? Anablayse cannot be identified, but in some versions seems to be an alternative name for Carhaix.

Nennius writes that Arthur's 11th battle was fought at 'Agned' (in some manuscripts of the Historia 'Breguoin' is substituted), and some have speculated that this may be a corruption of Andegavum – ie Angers. Wace, writing in the 12th century, tells us that Arthur took Angers and bestowed it upon Kay, but the only battles we know of at Angers were the Saxon capture of the town in 463, followed by their expulsion by Childeric in 464. There is no historical record of Clovis losing Angers, but there are very limited sources on Clovis' campaign in Brittany, so we cannot be sure that he did not.

The sensible approach must be to strip the Arthurian legends back to the bare, historically attested, bones, and then see if there are any elements of the legends related to the historical parts that add to our knowledge. And in one respect, the legends are quite instructive.

7.5 The Geography of the Border in Brittany post 496

Virtually the whole of the area between St Brieuc and Auray was a dense forest, substantially isolating the Brittany peninsula, and although roads traversed this forest at Loudéac and Pontivy, these routes offered too much scope for ambush to be of use to an invading army. So, in effect, access to the peninsula was confined to a northern route that passed near St Brieuc, and the old Roman road through Vannes and along the south coast towards Brest. From the point of view of the Bretons, the key strategic defences were located on the northern route, at Châtelaudren, and on the southern route at Rochefort-en-Terre and La Roche Bernard.

In terms of the place names in the Arthurian legends, the identification of Bourges and Berry is fine, and it is fairly easy to detect that Gannes was Vannes, which, following the treaty of 496 was near the southern end of the Breton border with the Franks. As we have seen, Trèbes (Thebe in some manuscripts) may have been Treves (now Trévé) near Loudéac. We are not told where Benoic was, but we are told that there was a castle in Benoic called Corbénic, and this is very helpful.

What does 'Corbénic' mean? Assuming that 'Cor-' means hill, we then need to identify Bénic, which is not hard because its name has barely changed. Bénic (or Binic as it is now called) is a fishing village on the Côtes d'Armor in Brittany, nine miles from Châtelaudren. There is a hill to the north side of the port, the port itself being formed by the mouth of the river Ic. The meaning of Bénic (pen-ic) is 'the head of the river Ic' (just as Bénodet is the 'head of the Odet river), and the toponymy of Corbénic is cor-pen-ic, meaning 'hill at the head of the river Ic'. At some point in the Middle Ages, the name was abbreviated to 'Bénic', and then in the 16th century it became 'Binic'. 'Benoic' is therefore entirely apt to describe the region around the castle.

The valley of the Ic has been occupied since 3500 BC and the town of Binic contains some interesting early archaeology. Finds of bronze swords, Roman coins and Gaulish cartwheels suggest that the site contained an Iron Age Celtic fort. On the southern side of the river are the remains of a castle built in the Early Middle Ages (late 5th century to the end of the 9th century), called the Camp de Bernains or the Camp de César. This triangular castle was defended by nearly 2,000 feet (600 metres) of walls and 7 towers, and set in the middle of it was a dolmen called the 'Table de Margot' (which was partially destroyed in a scheme of improvements to the port in 1816). The castle has at some point been reduced, and all that remains are some low sections of stone walls. Further construction at the foot of the promontory called La Banche (on the sea shore) was found in the 19th century, when allegedly more than 200 Roman coins were recovered from the site, but these were apparently dispersed. This site has been interpreted as a Roman bath.[28]

The Camp de Bernains is now a nature reserve and is completely overgrown. On the north side of the Ic, the cliffs rise 260 feet (80 metres) above the river, and the high ground has obvious strategic significance, but this area was heavily developed in the 19th and 20th centuries, so any archaeology here is likely to have been badly damaged.

The first recorded use of the name 'Binic' for the town occurred in 1545, prior to which is was known as Bénic. So it would have been known to the 13th century authors of the Arthurian tales as Bénic, or, I suggest, Corbénic.

A few miles ot the south-west of Binic was the castle of Cesson, which may have been on the Gallo-Roman/Frankish frontier at the end of the 5th century. In 479 St Brieuc set up a monastery there, and eventually the town took his name, but at the time there was no significant settlement around the castle.

Incidentally, 'Margot' is the name of a fairy in Celtic folklore, and various rocks, caves etc. are associated with this fairy throughout the Celtic world; so unfortunately this provides us with no assistance. 'Bernain' is a Basque place name and personal name, and since it is known that Basque units served in the Roman army in far-flung locations (for example, one unit was stationed on Hadrian's Wall), it is possible that Roman troops were stationed at Bénic and that some of these came from the Basque country. The name was often corrupted in the Christian era to Bernard, after the saint of that name.

In the Arthurian legends, we are told that Corbénic remained standing until the time of Charlemagne, who razed it to the ground *"when he invaded England"*.[29] The reference to Charlemagne (King of the Franks from 768 to 814), gives us two useful pieces of information: firstly that Corbénic was **not** in fact in Britain, and secondly that it was destroyed during Charlemagne's

28 Pierre Merlat, 'Ve Circonscription. In: Gallia, tome 15, fasciscule 2' (1957)
29 Vulgate Lancelot, Vulgate Queste del St Graal, Vulgate Estoire del Saint Graal, Third Continuation of Chrétian's Perceval, Post Vulgate Quest del Saint Graal, Sir Thomas Malory La Mort D'arthur

reign. There is no record of any visit to Britain by Charlemagne, but he certainly campaigned in Brittany. He firstly established a militarised zone (the Breton Marches) to contain the Bretons, broadly in the area from Rennes to Nantes. And later he launched invasions of Brittany, one in 786, led by Audulf, and in one in 799 when Count Guy conquered the whole region. Charlemagne may have campaigned in Brittany himself in 811. So we can reasonably conclude that the fortress was destroyed in this period.

7.6   The Grail Castle Legend

Geoffrey of Monmouth (the monk who was the author of Historia Regum Britanniae) is believed to have been a member of the Baderon family, seigneurs of Dôl-Combourg, so it is likely that Geoffrey was familiar with the history of Dôl, and that this informed his writings.

Archbishop Baudri of Bourgeuil, in his 'Chronique de Dôl' written in the early 12th century reported a visit of Budoc, his predecessor (as Abbot of Dôl), to Jerusalem, in the 6th century. He wrote that *"Such was the saintliness of this man, Saint Budoc, that this is attested by the precious gift which he brought back from the sacred City of Jerusalem, that is to say the cup and plate that our Lord used at the last supper which he ate with his disciples."*[30] This may well be the basis of the legend that the Holy Grail was brought to Brittany. (There are similar stories of other holy relics being imported to France by pilgrims who visited the Holy Lands in the early Middle Ages, for example splinters from the cross).

St Budoc is a mysterious character in Breton history, who is said to have been the third abbot/archbishop of Dôl after Sampson and Magloire. Magloire is said to have resigned the archbishopric of Dôl to set up a monastery on Sark, according to Sarkese legend in 565. This would date Budoc's period of office to the late 6th century, and references to a Budoc who allegedly set up a church on the banks of the Tamar River in the early 5th century must refer to someone else. Indeed Geoffrey of Monmouth and Wace both tell of an earlier King Budec, who took care of Ambrosius and Uther Pendragon as children, during Vortigern's reign, but since 'budeg' simply meant 'victory' (hence Boudicca, meaning Victoria), this was a reasonably common name.

---

30 *"Quantae vero sanctitatis fuerit vir iste sanctus Budocus, pretiosa munera quae secum de sancta civitate detulit Jérusalem, scutella scilicet et scutellus quibus Dominus usus est in ultima Coena quam cum discipulis suis fecit testantur."* (Acta Sanctorum Ordinis Sancti Benedicti Saec. I, pages 223-225).

Taken at face value, Budoc collected the grail and the plate from which Christ ate the Last Supper, from Jerusalem, and it is possible that his visit to Jerusalem took place in Arthur's lifetime (but only towards the end of his life). We need not speculate on whether the objects brought back by Budoc were the real grail and plate. It is sufficient to know that the religious community of Brittany believed that the genuine grail and plate had been brought back to Brittany, and were in their custody.

What we need to remember is that, after 496, the land occupied by the Bretons was essentially the former territory of the Osismes and Veneti, and that the former territory of the Coriosolites was probably under the jurisdiction of the Franks. Dôl, in the latter area, was a Breton religious outpost established in Frankish territory by a gift from the Frankish king, but although the Franks and Bretons were at peace in the early 6th century, and indeed shared the same religion, the relationship between the Franks and the Bretons was to become increasingly strained towards the end of the century.

Moreover, there can have been little intermingling of the communities, because there are very few loan words from the Breton language in French. And certainly Magloire felt it necessary to remove himself and a large band of monks from Dôl to Sark in c. 565, possibly because of security concerns. If the Breton religious community at Dôl held objects that they regarded as sacred, they might well have chosen to keep them somewhere secure in the territory under Breton control. And what we know is that, in the 'Grail Quest' stories, the Grail was kept at Corbénic. 'Lancelot' (written 1215 – 1230), the 'Quest del Saint Graal' (1215 – 1230), the 'Estoire de Saint Graal' (1220 – 1235), the 'Third Continuation of Percival' (c.1230), and the post-vulgate 'Quest de Saint Graal' (1230 – 1240) all describe events concerning the Holy Grail. These stories were repeated and embellished in the later work of Thomas Malory 'Le Mort D'arthur' (1469 – 1470) and in the poetry of Alfred Lord Tennyson ('The Idylls of the King' (1859 – 1860)). We also know that Corbénic was located in a place that was foreign to the Norman French authors of the legends, or the Franks from whom they may have learned the story, because it is described as being constructed in 'Listenois' (the strange land) or 'Terre Foraine' (the foreign land). The rugged, rocky, forested landscape of north Brittany had little agricultural value, and the Franks might reasonably have regarded it as a wasteland.

In essence, the 'Grail Quest' tales recount the story of a time when Galahad was involved in a mission to heal a king, or possibly two kings, who were suffering from serious wounds – this monarch, or these monarchs, being called variously the 'Roi Pêcheur' (the Fisher King), the 'Roi Blessé' (the Wounded King), the 'Roi Méhaignié' (the Maimed King), Pelleas or Pellès. The wounded king, or both wounded kings, lived at Corbénic, a castle on the coast, where they spent their time fishing in a river beside the castle. The castle had been constructed in Listenois (the strange land), by two brothers, Alan and Joshua, followers of Joseph of Arimathea,[31] with the help of King Calafes. And the legends further tell us that the Holy Grail was kept in the Palace of Adventures, inside the castle.

In Arthur's day, according to some of the 13th century romances, the king at Corbénic was Pelles, who lived there with his daughter Elaine (the mother of Galahad) and his son Eliezer. The castle had, however, been enchanted, which meant that it was very difficult to find. Despite this inconvenience, the castle was visited by various knights, starting with Gawain and including Lancelot. Lancelot was, according to the legend, the son of King Ban of Benoic, the overlord of the whole area.

However, generally the visitors did not recognise the Grail for what it was. Gawain in particular was shown the door when his attention became diverted to the beautiful maiden carrying the Grail, rather than the cup itself. One particular story tells us that Lancelot brought the body of Amide (a sister of Percival) to the castle by boat, after seven months of wandering at sea. This tells us that the castle was on the coast (as well as by a river). In his several visits, Lancelot rescued Elaine from a boiling tub, killed a snake and recuperated after a period of insanity. Various magical events happened in the castle, but after Galahad took the Grail to Sarras (a kingdom in Arabia) (from whence it was drawn into heaven), the spell over the castle was broken.

There is an assumption among British authors that Corbénic, despite its obviously Continental style of name, was in Britain, and that these events happened after Arthur returned to Britain. For example some commentators have suggested that Corbénic was in the Lake District. Supporters of the Lake District theory suggest that a magical canal opened up to connect the Lakes to the sea for this purpose! Others believe that the castle was at Corbeny, near Laon in the Aisne Department in Picardy, which, according to this theory, was close to the monastery where the monk who wrote the stories lived. However, this idea shares the defect of the Lake District theory, because the Aisne Department is entirely landlocked. (Incidentally 'Corbeni' may mean 'hill of women').

We know from the Arthurian legends that Lancelot (if he existed at all) was a nobleman (and later possibly a king) living in France (could the name

---

31 Joseph of Arimathea, according to the Gospels, took Christ's body down from the cross, and interred it in a tomb hewn from rock, which had been prepared for his own burial

possibly derive from 'Lan celtoi', 'the Celtic shore'?). So it is absolutely consistent with the legends that events and places associated with Lancelot will be found, if they happened at all, in France. And it seems clear that Corbénic was the modern Binic for the reasons explained above. The 'boiling tub' from which Lancelot rescued Elaine could possibly have been in the Roman baths. And what better cure after a bout of depression than a seaside holiday with some gentle thalassotherapy?

In summary the case for the identification of Binic as the site of Corbénic is as follows:

- The toponymy clearly identifies this specific place.
- It is on the coast.
- It is by a river.
- Binic is in what the Franks would have called Listenois, or Terre Forain (ie Brittany)
- It was well known to the Franks, being a prominent border defence.
- According to the legends, Elaine, the daughter of the lord of Corbénic, had a relationship with Lancelot, who was brought up at Châtelaudren. Châtelaudren is nine miles from Binic.
- The castle was of impressive size, and probably existed in the Arthurian period.
- The castle had been destroyed before the 13th century, as described by the chroniclers of the Arthurian period.
- It is entirely probable that it was destroyed by Charlemagne, as described by Geoffrey of Monmouth.

While there are countless references to Corbénic in the Arthurian tales, they are almost all fictional or imaginative, and we need not spend time trying to detect any historical substance behind them. But we have noted the story of the boiling tub, and the possibility that this was a reference to the Roman baths, and it is worth noting another connection. A few miles to the southwest of Binic is St Brieuc, which in the early Middle Ages consisted of a castle, the Castrum de Cesson and (from about 479) the monastery of St Brieuc. One particular story from the legends tells us that Pelles, the King of Corbénic, being aware of prophesies that Lancelot would father a child who would complete the Grail Quest, decided to trick Lancelot into sleeping with his daughter Elaine (knowing that Lancelot loved only Guinevere). Elaine's maidservant told Lancelot that Guinevere was waiting for him five miles away at the Castle of Case. Lancelot duly went to the Castle and climbed into bed with Elaine, believing her to be Guinevere, and thus fathered Galahad. It seems to me that the Castle of Case could be the Castrum de Cesson at St Brieuc. The same castle might also be the 'Castle of Enquiry' (ie Question), a castle inhabited by priests where pious knights made their confessions before approaching the Grail Castle. The only other significant building near the Castle of Cesson was the abbey of St Brieuc

Incidental support for this case may be provided by other personal names in the legends. According to 'Les Merveilles de Rigomer', one of Arthur's knights was called Barnaains (recalling the Camp de Barnains at Corbénic). And according to Malory, Elaine's father was called Bernard.

Finally, Geoffrey of Monmouth, Wace, the Vulgate Merlin etc. tell a story of Arthur's rescue of a damsel in distress from a giant at Mont St Michel. The Prose Brut and The Legend of King Arthur say this event took place at Mount St Bernard, which puzzled Christopher Bruce, the guru of Arthurian place names. It seems likely that the change of name was not a slip of the pen, and that the authors of the latter works meant the hill at Bénic.

But trying to match the legends with historical facts is certainly not easy, and we cannot now identify many of the names in the legends. In terms of the alleged kings of Brittany of the period, Hoël was certainly an historical figure, remembered in the names of some Breton communes (Huelgoat, Canihuel and Huelc), and we have already discussed his predecessor Audren. But there seems to be little trace of Ban or Bors, or for that matter Lancelot. The concept of multiple kings of Brittany is not problematic per se, because it is doubtful that the region was ever unified before the 8th century, and we know that there were groups of Alans and 'Romans' in the region who may well have had their own leaders. The problem lies in trying to connect the names which we are offered by the legends, with any particular area or 'tribe' in the absence of place name identification.

The best we can say is that there may have been a Ban and a Bors who were 'counts' (for want of a better term) in the northern territory of Benoic and in the Vannetais respectively, but we have no means of proving it. The names do not look like Brythonic names or Roman names, so they appear to have been corrupted, possibly by the Norman scribes who wrote down the legends. Like so many of the other figures of the Arthurian legends, they simply recede from our view, into the mists of time.

7.7   An Imaginative Reconstruction of the Life of Arthur

If we assume that there is historical substance to the tales of Arthur in Brittany, we can assemble the outline of a possible biography of his life, which needs to be treated as educated guesswork, not historical fact:

465 – 470	Arthur is born in Tintagel, the son of Uther Pendragon and the grandson of Constantine of Brittany. His mother is Igerna, the wife of Uther's enemy Gorlois (Gaulois – surely?). Uther is a British military commander, who has recently taken command after Vortigern was exiled.
468	Uther fights in Riothamus' army at Bourges, and escapes from the battle as the British are defeated by the Visigoths.
470	Childeric defeats the Visigoths and the Saxons and forces the Saxons to abandon their ambitions in the Loire Valley.
477	Ælle lands in Kent, with his sons, and three ships of men (perhaps a force of 270), to join the thriving Germanic colony there. He soon takes command not only of the colony in Kent, but also that of the Saxons in Essex and the Angles in East Anglia and Lincolnshire.
481	Clovis inherits the throne of the Salian Franks in Flanders, aged 15.
480s	In Britain, the Belgo-Romans fight the Anglo-Saxons in the east, especially in Lincolnshire, and the fortunes of war fluctuate – *"After this, sometimes our countrymen, sometimes the enemy, won the field"* (Gildas)
485	A significant victory for Ælle in England.
486	Clovis wins the Battle of Soissons, driving out the last Roman governor in Gaul.
Late 480s	The Belgo-Romans form an alliance with the Celtic British against the Anglo-Saxons, to defend a line down England along the River Trent and Watling Street to London. Arthur

becomes a commander of the British army.

490   Clovis seizes Blois.

491   Ælle takes Pevensey Castle, which was then an island, and slaughters the occupants, thus expanding the Kent colony along the coast into what became Sussex.

491 – 492   Arthur fights back and wins several battles against the Saxons, with support from the Bretons from Armorica.

493   Aurelius Ambrosius leads a combined British army, at the Battle of Mons Badonicus, possibly at Arbury Hill. Ælle and his sons are killed and their army is destroyed.

495   Clovis extends his empire westwards from the Avranches region, sacking Mont St Michel and taking Alet and Dinan

In response to an appeal for help from King Hoel, his cousin, Arthur takes a substantial infantry force to Brittany, possibly landing at Le Yaudet or Binic.

Clovis sends his Saxon vassal Chillon to take Nantes. With half of his army pinned down at the siege, but having secured Rennes, he leads the other half of his force towards Brest, by the northern route, with the aim of cutting off the Breton supply line for reinforcements from Britain. The eventual object is that the detached force should circle round the peninsula, through Quimper, to attack Vannes from the west. Meanwhile Clovis expects Chillon to take Nantes and move with the rest of his army to assault Vannes from the east, trapping Hoël in a pincer movement.

Arthur, newly arrived in western Brittany, learns that a Frankish force is approaching from Rennes along the northern route to Brest, and decides to intercept them. He joins up with units of the Breton army, including cavalry commanded by Lancelot, who was born and raised at the northern military command post of Châtelaudren, a fortress built by Arthur's great uncle Audren.

The combined force takes Clovis' army by surprise, and fights them to a standstill. Lancelot distinguishes himself in battle.

496   Clovis realises that he no longer has sufficient manpower to take Vannes, with Arthur's force arriving to reinforce Hoël. Indeed it is likely that Arthur will lift the siege at Nantes before Clovis can bring up reinforcements.

Clovis offers Hoël an alliance: Hoël is to abandon any claims to Rennes or the Loire valley east of Nantes, and Clovis will leave the Bretons autonomous in the peninsula – mainly in the former lands of the Veneti and Osismes. No hostages or tribute are required.

So the new border of Brittany runs southwest from Corbénic to Corlay, and then southeast through Mûr-de-Bretagne and Loudéac. From there it follows the present eastern boundary of the Department of the Morbihan, and includes the Department of the Loire Atlantique. Breton refugees from further east resettle within the new borders, for example at Ploërmel '(Plou Armel' – 'the parish of Arthur').

500 – 535   With the Saxon menace in abeyance, England enjoys a relatively peaceful period. However, this is punctuated both by occasional clashes with the Saxons, but more seriously by bouts of civil war, possibly between the Belgo-Romans and the Celtic British.

535 – 536   Years of no summer, resulting in famine across the world and a fight for resources in Britain.

537 - 542   Arthur is mortally wounded at the battle of Camlann, fighting against Celtic Britons led by Mordred (Medraut in Welsh or Modredus to Geoffrey of Monmouth, a name said to be derived from the Latin Moderatus). Arthur is taken to Avalon, where he dies.

7.8   The Substance Behind the Grail Quest Legends?

If the previous section was historical guesswork, this section is pure romance.

Before the war, Lancelot was an occasional guest at Corbénic, a castle near Châtelaudren, which was held by a lame baron called Pelles. The castle has been recently constructed on the site of a Gaulish earthwork fortification defending the port of the river Ic. The north wall ran along the river bank, and Pelles enjoyed fishing from the ramparts. Being disabled, his main recreational interest was fishing, which he could do from the castle walls, saving himself a painful climb down to the riverbank and back.

Pelles' daughter Elaine had taken a shine to Lancelot, and introduced him to the Roman baths on the foreshore in the hope of attracting his attention – naked girls he had seen before, but the baths were a real surprise! A tryst was arranged at the nearby Castle of Cesson, as a result of which Elaine became pregnant; but Lancelot refused to marry her. In later years he had an affair with Guinevere, which split the Breton Court. Nevertheless, he continued to see Elaine occasionally, especially when he stayed at Corbénic during a period of convalescence. She never married, but was immensely proud of their son Galahad.

In about 560, after renewed tensions between the Bretons and the Franks, Budoc, the Abbott of Dôl entrusted the baron then commanding Corbénic with the safekeeping of the treasures of the monastery. These included the cup and plate which Budoc had brought back from Jerusalem, and which he believed to be the cup and plate used by Christ at the Last Supper.

These were later removed to a safer location, when Charlemagne attacked Brittany. The castle was destroyed in this campaign, at the end of the 8th century or beginning of the 9th century.

7.9   A Big Question

Did Arthur visit the Channel Islands? Unfortunately, it is impossible to answer this question definitively, and there are no local legends to help us. We have only vestigial evidence that Arthur existed, and even less evidence that he visited Brittany, so it is almost pointless to speculate on how he might have got there. However, on the assumption that he did exist, and that he did fight battles in Brittany, I think we can speculate with more confidence on the route.

There were, as we have seen in other contexts, effectively two main routes across the western English Channel; the 'island hopping route' from Hengistbury Head (and later Poole Harbour and Clausentum (Bitterne, Southampton)) via Guernsey to St Malo, Binic or Le Yaudet. And the direct route from Plymouth to Le Yaudet, L'Aberwrac'h, Brest or Vannes. Other permutations were obviously possible, given the freedom of the seas, but these were the most logical and most frequented routes.

In c.500, the Belgo-Romans controlled the central southern ports of Poole Harbour and Clausentum, and the Celtic British controlled Plymouth. The Celtic migration of the 6th century was not yet fully underway, but some early migrants from Wales and Cornwall had reached Brittany to join peoples who had been there since the 4th century military migrations, probably descendents of soldiers from northern Britain. These early migrants appear to have taken the route from Plymouth to the western ports of Brittany.

The Franks controlled what was to become Neustria, and had raided as far west as Mont St Michel. It is unclear whether they controlled Alet (St Servan), but it seems they had limited, if any, authority over the Bretons, at least in the lands formerly occupied by the Veneti and the Osismes. The Saxons were allies of the Franks in Gaul, and, as we shall see, by the middle of the 6th century, the Franks were presenting themselves as allies of the Anglo-Saxons in England. And the Romans, on both sides of the Channel, were allied with the Celtic British against the Saxons/Franks. It is clear that any British force sent to reinforce the Bretons against the Franks would therefore have disembarked at St Malo or somewhere further west, and I think that St Malo would have been unlikely because it would have put the arriving troops too close to the Franks in Rennes, if not in St Malo itself.

The choice of route would have depended mainly on where the British force was raised: if it was primarily a force consisting of Celtic troops from Wales and Cornwall, it would have undoubtedly sailed from Plymouth, and arrived at Le Yaudet or a port further west. But if the British force was mainly comprised of 'Belgo-Roman' troops, the natural port of embarkation would have been Southampton. What we can assume is that Arthur's army would have included many veterans of the battle of Mount Badon.

Either option could have landed the British force close to King Hoël's base in northern Brittany at Châtelaudren, the Plymouth route by sailing to Le Yaudet and the Southampton route by sailing to Binic. It is hard for us to tell which of the French harbours would have had better port facilities, since both were essentially small fishing villages, but both had late-Roman fortifications and would have provided a secure base for disembarkation.

So, in the end, the answer probably depends on what forces were available for the British expedition, and that is something we may never know. Moreover, even if the British fleet did anchor off Guernsey to wait for the tide down to Binic, it does not follow that the troops would have disembarked. Nor can we know whether any men from the Channel Islands joined them. But would Arthur have wanted to visit Guorthigern's castle, either on the way out or the way back? That is another question.

Chapter 8:
The Power Struggles of the Sixth Century

8.1   The Saxon Conquest of Belgo-Roman England

The 6th century dawned with northern Europe enjoying a period of relative peace. The British had decisively defeated a Saxon army at Mount Badon, and the Saxon leader Ælle appears to have disappeared from the record around the same time. The Bretons had concluded a treaty with Clovis in Armorica, and his successor was sufficiently well disposed towards them that, in the middle of the century, he gave lands to St Sampson to endow his monastery at Dôl. The Western Roman Empire had disappeared in all but name, but the resulting political settlement restored an element of stability to Western Europe, after a century of turbulence. Italy was under the control of the Ostrogoths. The Alamanni and the Huns had been defeated, the Visigoths had been settled in the south of France and Spain since 415, and the Vandals were occupied in unsuccessful wars with the Berbers in Africa.

The mass-migrations that continued were migrations of Slavic peoples into Eastern Europe, a long way from Britain and Gaul. These were later to have an indirect consequence for Britain, because they severed the connections between the Germanic tribes of Central and Northern Europe and the Eastern Roman Empire, but this would have concerned no one in Britain in the early years of the century.

Unfortunately the period of peace was not to continue: the old tensions between Bretons and Franks and between Britons and Saxons remained, and there were further Saxon migrations into eastern England, either from their homelands in north Germany or from their colonies in northern Gaul. Like the earlier Saxon settlers, and most peoples of the period, these would have been primarily peasant farmers, who engaged in some fighting in the idle months of summer. They brought their womenfolk with them, which meant that they were able to preserve their language and culture, but this also increased the pressure on the land resources of eastern England.

There was some cultural exchange, and even intermarriage, with

163

the indigenous Belgo-Roman tribes of the east, but to the Saxons the local population were all 'wealas', meaning either foreigners or slaves interchangeably, regardless of what language they spoke.

The view from the west was rather different; the enigmatic 'First Address of Taliesin', one of the surviving 6th century poems from Wales, names England as 'Lloegyr' and the Angles and Saxons as 'Allmyn' (Germans). The 'Y Gododin' (a poem written any time between 600 and the early 11th century), employs the term 'Lloegrians' to describe the indigenous population of England, who I refer to as the Belgo-Romans. This term was widely used by historians for many years: for example the Cambridge Essays of 1855 (of the peoples of Scotland) say that *"the present differences observable in the dialects [of Scotland] are due to the fact that the Lloegrians gradually absorbed the entire population to the south of the Clyde and the Forth and their dialect became the paramount idiom in the whole country, just as the Teutonic idioms subsequently overpowered the Lloegrian British".*

The reason why I do not use the term 'Lloegrians' is that it has acquired ethnic associations that I regard as spurious. According to several old commentaries, the Lloegrians came from Gascony, whereas I am confident that the people referred to by that term came from Belgic Gaul.

The 'Book of Taliesin' tells us that:

"Three races cruel from true disposition,
Gwyddyl and Brython and Romani
Create discord and confusion;
And about the boundary of Prydain, beautiful its towns
There is a battle against chiefs above the mead vessels."

The meaning of 'Brython' and 'Romani' is clear, and William Skene ['Celtic Scotland, A History of Ancient Albany', 1890] explains the meaning of 'Gwyddyl' *"Although the word Gwyddyl is in modern Welsh usually translated 'Irish', yet there can be no doubt that it was originally used in a much wider sense as the equivalent of the Irish word 'Gaidheal', and was applied to the whole Gaelic race, wherever located. Of this there is ample evidence in the old Welsh poems."*

So quite clearly, from a Celtic perspective, the British Isles had been populated by Gaels, Britons and 'Romani', before the 'Germans' arrived, and the Welsh authors perceived a clear distinction between Britons (in which they included themselves) and Romani. The story of the 6th century in Britain is essentially then very simple: the Anglo-Saxons found the agriculturally valuable lowland areas of England occupied by 'Romani', who they were easily able to subdue, but they later came into conflict with the Britons and Gaels in the west and the north.

The total number of Saxon immigrants has been estimated to have been in the order of 100,000 to 200,000, and although the indigenous population of the British Isles was much depleted by the middle of the 5th century, it is generally estimated there remained at least 2 million natives. The Saxon genetic influence was therefore limited, and to some extent quarantined within the immigrant communities. This left their genetic legacy exposed to ethnically selective external threats, as we shall see in Chapter 12, but for the next 500 years the Saxon warlords became established as a ruling aristocracy in England and introduced the first effective government into the country.

Their expansion was initially slow, and in the century after the arrival of the first settlers, the Saxons had not progressed far from their 'kingdoms' between the Humber and the Thames (established in the early 5th century) and in Kent and Sussex (established in the second half of the century). So the Anglo Saxon 'empire' in Britain consisted of a group of colonies along the eastern seaboard, divided by the Belgo-Roman salient in London. The northern umbilical cord of this peninsula was Watling Street, which connected London to the Midlands, but the road network also linked London to Bath, Winchester etc. Early attempts by the Angles and Saxons to break out of their east coast domains, and in particular to unite them, met with failure at the Battle of Mount Badon, and for a generation they accepted the status quo.

Natural events then took a hand. In the years 535 and 536, there was a vicious cold snap, probably caused by the eruption of Krakatoa or of volcanoes in South America. In the years with no summers, the crops failed and famine ensued across the globe. The weakened condition of populations everywhere may have contributed to an epidemic in 541 – 542, which appears to have started in China, and which became known as the Plague of Justinian because it wiped out a quarter of the population of Constantinople. Over the next century, it was to kill between a third and one half of the population of Europe, with far-reaching consequences: for example it may have contributed to the rise of Islam, by weakening the Eastern Roman Empire in the 7th century.

This plague was similar to the later Black Death, a contagion borne by fleas living in the fur of rats, and it was imported into Gaul by rats on ships arriving from Egypt. We know from finds of Mediterranean pottery in western Britain that the Atlantic trade routes were operational during this period. The New Cambridge Medieval History comments *"the discovery of a significant quantity of fifth- and sixth- century jars, bowls and amphorae (the so called 'A' and 'B' wares of the archaeologists) from the eastern, central and western Mediterranean in several aristocratic and/or princely sites in Ireland (Garranes and Clogher) and the British far west (Tintagel in Cornwall, Dinas Powys in Wales) and north (Dumbarton Rock) proves that such connections lasted during the Dark Ages."*[1]

These links now cost the Celtic British dearly. The 'Liber Landavensis', or 'Llyfr Teilo', describes how a 'yellow plague' swept through Wales in the 540s, causing massive loss of life. But it is possible that the Saxons were less affected because we have no reports of an epidemic among them. Possibly they were simply resistant to the strain of the disease, but more plausibly they had no trading links with the eastern Mediterranean.

The resulting depopulation of the Celtic lands may have been a trigger for renewed expansion by the Saxons, but we know little of the process by which they came to dominate England. By 547, the Angle kingdom of Bernicia had been established in Northumberland, Durham and southern Scotland, and in about 560 the Saxons had control of the whole of East Yorkshire, where they established the kingdom of Deira. We do not know of any battles that took place in this process. The first 6th century battle that we know of in England was the Battle of Bedcanford in 571, which was won by the Saxons. This gave them control of Aylesbury, Bentham, Eynsham and Limbury, which therefore meant that they had broken through any defensive line based on Watling Street (which broadly followed the course of the modern A5). London must have fallen under Saxon control shortly after this, if it had not already done so. The Saxons had by then united their kingdoms in Sussex and Kent with those in East Anglia, East Yorkshire and Northumberland, so they ruled the whole of central and eastern England.

The Celtic west and the Belgo-Roman centre of the country may have formed alliances against the Saxons, but they also fought among themselves, for example at the Battle of Arfderydd in Cumbria in 572. This cannot have helped their cause. In 577, the Saxons defeated a British army at Dyrham in South Gloucestershire (the meaning of 'durum' in Belgic is discussed at 9.3 - the word meant castle or fort, and Dyrham was probably originally constructed to defend Bath from the Celts), and gained control of the Belgo-Roman south. Gloucester, Cirencester and Bath fell to the Saxons, and the

---

1 Stéphane Lebecq. "The Northern seas (fifth to eighth centuries)" page 642, in Paul Fouracre (ed), The New Cambridge Medieval History, Volume 1. (2005) © Cambridge University Press, reproduced with permission.

land bridge between Wales and Cornwall was broken when the southern crossings of the River Severn came under Saxon control.

In 584 there was a battle at Fethanleag (Faddily in Cheshire) where one of the Saxon leaders was killed, but the British were ultimately defeated, and in consequence the Saxons cut the land bridge between Wales and the Celtic north. So by the end of the 6th century, and with only three recorded battles, the Saxons had control over virtually the whole of the former Belgo-Roman England.

All of the future battles between the Saxons and the Celtic British occurred in the time-honoured boundary zones. The first of these took place in c. 600 at Catterick in Yorkshire where 300 Celtic warriors mounted a suicidal attack on the Saxons established in the town, and were annihilated. The Celts possibly launched their attack from Durham, 28 miles to the north.

Bede tells us that the last battle between the Angles and the Irish in England took place in 603 at Degsastan (location unknown), when the Irish King Aiden of Dál Riada (western Scotland) was defeated by the Bernician King Ethelfrid (Northumberland). Some Angle rebels fought with the Irish, but in conflicts between the Anglo-Saxons and the Gaels, the Celtic Britons appear to have sat on the side-lines, as illustrated by the dismissive comments in the Welsh poem 'The First Address of Taliesin':

"Angles and Gallwydel
Let them make their war."

The Anglo-Saxons broadly inherited the time-honoured frontiers between Belgo-Roman England and the Celtic west and north, so the front line ran through Cheshire in the north-west. Unsurprisingly, the next battle took place at Chester in about 616. Another battle in the same year, near Leeds, shows that Yorkshire was still hotly contested, and there followed conflicts along the ancient Celtic boundaries until the end of the Saxon era. The Cornish were confined to the land west of the Tamar in 936, the Saxons were battling the Picts in Strathclyde in 946 and they were still fighting the Welsh in 1063, three years before Hastings.

In considering this period of conquest, it is important to bear in mind the scale of the war. In the case of a battle in 614, we are told that 2,066 Britons were killed, but as we have seen there were only 300 British warriors in total at the Battle of Catterick. By the standards of the wars being fought on the Continent in that period, these were mere skirmishes. And the populations from which the opposing forces were drawn were also very small. Bede tells us that the Kingdom of Mercia (one of the main Anglo-

Saxon kingdoms, but the latest to develop) comprised 12,000 hides of land in the middle of the 7th century. A hide was the area of land considered necessary to support one family, so if Bede is correct, about a century after the Anglo-Saxon 'annexation' of England, one of their kingdoms consisted of 12,000 families.

By the end of the 6th century, the Anglo-Saxons kingdoms were starting to emerge, the earliest being that of Kent. Here King Æthelbert, a 'high king' of England, who had accepted Christianity in 597, promulgated the first legal code in Europe which was not written in Latin: these laws are the earliest surviving documents written in Old English.

It is indeed in the area of government that the Anglo-Saxons made some of their most enduring contributions to the development of England. Over the 500 years of their imperium, England was forged into a country which, if not exactly a nation state, shared in large measure a system of government and a national identity which were well-advanced for their time. Traces of that system of government are still reflected in the administrative regions of Britain today. The first kingdom to be organised in this way was that of Wessex, which included Hampshire (the district around South Hampton), Devonshire, Dorset, Somerset and Wiltshire. And as the kingdom of Wessex took over other Saxon kingdoms, they too were organised into shires, each with an Ealdorman (Alderman) and a Shire Reeve (Sheriff) responsible for law and order. No other country of the period was as cohesively administered, and few kings were as enlightened as Alfred the Great (849 – 899), who did so much to encourage learning in an age of barbarism.

However the Anglo-Saxon system of government entrenched a system of 'apartheid', which suppressed the British majority (who today are almost invisible in archaeological terms). The laws of King Ine of Wessex (which date from 688 to 694) mention six classes of 'wealas' and confirm their lower social status. Although the later laws of King Alfred do not make the same distinctions, they incorporated the laws of King Ine by reference. The subtle difference between the two legal codes suggests that, by the 9th century, the Anglo-Saxons had absorbed the British elite, and a common 'English' identity had emerged. But it is unlikely that the ordinary British peasants felt like equal members of this nation.

8.2   The Celtic Migration

As the Anglo-Saxons reached the west of England, an increasing number of Brythonic-speaking Celts migrated south to Brittany, especially in the second half of the 6th century. Others went to Galicia in northwest Spain, where a bishopric of Britonia was established (now the parish of Bretoñia). Unlike the earlier British migration to Gaul, which was essentially a migration of troops from the north of England, this second wave was a civil migration, apparently supervised by Celtic nobles and clergy, and therefore with a religious undertone. The people concerned probably thought that they were sailing to a 'promised land'. The earliest migrants included St Brieuc (c.409 – 502), but most of the founding saints of Brittany arrived in the 6th century

Estimates of the total numbers involved in the second wave of migration vary from 30,000 to 100,000. While it appears from both the testimony of Procopius and the fact that these migrants became culturally dominant in Brittany that the peninsula was substantially depopulated before their arrival, the immigration would have resulted eventually in pressure on space. The bulk of this immigration seems to have occurred in the years after the renewal of the Anglo-Saxon campaigns in England, so say from the 540s onwards, and the surge in numbers may have started to result in a shortage of usable farmland by the 560s.

Brittany and the south-west of England were almost symmetrical in their anthropology, with closely related Celtic tribes, originally from Devon and Cornwall, occupying both peninsulas, increasingly compressed on the north side of the Channel by the Anglo-Saxons, and on the southern shore by the Franks, to their east. The parallels can be helpful in explaining events, but can also result in confusion, especially because the settlers in Brittany renamed many parts of their territory after the equivalent locations in Devon and Cornwall. This problem, which we encountered when discussing the Arthurian romances, often makes it hard to distinguish between Cornouaille in Brittany and Cornwall in England.

As we shall see, it appears that the early settlements In Brittany were established in the west and south of the peninsula, but later on the migrants colonised lands further east, including territories formerly occupied by the Coriosolites. This brought them into conflict with the Franks at the end of the century, but the early settlements were peaceful, and the Franks maintained to the outside world that they had invited the Bretons in.

The main written records relating to the period are later hagiographies of the Breton saints, typically written in the 10th and 11th centuries, and it is hard to know how much history underlies them. But some of these date from earlier periods, including a few rare examples from the 7th or 8th centuries, and the earliest Life of St Sampson may date from as little as 50 years after his death. Moreover we have a contemporary witness in the person of Gregory of Tours, who continued writing until his death in 594.

Born in the Auvergne into a Senatorial family, Gregory was not a Frank, but lived among them and recorded a great deal in ten books collectively known as 'The History of the Franks'. From his home in Tours, he had a relatively close knowledge of Brittany, although there is no evidence that he ever visited the province. In addition to the sources available in what is now France, most of the early Breton saints came from Wales, and there is a certain amount of source material in the ancient records of Welsh churches that can be of assistance.

8.3   The Role of the Channel Islands in the Migration

We know that the Channel Islands (or at least most of them) were under Frankish rule by the middle of the 6th century, because when St Sampson asked Childebert for more lands to augment his small estate at Dôl (which had been carved out of the See of Alet), Childebert gave him four of the islands. This probably took place in about 557. Bertrand d'Argentré (1519 – 1590), a court official in Rennes, wrote: *"To this archbishop, Childebert gave some islands and lands in Normandy: Rimoul, Augie, Sargie and Vesargie, which were islands off the coast, for so I find in the old documents".*[2][3]

And there seems to have been a Frankish system of government in the islands, based on the old Roman system of regional 'counts', a system which reflected the regimes in the adjacent parts of France. Gregory of Tours reports that *"from the death of King Clovis onwards the Bretons remained under the domination of the Franks and their rulers were called counts and not kings".* A *"chief and prince"* Withur probably ruled in Dumnonée in such a capacity, and St Magloire is reported to have cured the leprosy of the 'Count of the Islands' *('Comes Insularum'),* one Count Lojesco, or Loïescon. Presumably, after Childebert's gift to him, St Sampson had an interest in the rental income from his islands as a landlord, while the Count had administrative control and was responsible to Childebert for their government. There was also a regional ruler in Brittany called Judual, who seems to have had an intermediate status. He is described as a 'king' in the

2 *"A cest archivesque Childebert donna quelques isles et terres en Normandie: Rimoul, Augie, Sargie, et Vesargie, qui estaint isles en la coste; carje trouve cela aux vieilles lettres".*

3 Bertrand d'Argentre: L'Histoire de Bretaigne, des rois, ducs, comtes, et princes d'icelle, depuis l'an 383 jusques au temps de madame Anne Reyne de France dernière Duchesse. Troisième édition revue et augmentée par messire Charles d'Argentré. Paris, by Nicolas Buon (1618)

'Life of St Magloire', but the Breton tradition in titles suffered from a certain amount of inflation, and it seems more probable that he held a position subordinate to Childebert, but senior to Withur and Lojesco. 'Prince' might be a more apt title for him, and so we should demote Withur to 'Count'.

It is not clear exactly which islands were under Lojesco's control, because in the 'Life of St Magloire' we are told that Lojesco 'owned three of the Channel Islands' and that he gave Sark to Magloire. Sark had been settled from Jersey, so it would be reasonable to assume that Jersey was one of the other islands under Lojesco's rule. And Brecqhou, the same work tells us, belonged to one Niro or Nivo, so my guess is that the third island in Lojesco's control was Alderney, which was the other island in Childebert's gift to St Sampson. In other words, Sampson's title as overlord covered the same four islands as Lojesco's and Niro's governorships combined.

The names of the islands in the gift to St Sampson, as recorded, are curious, being evidently the Frankish names for them, but also in the omission of one of the Channel Islands. We can presume that Rimoul is Alderney, Augie is Jersey, Sargie is Sark, and in my opinion Vesargie (or Bis-Sargia in some manuscripts) is Brecqhou; which leaves the question of what happened to Guernsey?

We can be fairly confident of the name of Jersey, because in the later reign of Charlemagne, Geroaldus, Abbot of Fontenelle in Neustria, was sent to Jersey with an imperial commission, and the account of the mission identifies 'Augia' as an island near Coutances.[4]

A rather more problematic reference, which may or may not provide corroboration for the name of Jersey at this time, is found in the 'Life of St Marculf', a monk who had been given land at Nanteuil by Childebert. He is thought to have been born in about 500, in Bayeux, and to have died in 588, and he is said to have been the man who sent St Helier to Jersey. But the oldest history of his life tells us that he himself visited an island called 'Agna', which he found to have only thirty inhabitants, one of whom was a hermit called Elitus. It seems very improbable that Jersey would have had so few inhabitants, but conceivably the population had been devastated by the plague. Or alternatively, was Agna another island, perhaps Chausey?

Some writers have said that Vesargie was Guernsey, but this simply cannot be the case. For one thing it would make no sense to call Guernsey 'West Sark' – it was, and is, much larger and more commercially significant. In any case, there are islands between Sark and Guernsey, and 'West Sark' must imply some measure of proximity. Sargia' is also said to refer

4 Francois de Beaurepaire – Les Noms des Communes et Anciennes Paroisses de la Manche, 1986

to Guernsey, being said to mean 'twice Sark' in a reference to the relative sizes of the islands, but that makes little more sense. It would be like calling Britain 'twice Ireland'. And 'bis' in modern French is used to mean 'extension', an apposite description of Brecqhou, which is separated from Sark only by the narrow Gouliot Passage.

Guernsey may have been called Lisia in the middle of the 6th century, or it may have started to acquire is modern name (eg as Guerneri), but it is very unlikely that it was ever Vesargie. The island directly to the west of Sark is Brecqhou, the name of which is Norse and therefore of much later origin (Brenk Hólmr means 'steep island'), and in my opinion that is the island which was called Vesargie in the 6th century.

So why was Guernsey omitted? Clearly one possibility is that d'Argentré simply forgot the gift of Guernsey (after all, he seems to be recalling the original documents which he claims to have read, rather than copying them down, and they have not survived). But the same four islands seem to have formed parts of the estates of Lojesco and Niro, so I suspect that the omission of Guernsey was deliberate. Another possibility is that Guernsey had already been given to St Sampson, and Childebert later added the other islands to his estates. St Sampson, according to local legend, visited Guernsey and converted the population, so it is possible that he had asked Childebert for Guernsey along with the land at Dôl after he first arrived in Brittany.

But more exotically, perhaps Guernsey was not Childebert's to give. Had the 'kingdom of Guorthigern' remained an independent kingdom, or was it a dependency of some other power? Was it perhaps a holy place, which was considered autonomous (perhaps a little like Tours in the 6th century)? Unfortunately there is so little recorded history for this period that we will probably never know. But it does seem clear that Guernsey had a status which was different from that of the other Channel Islands.

The migration story also brings into question the route taken by the British emigrants. The ships of the period were more capable than pre-Roman era ships (having rudders for one thing) and there is no doubt that they made voyages far longer then the direct Channel crossings. But the association of St Sampson with Guernsey and the other Channel Islands suggests that the route via the islands was still in use. This evidence is not conclusive, because we cannot know whether St Sampson came to Guernsey from Brittany, having originally arrived in the west of the peninsula. But if he first arrived in France near Cancale, as Breton legend suggests, it would be highly probable that he travelled via the Channel Islands.

Despite having lived under Frankish rule for a few decades, I think we can assume that the Channel Islands of the mid 6th century would still have been culturally 'Roman'. But Frankish influence was increasing, especially in Jersey, which was converted to Christianity by St Helier, a monk from Frankish Belgium. This influence is reflected in the dedication of several parishes in Jersey to Frankish saints (St Clement, St Martin, St Ouen and St Helier), a pattern that is not generally seen in the other islands (St Martin in Guernsey being the exception).[5]

It is very likely that the local populations spoke Gallo-Roman dialects, after 500 years of existence on the periphery of the Roman Empire, and these would probably have been intelligible to the Franks after their 200 years as Roman fœderati. The people of Devon and Cornwall spoke Brythonic, and there is virtually no evidence of Brythonic in Channel Islands personal or place names, excepting the personal names which can be traced to later immigrations of agricultural labourers from Brittany. This may indicate that, before the main Celtic migration of the 6th century, the population of the Channel Islands had limited contact with Brythonic speakers.

Very little is known of the ephemeral St Helier, but legend has it that he was killed by Saxon pirates in the course of a raid on Jersey. We do not know of organised Saxon raiding fleets (like those of the later Vikings) at this time, but a drunken robbery by a rogue crew is certainly a possibility. The legends suggest that St Helier's body was taken to Normandy for interment, which reinforces the impression that Jersey's connections with the Côtentin were strong.

It is unclear to what extent the Channel Islands were still involved in International trade at this time, but the archaeological evidence suggests that the main Atlantic Coast trade probably crossed the Channel at the western end. For example shards of 'B2' amphorae have been found at nine places in Devon and Cornwall, five places in Somerset, one in Glamorgan, one at Dumbarton Rock in Scotland and five in Ireland. These amphorae originated in the north-eastern Mediterranean, some from Rhodes and Cyprus, but most from Asia Minor (Cilicia) and Antioch, and they date from the 5th to the 7th centuries. This kind of pottery has not been unearthed in the Channel Islands, and an outlier found at the Île Lavret, near Bréhat is the only evidence that the traffic in these containers and their contents came anywhere near the Islands.[6]

Further evidence that the Atlantic trade route was still operational is

5 It occurs to me that this influence may be responsible for the 'South African' accent detectable in the speech of the indigenous population of Jersey today.
6 Pierre Roland Giot and Guirec Querré, 'Le Tesson d'Amphore B2 de l'Île Lavret (Bréhat, Côtes du Nord) et le Problème des Importations', Revue Archéologique de l'Ouest, 1985,

found in the 'Life of St John the Almsgiver', where one of the miracles the saint is said to have performed related to a sea-captain who sailed to Britain to collect tin. This demonstrates that in Cyprus at least (which is where the book was written by Leontius, sometime after 641), Britain was still known as a source of tin. But there is no reason to suppose that ships which regularly crossed the Bay of Biscay would have sailed to Guernsey to collect it.

Whatever the trade route for freight, it seems that some of the Britons migrating to Brittany sailed via the Channel Islands: St Sampson (d.565) and St Magloire (who settled in Sark in 565) apparently arrived in Brittany together, near Cancale, and according to the Life of St Malo (d.620), that saint arrived at the Île de Cézembre (now St Malo) *"after seven years of navigation"* (this is a story that we will explore further in section 8.6). But St Brieuc (c.409 – c.502) landed at L'Aberwrac'h; St Tugdual (d.563), a Welsh monk who became Bishop of Tréguier, landed at Trébabu in the Léon district (with 72 followers); and Paul Aurélien also arrived in the west with a party of 24. Similarly, St Paterne of Vannes may have arrived at that port in south Brittany.

The general impression is that both routes were used, and that the earlier migrations arrived in the west of the peninsula. It also seems that the Bretons only landed in the Bay of St Malo after the treaty of 496 – 499, and we may therefore conclude that this treaty had the effect of reopening the Channel Islands route. The later arrivals probably chose locations further east because the west had already been settled and because the land east of the great forest, which stretched from St Brieuc down to Auray, was more easily cultivated.

From the point of view of the Channel Islands, their relative isolation from the Atlantic trade route may have had a silver lining, if it saved the Islands from the worst effects of the plague. But then we are drawn back to the troublesome reference to 'Agna' in the 'Life of St Marculf', and have to wonder whether the Islands really did escape the contagion.

8.4   The Bretons

The records of this period explicitly distinguish between the 'Bretons' and the 'Romans' living on both sides of the Channel (eg Canon 9 of the Second Council of Tours, in 567, which prohibited the consecration of Breton or Roman bishops in Armorica without the written permission of the central authorities, and the first Vita Samsonis[7] (early 7th century) which says that the saint's feast day was celebrated by *"numerous Bretons and Romans on one side of the sea and on the other")*. It is therefore clear that there were people in both England and Armorica who were not Bretons but who were not Saxon or Frankish either.

In Gaul, we know these people as Gallo-Romans, and in this book I have used the term Belgo-Romans for the Britons, but it is probable that they all considered themselves to be Romans. This is especially likely to have been the case in northern Gaul, where there was a Roman administration until 486, whereas England had expelled its Roman officials at the start of the century. England was in any case less Romanised throughout the period of the Empire. In fact, we are told by Gregory of Tours that the Bretons still adopted Roman hairstyles and dress in his day, and that the Saxons sent to reinforce them were ordered to adopt the same costumes to distinguish them from the enemy.

In 554, the Eastern Roman Emperor Justinian wrested control of Italy back from the Ostrogoths, after 20 years of war. This created a new competition for hegemony in Western Europe, with the Eastern Empire now in close proximity to the rising superpower of the Franks. The Franks, in their usual way, fluctuated between diplomatic efforts to form an alliance with Justinian on the one hand and providing surreptitious support for a last Ostrogoth uprising against him in the late 550s. They sent ambassadors to Constantinople to convey the message that they were the imperial power in most of Gaul and western Germany, and that, through their Saxon allies, they also ruled in England. In respect of the latter claim, it was essential that they should conceal from Justinian that there were still 'Romans' in England, who did not regard the Saxons as the legitimate heirs to the Empire. So to bolster their claims, they sent Angles along with their delegation, as witnesses to the alliance between the Anglo-Saxons and the Franks. We know what they told Justinian, because Procopius (500 – 565) was on hand to record their presentations:

"The island of Brittia is inhabited by three very populous nations, each having a king. And the names of these nations are Angiloi, Frissones and those of one name with the island, Britones. And so great appears to be the population of these three nations, that every year they emigrate thence in large companies to the land of the Franks. And the Franks allow them to settle in the part of their land which appears to be more deserted; and by this means they say they are winning over the island. Thus it actually happened

7 Book II, 11

that, not long ago, the king of the Franks, in sending over some of his intimates in an embassy to Basileus Justinian in Byzantium, sent with them some of the Angiloi, thus seeking to establish his claim that the island was ruled by him."

Thus we know that the Franks claimed to have invited the Britons to settle in Armorica 'to win over the island', but the reality is that the Franks would not have known much about what was going on in Brittany, which was largely cut off from the rest of France by a vast and dense forest.

We know little of the individual migrants, because most of the genealogies of the Breton saints and kings date from the 10th and 11th centuries, and cannot be regarded as reliable. But the 'Lives' of various Saints do offer us some clues, in particular the two 'Lives of St Sampson', one of which probably dates from the 7th century. St Sampson was educated in Wales, and had studied at a monastery on Caldey Island off the coast of Pembrokeshire. He became abbot of this monastery when his predecessor, Pyro, had got drunk and fallen down a well. He had been consecrated a Bishop in 521. He visited Cornwall and then sailed for Brittany, arriving, according to Breton legend, at the River of Guyout (possibly Vivier-sur-Mer, near Cancale).

The earlier 'Vita' tells us that when Sampson arrived in Brittany, one Commorus, an 'alien chief' had bought the support of Childebert and killed Jonas, the rightful ruler of the area. Jonas' son Judual had been sentenced to death and was in prison awaiting execution. Sampson went immediately to Childebert, and having overcome a hostile reception by performing miracles, he persuaded Childebert to grant Judual his freedom. He then went with Judual to the islands of Guernsey ('Lesia') and Jersey ('Augie'), where the people were *"well-known"* to Sampson, and raised a fighting force. This party sailed to Brittany, and Judual *"with a single stroke knocked down the unjust and violent Commorus".* Childebert then gave Sampson the land to found a monastery at Dôl-de-Bretagne ('dôl' means grief), which became one of the most important religious centres in Brittany.

Others have speculated that Commorus was the Breton Count Chonomor, recorded by Gregory of Tours in a story dated to about 550. Gregory writes of an episode when a Count of the Bretons, Chanao, had killed three of his brothers, and had imprisoned a fourth, Macliau. Macliau was freed on the intervention of Felix, the Bishop of Nantes on condition that he swore an oath of allegiance to his brother. Later Macliau broke his oath, and was pursued by his brother Chanao, taking refuge *"near another count of this region named Chonomor",* who hid him and told Chanao he was dead. Chanao was delighted at the news, and took possession of the whole kingdom, while Macliau took refuge in Vannes where he was consecrated a Bishop. But when Chanao died, Macliau renounced his religious vows, taking back the wife he had deserted to become a man of the cloth, and seized his brother's kingdom. For this he was excommunicated.

Chanao was killed at the Battle of Nostang in 558, as we shall see presently, so it is plausible that Sampson encountered Chonomor/Commorus in c.550. And the description of Commorus as an 'alien chief' suggests that he was a British Dumnonian who had settled in Domnonée – some have speculated that he was the British Marcus Conomorus (the 'King Mark' of Tristan and Isolde).

Bernard Merdrignac and Philippe Guigon ('The British Settlement of Brittany', 2003) consider it likely that Macliau ruled the area around the Morbihan, and that his surviving brother Budic controlled Cornouaille (on the basis of the many 'Budic' place names in that area). Macliau and Budic made a pact that when either of them should die, the other would protect the interests of the deceased brother's children. But when Budic died in 577, Macliau seized his 'kingdom' and drove his son Thierry into exile. According to Gregory of Tours, Thierry, after *"a long time fugitive and wandering"* returned to Brittany and killed Macliau and his son Jacob. As with St Malo's *"seven years of navigation"* to reach Brittany, one cannot help wondering whether Thierry's period in exile took him to the Channel Islands.

But in the 'Vita' of St Melor, the son of Macliau, we are told that Macliau, was murdered by 'his brother' Rivod, who had taken control of Cornouaille. Macliau had escaped to the court of Conomor at Léon, but Rivod pursued and slew him. This suggests that Judual did not kill Commorus, because he still had a court at Léon at some point after 558. One version of the 'Life of St Lunaire', which may date from the 9th or 10th centuries, tells us that a Briton called Riwal came to Brittany, and was a leader *("dux")* of the peoples on both sides of the sea. In other 'Vitae' of the period, Riwal is described as a *"king of Cornouaille"* or a *"chief of Dumnonia"*, so we really do not know what his rank was or what area he ruled, but the 'Vita of St Winnoc' dates his arrival to the reign of Clotaire I, (558 – 561), which would mean that he was a contemporary of Macliau. The only problem then is that Gregory tells us that Thierry killed Macliau, whereas the Vitae tell us he was killed by Riwal.

Fortunately we do not need to concern ourselves with this issue, since the salient points from the Channel Islands perspective are the dates of the arrival of St Sampson in Brittany, which seems to have been c.550, and the Battle of Nostang and subsequent conflicts between the Bretons and the Franks, which are confirmed by Gregory.

There is corroboration for the date of arrival of St Sampson in the Welsh ecclesiastical history too, because the 'Liber Landavensis, Llyfr Teilo' tells us that, after the plague swept through Wales in about 549, St Teilo, a monk of royal blood, took the survivors of his community to Dôl, where he and St Sampson planted an orchard of fruit trees between Dôl and Cal. So this story supports a date of about 550 for the foundation of the monastery. St Teilo is reported to have stayed in Brittany for 7 years and 7 months, possibly returning to Britain because of the conflict which arose in 558.

When Sampson arrived in Brittany, the Vitae tell us that the *"chief and the prince of this region"* was Withur, who governed in the name of Childebert ('this region' being Dumnonée). Another early Breton saint was Paul Aurelian, known as 'the Dumnonian' (possibly a relative of the Ambrosius Aurelianus mentioned by Gildas as the British king at the Battle of Mount Badon). He is said to have been a cousin of Withur, who gave Paul his house on the Île de Batz and a deserted oppidum on the mainland. Paul landed at the 'Port of the Oxen', and took possession of a Villa Petri in Ploudelmazeau. He was then sent by Withur on a mission to King Childebert, who ordered that he be consecrated 'at Lutetia', and settled lands on him *"in the two countries of Ac'h and Léon"*, in the furthest extremities of Brittany.

Childebert's gifts to Paul and Sampson, and his appointment of Tugdual as Bishop of Tréguier, confirm that by the mid-6th century he ruled over the whole of northern Brittany; and we can guess that the appointment of Clovis as a Roman Consul in 508 had given him that authority (although Gregory dates it from the death of Clovis in 511). But to what extent the Frankish kings exercised local control is less certain. When Count Leudaste later fell out with King Sigebert in Tours, he fled into 'exile' in Brittany (according to Gregory), which suggests that the writ of the Frankish kings did not run far below the constitutional surface. And we know that the Franks were not present in the peninsula in numbers sufficiently large as to significantly affect the DNA of the population (see Chapter 1).

In terms of the church, the clergy of Brittany seem to have become more integrated into the episcopate of the Frankish kingdoms as the century wore on. Eumerius, the Bishop of Nantes attended the Second Council of Orleans in 533, although Nantes may by then have been in Frankish hands. But the decidedly Breton Sampson attended the Council of Paris in 557. It appears that he received the donation of four Channel Islands at this time, and it was as well for him that he took this opportunity, because a year or so later Childebert was dead and the Bretons were at war with the Franks.

The Bretons came not only with their own language, but also with their own tradition in names – for people and places. *"By Tre- Pol- and Pen- may you know the Cornishmen"* goes a British saying, and these stems are to be found in the names of many people and places in Brittany. 'Tre' means estate or homestead, 'pol' means pond or pool, and 'pen' means head. In particular the word 'Poul-' (pool) and the word 'Ker' (city) are very indicative of the spread of the Breton culture, and Frankish names like 'Guerche' (fortified place) mark the places on the other side of the boundary. If I am right that the later arrivals settled in the east of the peninsula, these newcomers will have put additional pressure on the ill-defined boundary between Brittany and the Frankish kingdom of Neustria, and it is easy to see how competition for land could have flared into violence.

At some point in the early 6th century, the Bretons had become subjects of the Frankish kings, and I have suggested that this followed from Clovis' appointment as a Roman Consul in 508. So the areas described as 'kingdoms' in the Vitae of the saints were no more than counties in constitutional terms. However, there was an area around Vannes that may have maintained a greater degree of independence. This was called the Bro Waroc'h or Broërec, after an early Breton chieftain called Waroc'h or Erec, who is said to have died in c.550. It was this chieftain who is said to have given Gildas the land on which to construct his monastery on the Rhuys peninsula. And it was this area which was to prove the focus of the conflicts between the Bretons and the Franks which ignited from 558 onwards.

8.5   Renewed Conflict Between Bretons and Franks

Clotaire I (Lothar) was one of the brothers of Childebert, and the ruler of north-east Gaul from his capital in Soissons, about 60 miles from modern Paris. He had annexed the kingdom of one of his brothers, Chlodomer, who died in 524, instigating the murders of Chlodomer's three young children in the process, and he had subjugated the Burgundians in 534. And when his great nephew Theodebald died in 555, he seized the territory of the Ripuarian Franks (after a bloody battle), and took Theodebald's wife to bed. So at the time when Sampson was arriving in Brittany, Clotaire ruled three-quarters of the Frankish empire, and his only rival was Childebert, ruling in what was to become Neustria (roughly modern Normandy, west of the Seine).

Clotaire had seven sons by several wives (two of them sisters), but three of them did not survive him. One of these sons was called Chramn, the only son of Chunsina, Clotaire's last wife. Clotaire sent Chramn to Clermont-Ferrand where he lived a life of dissipation, while his father fought against

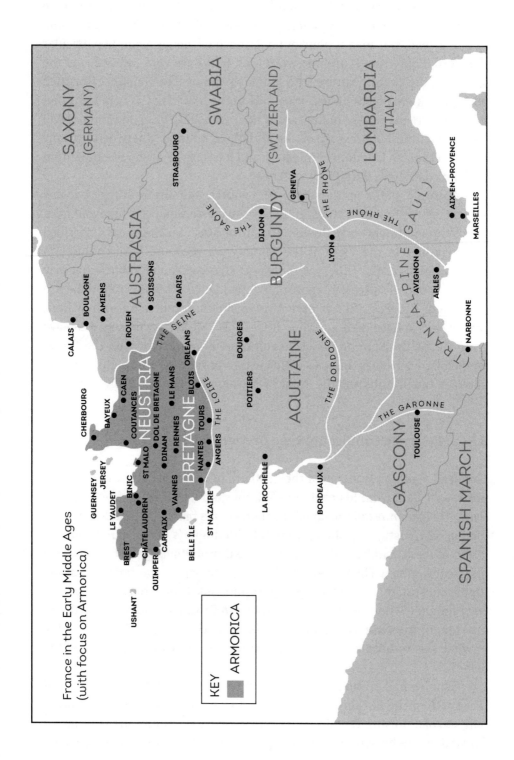

France in the Early Middle Ages
(with focus on Armorica)

KEY

ARMORICA

180

the Saxons in Thuringia. Chramn made himself unpopular in Clermont, notably by issuing a royal decree that the daughters of certain senators should be abducted for his entertainment. So when he became seriously ill and all his hair fell out, this was probably seen as divine retribution, and Chramn decided to move to Poitiers to escape the succession of plagues which then ravaged Clermont.

He resolved to get close to his uncle Childebert, and the two of them began to conspire against Clotaire. Clotaire visited the Limousin, part of his father's kingdom, and behaved as if he ruled it. His actions were reported to Clotaire who sent two of his other sons, Charibert and Gontran, to deal with the miscreant, but before battle could be engaged. Chramn sent a messenger to his half-brothers to say that their father had been killed in battle, which caused them to head for Burgundy.

Incidentally, Charibert's daughter Adelberg (also known as Bertha) married King Æthelbert of Kent, to cement the alliance between the Franks and the Saxons, but only on condition that she should be allowed to continue to practise her religion. We will return to this couple in 8.6.

With Clotaire tied up fighting the Saxons, Chramn pursued his brothers, and Childebert, who had also been told that his brother had been killed, marched into Clotaire's territory, pillaging the area around Reims. But Childebert then fell ill, and after a long decline he died in 558, leaving two daughters but no sons.

Chramn was already in revolt against his father, and had assembled an army drawn from Aquitaine and the Arverne. He decided to form an alliance with the Bretons, who clearly must have felt concerned at the prospect of becoming subjects of Clotaire, and Chramn took himself and his forces to the area around Vannes. Clotaire realised that a potential insurrection had to be nipped in the bud, and pursued Chramn to Brittany. The result was the Battle of Nostang in the same year, near Lorient, which resulted in a complete victory for Clotaire. The Breton king Chanao was killed in battle, and Chramn, his wife and daughters were captured. Chramn was strangled and his family were shut in a cottage which was torched.

The battle put an end to the alliance that Clovis had formed with the Bretons, and the area formerly occupied by the Veneti became disputed. To the Franks, this territory was theirs by conquest, but the Bretons considered they had a prior claim. And the potential for further Breton revolt was clear, because the Breton leadership was not annihilated in the battle: Chanao was succeeded by his brother Macliau, the former Bishop of Vannes.

Clotaire was already 61 in 558, and he died in 561. Just as his father had done, he divided his kingdom between his four surviving sons, and the new western kingdom of Neustria and Aquitaine passed to Caribert I. Charibert, in the family's tradition, practised 'serial monogamy', but despite having a succession of wives and mistresses, when he died in 568 he left no sons. Daughters, such as Charibert's daughter Adelberg, the Queen of Kent, were unable to inherit under Frankish law.

This resulted in a second 'partage' of the kingdom, and Chilperic inherited the Kingdom of Soissons, which included Neustria and the disputed territory around Vannes. Oddly, an enclave around Coutances formed part of the Kingdom of Reims, and since the Channel Islands were later to form part of the diocese of Coutances, it is not absolutely certain to which Frankish kingdom they belonged. However, the Bretons took full advantage of the family feuds that inevitably followed the partage, and Chanao's son Waroch II (grandson of the founder of the Bro Waroc'h) seized Vannes in 578.

This provoked a response, and Chilperic assembled an army recruited from Poitou, Maine, and Anjou together with Saxons from the Bessin, and marched westwards to be confronted by Waroch on the Vilaine River in 580. The armies fought for three days to a standstill, and in the resulting negotiations, Waroch agreed to nominally hand back Vannes on condition that he governed it 'by order of the king', and that he would pay tribute and hand over his son as a hostage.

The Bretons then began to pillage the area around Rennes and seized the vineyards of Nantes at the time of the vintage. Waroch steadily siphoned off the production back to the Vannetais over the next few years. Chilperic was assassinated by an unknown assailant in 584, leaving Neustria in the care of his widow Queen Fredegund, as regent for his unborn son Clotaire II. In 588 the Bishops of Nantes, Angers and Le Mans appealed to King Gontran of Burgundy, whose capital was at Orleans, for help against the predations of the Bretons, with the result that, in 590, Gontran sent an army against Waroch led by two generals, Beppolen and Ebrachaire. But this initiative clearly offended Fredegund, who was not a woman to be ignored, and who in any case detested both Gontran, her brother-in-law, and Duke Beppolen. So, rather surprisingly, she sent some Saxons in her service to support the Bretons!

Waroch also benefited from disunity in Gontran's army, because Beppolen and Ebrachaire quarrelled on the way to Brittany, and their forces set up separate camps. In the resulting battles, Duke Beppolen was killed in action, but Ebrachaire succeeded in capturing Vannes. To recover the city, Waroch handed over hostages and declared his loyalty to Gontran, but as soon as Ebrachaire had gone, Waroch instructed his son Canao to attack the Frankish rearguard as they retreated across the River Vilaine (possibly to free the hostages?). In a rage, Ebrachaire devastated all of the places he went through on his return journey, as far as Tours, with the result that he was banished by Gontran.

So by the end of the 6th century, as the Belgic Britons in England were being subsumed into Saxon kingdoms, the Bretons had reclaimed their de facto independence from the Franks. The territory of the Veneti was once again Breton, but Nantes seems to have remained under Frankish control. The Franks decided to quarantine the Bretons in their peninsula and established a border zone based on the Vilaine and Oust rivers - a contemporary account refers to *"the Limes of the Bretons"*, effectively the ancestor of the Breton Marches.

8.6   The Celtic Saints

The churches in Britain suffered during the collapse of the Western Empire, both from the general economic and social malaise and from internal divisions over Pelagianism, the 'heresy' taught by a British monk called Pelagius in Rome. This doctrine had obviously caught on in Britain, because in c. 429, the Bishops of Gaul sent Bishop Germanus to Britain, *"to go to the Britons and confirm their belief in God's grace"*[8] (ie to renounce Pelagianism), which he did by holding a public debate. While in Britain, Germanus also led a British force in a battle with Picts and Saxons, and castigated Guorthigern for his sins.

At about this time, St Patrick was helping to establish the church in Ireland. He was the son of a Roman official who lived on the west coast of Britain, or possibly Armorica. He was captured by Irish raiders when he was about 16, and taken to northern Ireland where he was forced to work as a shepherd. But he managed to escape in about 420 and boarded a ship bound for Gaul, which was carrying a cargo of hunting dogs. When he arrived in Gaul, he absorbed the teachings of the Marmoutier community, and when he returned to his parents, he told them that he wanted to become a Christian missionary in Ireland, where the seeds of Christianity had not yet taken root. Pope Celestine had sent Palladius as the first bishop *"to the believers in Ireland"* in 431, but his mission had been unsuccessful, and Palladius had soon returned to Rome.

8 Bede

Patrick was appointed a bishop in 432, and, with the benefit of being able to speak the native Gaelic language, he won many converts, despite the fierce opposition of the Druids. The Christian establishment that Patrick founded in Ireland later exported the religion to other parts of the region: Brendan (486 – 578) is reported to have voyaged in a curragh in the Atlantic, and it is known that the Irish religious community had strong ties to the church in Wales. The Irish also exported Christianity to the west of Scotland, when a monastery was established by Columba on the island of Iona in 563. From there, missionaries went out to the Picts, Angles, Saxons and Jutes, and a member of the Iona community, Aiden, established a monastery on Lindisfarne off the coast of Northumberland in c.635.

Meanwhile the Roman church, having baptised Clovis in 496, had established its control over Gaul on the back of the military successes of the Franks. The Arian Visigoths had been expelled from Aquitaine after 508, and the Burgundians, who were also Arians, had been defeated in 534. So, towards the end of the century, Pope Gregory (540 – 604) decided it was time for the Roman church to reach out to the barbarians in England. We know that he was aware of the British, because he had once seen some beautiful English slave boys for sale in the Forum, and had made a pun about Angles and Angels to his companions at the time.

He therefore sent St Augustine of Canterbury to Britain with a party of 40 supporters, to convert the Saxon King of Kent, Æthelbert, a mission undertaken with considerable trepidation because of the fearsome reputation of the heathen Saxons, as conveyed to Rome by the Frankish clergy. Kent was chosen for the destination of this mission, partly because it was known that Æthelbert's wife was the Christian Adelburg (or Bertha), daughter of King Charibert of the Franks. The missionary party halted in southern France, and sent Augustine back to Rome to beg to be recalled, but Pope Gregory encouraged them to persevere. However, Augustine and his companions did not meet with the martyrdom they possibly expected, because, when they arrived at Canterbury, they discovered that there was already a Christian community there. Adelberg had had a chapel constructed, where she regularly celebrated Mass with the priest who had accompanied her from Francia, along with a growing congregation. As Thomas Hodgkin put it *"It was the opinion of the Pope Gregory that the Frankish ecclesiastics of Gaul had been somewhat neglectful of their duties in reference to their heathen neighbours of Britain."*[9] The mission was successful, Æthelbert was duly converted, and thousands took part in a mass-baptism on Christmas

[9]'Longman's Political History of England', 1906.

Day in 597. Further missions followed, the first in 603, when Augustine summoned the bishops *"of the nearest British province"* to a conference. But the Celtic bishops of the north and west, many originating from Iona, were reluctant to submit to the jurisdiction of the church in Rome. The schism was only healed at the Synod of Whitby in 664, when differences over the calculation of the date of Easter and the hairstyles of monks were resolved in favour of the Roman doctrine.

In Guernsey, as we have seen, the local legend is that the island was converted by St Sampson in c.550, and Jersey is said to have been converted by St Helier at a similar point in time. But some have speculated that Christianity may have come to the Channel Islands before that. Certainly it is hard to imagine that no one in the Channel Islands had heard of Christianity, if it had been widespread in Britain and Gaul in the 4th century and the official religion of the Roman Empire since 391. St Martin of Tours had been preaching relatively near by from 373, and the influence of the monastery at Marmoutier is visible in the dedication of parishes in both Guernsey and Jersey to the saint. So it is certainly possible that missionaries had reached the islands long before the arrival of St Sampson and St Helier, despite the fact that the Vitae Samsonis tell us that Lisia was still pagan before Sampson's visit.

Possible evidence of an earlier mission is found in the Life of St Brendan. This Irish saint (c.484 – 587) undertook a 'seven-year voyage' with a group of companions, one of whom was St Malo, to the 'Isle of the Blessed', sometime between 512 and 530, before his visit to Britain. The 'Isle of the Blessed' is described in the usual lyrical terms as a fertile place, covered in vegetation, but no other description is provided. However, in one of the most frequently cited tales of his voyage, he landed on an island that turned out to be a sea monster called Jasconius or Jascon. Could this be our old friend the leper Count Lojesco?

According to various theories, his voyage (in a curragh, remember) took him to the Canary Islands, the Azores or North America, but many writers have expressed doubt as to the historical value of the legend. My observations are that Malo, the person, ended up in St Malo, the town, and that none of the Azores, Canary Islands, or North America are located on any reasonable route from Ireland to this destination. So it seems to me fairly likely that Brendan and his party sailed to the Channel Islands, probably specifically Guernsey, 20 years before St Sampson arrived. They may even have established a monastery there, because there are traces of an ancient religious settlement near the Vale Church in the north of the island, which are generally attributed to events in the 10th century, which we will discuss in Chapter 12.

Previously, the people of the Channel Islands had worshipped various gods of an astronomical or natural origin, and in Guernsey in particular there appears to have been a cult around a female figurehead, perhaps a goddess. Two granite statues of female figures are located in local churchyards, and one early consequence of the island's conversion to Christianity may have been the resculpting of one of them, now known as La Gran' Mere du Chimquiere ('the grand-mother of the cemetery'). This statue is today located at the entrance to St Martin's Church. It is about 4000 years old in origin, but facial features and clothing across the shoulders, in a Roman style, were added at a later date. A sister statue at Castel church has not received this treatment, but we know nothing more about the origins of either monument or the religion that they may represent.

Chapter 9:
The Origins of English

9.1   Belgic

In my view, the key to understanding the England of the Dark Ages lies in the development of the English language. A large component of this language is of course the Anglo-Saxon of the Germanic invaders from the east, but there is a great deal of the language which is not of Anglo-Saxon origin, but which is not of Brythonic origin either. I have expressed my view that, when the Romans arrived in Britain, the population of south-eastern England spoke a language which derived from the language of the Belgae in north-western Gaul, and I believe that, by the end of the Roman era, most of the common folk of England spoke this language with a Latin gloss. I therefore prefer the term 'Belgo-Romans' for these people, to the more commonly used 'Romano-British', which is both ambiguous (because it could include Celtic-speaking Britons), and misleading because it implies that they spoke Latin. And I also reject the Welsh term 'Lloegrians', because this is associated with 'a people from Gascony', which they were not.

The languages of the Belgae and Anglo-Saxons were very similar. As Henri Guillaume Philippe Moke observed[10] *"it is easy to recognise a close relationship between this coastal idiom, which is the real Flamand, and the language of the Anglo-Saxons who previously occupied the area north of the Elbe and who would later conquer England. These are dialects so close that their common origin seems incontestable."*[11] The former existence of this intermediate linguistic group explains the near total absence of Brythonic loan words in English. *"This absence is perplexing, and extremely atypical in situations of cultural contact"*, Chris Wickham writes in 'Framing the Early Middle Ages' (Oxford University Press, 2005). There is no mystery once

10 'La Belgique ancienne et ces origins gauloises, germaniques et franques', 1833:

11 *"Un rapport étroit est facile à reconnaitre entre cet idiome du littoral, qui est le vrai flamand, et la langue des Anglo-Saxons qui habitaient autrefois au nord de l'Elbe et qui conquirent plus tard l'Angleterre. Ce sont des dialects se rapprochés que leur origine commune parait incontestable."*.

we recall that Caesar tells us that the Gallae and Belgae spoke different languages, and appreciate that the peoples of south-eastern England were Belgae. But the legacy of the Belgae has been forgotten. One reason for this oversight is that Bede, writing between 701 and 731, tells us that *"There are in Britain today five languages and four nations: English, British, Scots and Picts: each of these have their own language but all are united in the study of God's scriptures by that fifth language, Latin."* So the 'English' Bede was unaware of any Belgic influence or Belgic language, but it is not clear what he meant by 'British'. Was this the language of the Welsh, the Cornish, the Celts of Strathclyde or the peasant classes in England? Indeed, was Bede even aware of any distinctions between these languages? To understand his perspective, we need to know his background.

Bede was a Northumbrian who never left Northumbria. His native tongue was Anglo-Saxon, which he called English, possibly in a Northumbrian dialect. However, we know little about his dialect because, although we are told that he translated Latin into it for *"unlearned priests"*, and it is said that he was *"learned in our native songs"*, only five lines of his verse in Anglo-Saxon survive (Bede's 'Song of Death').

Anglo-Saxon was very different from modern English, and the Northumbrian version was different from the dialects of other Anglo-Saxon kingdoms. For example Bede uses the Anglo-Saxon word for 'wise' ('snotturra'). 'Wise' comes from the Proto-Germanic 'wisaz', and ultimately from Proto Indo European, but probably, in my opinion, via Belgic. And we can see why this word might have been preferred, in due course, to the Anglo-Saxon alternative! He uses 'yflaes' for 'evil', when the Kentish equivalent was 'evel' – again a word from Middle Dutch, or, in my opinion, Belgic. So the Belgic influence in central and southern England had clearly not reached Northumbria to the same extent. Bede corresponded in Latin with clerics in other Anglo-Saxon kingdoms, particularly Kent, and he may have been aware of differences in the Anglo-Saxon dialects in use at the time. But he had no correspondence with the British of any region.

Bede was a member of the gentry, and probably only had a passing acquaintance with the languages spoken by the 'wealas', even in Northumbria. He was obsessed with kings and the aristocracy, and did not consider the ordinary people worth a mention. It may be that when he referred to the British he meant the peasant classes in England rather than the Welsh or Cornish (if in fact he was aware of any distinction between any of these groups). He was certainly very ignorant of these peoples, but his knowledge of them has been unfairly derided for one remark: he tells us that *"At first the only inhabitants of the island were the Britons, from whom it takes its name, and who according to tradition, crossed into Britain from Armorica."*

Many have assumed that he was under the impression that Britain got its name from Brittany, but that is to distort Bede's words. He says that Britain got its name from the Britons (which is debatable) and that the Britons crossed into Britain from Armorica. I think it is clear that he knew of an early migration to Britain from 'Armorica', in fact the migration of the Belgae, and his only error lay in their place of origin. They came not from Armorica (broadly west of the Seine) but from Belgic Gaul (east of the Seine). The logical conclusion is that when Bede wrote of "the Britons", he was referring specifically to the Belgo-Romans. No doubt, in his mind, the term also embraced the Celtic peoples of the West, but he was probably unaware of the ethnic and linguistic differences between these groups of people. He probably had no direct contact with the Welsh or Cornish, or even with the peoples of Strathclyde, with whom the Angles were often at war.

Indeed, Bede was not particularly interested in the backgrounds of the indigenous peoples, because his central concerns were religious. To him, the crucial distinction was that the people of England followed the Roman faith, whereas the western British refused to eat with 'the Roman party' and, worst of all, celebrated Easter on the wrong day.

But to the people of Wales there were clear ethnic distinctions, even among the pre-Anglo-Saxon population, and from their perspective, the British living under Anglo-Saxon rule were almost as foreign as the invaders. By the 8th century, all of the people to the east of their lands were 'Germans' ('Allmyn'), and Bede would have been one of them.

The migration of the various cultures across the island is visible in place names, which tell us not only that particular linguistic groups attained dominant status in particular regions, but also that they did not entirely erase the pre-existing population or culture. Going back to pre-Roman times, the toponymic evidence shows that insular Celtic was spoken in the west and north of England (ie the uplands as opposed to the lowlands), but that even after those areas came under Belgo-Roman control, many original Celtic place names were preserved. For example rivers like the Severn and the Avon, hills like the Malvern Hills and the Pennines and forests like the Arden and the Wyre all have Celtic names. In turn, the displacement of Belgic place names by Anglo-Saxon names is heaviest in the extreme south and eastern regions of England, but many still survive. The pattern is one of layers of linguistic influence, consistent with the view that the Belgo-Roman and subsequent Anglo-Saxon hegemonies were primarily invasions of culture and language, and not wholesale displacements of the pre-existing populations.

If I am right, and the pre-Roman population of central and southern England spoke a separate language (which I have called Belgic), why has this language disappeared from our view? Mainly, this is due to the lack of a written record of 'Belgic'. In the Early Middle Ages, the few literate people in Celtic Britain wrote in Latin, the lingua franca, and the Anglo-Saxons wrote in runes, to the extent that they recorded anything. But the Anglo-Saxons did learn to write in the 8th and 9th centuries, whereas the indigenous peasant population did not. What survives to us, therefore, are Latin texts from the 'Celtic fringe', and Anglo-Saxon texts written in Old English. There is no written legacy of the language of the ordinary people of England.

However, there is ample evidence of the former existence of 'Belgic', both in English place names and in the English language, evidence which has been largely overlooked. This has happened because the Belgic influence is in some cases hard to distinguish from other Germanic sources or indeed from parts of the later Norman French. About half of the modern English vocabulary is said to derive from French, and it is generally assumed that this is explained by the Norman Conquest. But I think that some portion of this 'French' influence was already present in England before the Normans arrived, and I think that many words of Belgic origin have been attributed to other Germanic roots. In other words, I think that the evidence for this 'missing link' language, has been masked by subsequent linguistic overlays.

This hypothesis is consistent with the archaeological and genetic evidence that the indigenous population of Britain was not simply displaced by the Saxons. While Belgic may have had limited influence on Old English, the language of the Anglo-Saxon overlords, it continued to be spoken by the indigenous underclass, and it emerged in Middle English when the Anglo-Saxon imperium was removed. Of course, the common people of England had to learn some of the Anglo-Saxon languages (and later, in the north, some Old Norse), and indeed they soon discovered that the Anglo-Saxon languages contained a large number of short and useful words. Nearly all of the most commonly used words in modern English are of Anglo-Saxon origin – eg nouns like 'bed', 'body' and 'book'; verbs like 'to be', 'to do', 'to eat' and 'to drink'; adjectives like 'bad', 'black' and 'light', and conjunctions like 'and', 'but' and 'however'. But the grammar of Anglo-Saxon was fiendishly complex, and highly reflexive, with three grammatical genders and numerous 'cases'. A mastery of word suffixes was required to speak it well, and the system for conjugation of verbs was complex. So, by and large, the British peasants simply could not be bothered to learn it.

9.2   Belgic Grammar

In the ethnic melting pot, which England had become in the Early Middle Ages, the peasants adopted a large part of the vocabulary of the Anglo-Saxon language, but abandoned most of its grammar. Of course we do not know much about the grammar of the unwritten Belgic substratum, but there are some clues in the languages spoken today.

For example, take the word order of sentences. Most Celtic languages rigidly apply a verb-subject-object word order ('hit – I – you'), but some Germanic languages adopt the subject-verb-object ('SVO') format of modern English ('I – hit – you'). Old and modern French use a 'verb last' order ('I – you – hit'), and, crucially, early Anglo-Saxon also used a 'verb last' structure, as illustrated in the first three lines of the epic Anglo-Saxon poem 'Beowulf'. However the later Anglo-Saxons converted to the SVO order.

Further, the SVO order must have been present in the language of British England before the Celtic migrations of the 6th century, because the SVO word order is used in both Cornish and Breton, which are aberrations in the Celtic world. It seems obvious that the Cornish learned this structure from the Britons of England (Welsh has fluctuated between verb first and SVO), and that they did so before the Celtic migration to Brittany. Given the early conversion of Cornish to SVO, it is extremely unlikely that the Cornish learned this structure from the Anglo-Saxons (a) because they had as little to do with the Anglo-Saxons as possible and (b) because the Anglo-Saxons themselves did not adopt the SVO word order until later.

In other words, the SVO structure of modern English did not come from either old Anglo-Saxon or French, but it is known in some Germanic languages. It appears to have been adopted into both Cornish and Old English from another source, and in the case of Cornish, before the 6th century. I therefore conclude that SVO was the structure of Belgic.

Another striking feature of modern English is the absence of grammatical gender (the assignment of a gender to inanimate objects, as seen in Latin and most European languages). Anglo-Saxon, Old French and Old Norse all used grammatical genders, but by the 11th century (for reasons which we will see, the first period in which the language of the British peasants started to be reflected in writing), the English had already started to abandon it. Today, English uses only natural genders (ignoring conventions relating to ships, countries etc). We do not know precisely when this process started, or under what influences, but it must have developed in the spoken language of an illiterate underclass, and before the 11th century.

So it appears that the ordinary indigenous people of England, the 'wealas' as the Saxons called them, synthesised a language out of Belgic and Anglo-Saxon, by stripping both down to their strongest elements and discarding words and rules of grammar which seemed ugly or inconvenient. The resulting language was analytical, using word order instead of suffixes, and it had a greatly simplified grammar. It was in fact a work of genius, and the technical strengths of the foundations of English have helped to make it the world language that it has since become.

9.3   Belgic Place Names

Belgic survives not merely as a grammatical admixture in English. While many of the words in its vocabulary were less attractive or less useful than their Anglo-Saxon equivalents, the Belgic language survives in English place names and a number of words in our lexicon, especially verbs. Let us start with place names.

The textbook explanation of the name Durham is that it comes from the Anglo-Saxon word 'dun' meaning hill and the Old Norse 'holme', meaning island. It is true that 'dun' was an Anglo-Saxon word meaning hill (as in 'down'), but it was also a word of pre-Anglo-Saxon origin meaning 'town' (London, Caesarodunum, Lugdunum, Dundee, Dunkirk etc). And Durham is certainly not an island. 'Durum' is a Latin word meaning 'hard', but place names containing this word appear to derive from a similar pre-Roman word meaning 'fortress' (a root visible in the ancient name of Metz in north-eastern France, Divodurum, and in the Roman Augustodurum (Baveux in Calvados), Autessiodurum (Auxerre) and Octodurum (Martigny in Switzerland)).[12] Auguste Vincent ('Les noms de lieux de la Belgique', 1927), was adamant that place names ending in 'dunum' or 'durum' were Celtic, but this was based on the misapprehension that the Celts originated from a Central European heartland. Since it now appears more likely that they migrated up the western seaboard of the Continent, the origin of these words appears to be Germanic.

Cambridge is said to be derived from the Anglo Saxon 'Grantebrycge'. 'Bridge' comes from the assumed Proto Germanic 'brugjo', as does the Belgic

---

12 See 'Les noms de lieu de la France; leur origine, leur signification, leurs transformations', Auguste Longnon, 1923.

word 'brugge', but the traditional view would have us believe that 'cam' is a contraction of 'granta', the ancient name of the river. Is it not more likely to derive from the word 'cambo' meaning curve? Louis Davillé wrote a book entitled 'Le mot celtique "cambo"' in 1929, asserting a Celtic origin for 'cambo', which formed a root of the name of Cambodunum, now Kempten in Bavaria. However this theory again depended on the hypothesis that the Celts came from Central Europe, and if that is incorrect, 'cambo' is plainly of Germanic origin. Then Cambridge would mean 'the bridge at the bend in the river', presumably the ancestor of Magdalene Bridge (and those with light blue loyalties may be pleased to learn that the Belgic name of Cambridge is considerably older than the Anglo-Saxon ox and ford!)

Perhaps most controversially, I do not believe that all of the places recorded in the Domesday Book (1086) as 'tone's or 'tune's derive their names from the Anglo-Saxon word 'thun' meaning town. I think there was a Belgic word, from the same Proto-Germanic source, which was closer to the modern word 'town'. How else can we explain a name like Ingleton in Yorkshire, which was Ingletune in the Domesday Book? This is obviously not an Anglo-Saxon name, but the name given to a town of Angles by someone else. The 'tone' names are often found in Belgic contexts in the Domesday Book, like Meretone (now Marton) and Neutone (now Newton by Chester), both in Cheshire. And I would particularly refer to two places called Ferentone in the Domesday Book, one now called Farndon in Cheshire and one now called Farrington Gurney in Somerset, which are both close to the probable borders of Belgic Britain. I think that 'Ferentone' meant 'foreigner's town', and that these were towns with Celtic inhabitants within the borders of Belgic Britain. The very similar Ferenberge in Somerset (now Farmborough) meant 'foreigner's hut', in my opinion, and the meaning of Celtetone (now Cheddleton is Staffordshire) is clear. The people who named Ingleton and Celtetone were neither Angles nor Celts.

There are many places in England called Caldecote, or some variant of the spelling of the name, and this name is traditionally explained as deriving from the Anglo Saxon for 'cold cottage'. There can have been nothing remarkable about cold cottages in the Middle Ages, but we are supposed to believe that some were so cold that they deserved to be singled out as exemplars of the type. I think there is a better explanation. 'Cal' meant stone (a root visible in the French word for limestone 'calcaire'), and the Latin 'costa' means coast, or side (as in riverside – eg Côtes du Rhône). So therefore 'de cote' means 'at the side', and it follows that 'cal-de-cote' meant 'stone at the side', or 'milestone' – a perfectly sensible place description.

The interesting point about the Caldecotes is that, despite the

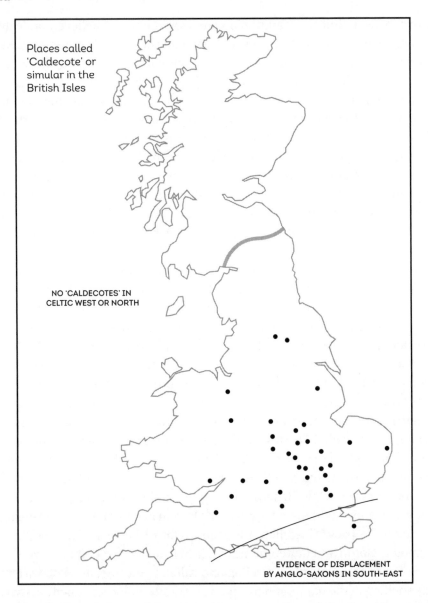

Places called
'Caldecote' or
simular in the
British Isles

NO 'CALDECOTES' IN
CELTIC WEST OR NORTH

EVIDENCE OF DISPLACEMENT
BY ANGLO-SAXONS IN SOUTH-EAST

superficially French form of the name, it appears to have been in widespread use in England before the Norman Conquest. Moreover, there are no Caldecotes in France (or Belgium), and, as we shall see, the name does not seem to have been recognised by the Normans. But it was clearly not an Anglo-Saxon term either, and I therefore conclude that 'caldecote' was a word in use among the peasant British before the Norman Conquest, in fact a 'Belgic' word.

The following are some of the Caldecotes which I have been able to identify (there are no doubt many others):

Present name	Name in the Domesday Book	County
Calcot	Colecote	Berkshire
Caldecote		Bedfordshire
Caldecote	Caldecote	Buckinghamshire
Caldecotte		Buckinghamshire
Caldicot		Buckinghamshire
Caldecote	Caldecote	Cambridgeshire
Caldecott	Caldecote	Cheshire
Calcot		Essex
Caldecott	Caldecotan	Essex
Calcot	Caldecot	Gloucestershire
Caldicot	Caldecote	Gloucestershire
Caldecote	Caldecota	Hertfordshire
Caldecote	Caldecote	Huntingdonshire
Calcott		Kent
Chilcote	Cildecote	Leicestershire
Collow	Caldecote	Lincolnshire
Caldicot		Monmouthshire
Caldecote	Caldachotta	Norfolk
Caldecott		Norfolk
Coldcoates	Caldecotes	Nottinghamshire
Caldecote		Northamptonshire
Caldecott	Caldecote	Northamptonshire
Chilcotes	Cildecote	Northamptonshire
Yelvertoft	Celvrecot	Northamptonshire
Caldecott		Oxfordshire
Caldecott	Caldecote	Rutland
Calcott		Shropshire
Catcott	Caldecote	Somerset
Calcutt	Caldecote	Warwickshire
Caldecote	Caldecote	Warwickshire
Calcutt	Colecote	Wiltshire
Calcutt		Yorkshire
Coldcotes	Caldecotes	Yorkshire

The geographical outliers among the above names are the two in Yorkshire, Caldicot in Monmouthshire, Catcott in Somerset (Caldecote in the Domesday Book) and Caldecote in Cheshire, which again help to define the limits of the Romano-Belgic culture by the Early Middle Ages. We can see that the boundary lay in Somerset in the South West, passing up through Monmouthshire, Cheshire and then across to the north-east to include Yorkshire. Before the Anglo-Saxon settlement I believe there would have been many other 'caldecotes' in the southeast of England, but that these have been displaced by Anglo-Saxon names.

The Normans who prepared the Domesday Book did not consistently spell 'caldecote' correctly (eg Caldachota, Caldecotan, Celvrecot etc), which suggests that they were unaware of its meaning. Moreover, as we shall see, the 'cote' element appears in many other English place names, sometimes combined with Latin or Anglo-Saxon words, so it appears to have been a word in widespread use on its own – and again of neither French or Anglo-Saxon origin.

The word 'cote' appears in literally dozens of English place names (eg Bodicote (Oxfordshire), Boycott (Boicote in the Domesday Book) in Buckinghamshire, Codicote (Hertfordshire), Draycote (Warwickshire), Littlecote (Wiltshire. Yorkshire), Merecote (Solihull), Ashcott (Aissecote in the Domesday Book) in Somerset etc). As already mentioned, the standard explanation for the word 'cote' is that it derives from the Anglo-Saxon word 'cott' meaning cottage. And it is true, 'cote' with a short 'o' can have this meaning (as in dovecote). But clearly the word had other meanings as well, especially when pronounced with a long 'o'. And in fact the 'cott' explanation is the least likely of the possibilities, as evidenced by the fact that the most Anglo Saxon areas of England are regions where the '-cote' names appear very rarely. There are no '-cote's in Kent, Sussex, Essex, Surrey or Middlesex – clear evidence, I believe, of the displacement of an earlier language by that of the Anglo-Saxons.

One sense of the word 'cote' appears to have related to a roadside or riverside location. Possible examples of this usage are Southcote (Sudcote in the Doomsday Book) in Berkshire, another Southcote in Buckinghamshire, Norcote in Gloucestershire, Hillcote in Wiltshire etc. And there are two places in Oxfordshire which have particularly intriguing names: Nethercote was called Altera Cote in the Domesday Book, and the very similar Nethercott was called Hidrecot. Altera is clearly derived from the Latin 'alter' meaning 'other', so the name obviously means 'other side'. While 'nether' simply means 'lower', so 'nethercote' was presumably a lower piece of land, it is curious that one of the 'Nethercotes' appears formally to have been 'the other side' ('alteracote'). But either way their names seem to indicate a location on one side or the other of some geographical feature.

But the toponymy is complicated by the fact that 'cote' also seems to have become a general term for 'land' in Norman French. Examples here include Kingscote in Gloucestershire, which was given as a dowry to William I's niece on her marriage to the grandson of the King of Denmark, and recorded in the Domesday Book as Chingescote (therefore presumably 'king's land'), and Biscot in Bedfordshire, which was Bissopescote in 1086. While the Normans may have been responsible for some of the 'cote' place names, there are literally dozens of them in the Domesday Book, which was written only 20 years after the Norman Conquest, and it is very unlikely that all of these places were renamed in that interval.

There are also many places in England called Draycote (generally 'draicote' in the Domesday Book), Draytone, Drayford etc, but the meaning of 'drai' is uncertain. It might be thought that it relates to drain and dry, but 'Drayford' would make no sense in that case (eg Drayford in Devonshire). I suspect it is the Belgic source of the Middle English word 'dray' meaning cart. For example, one Draitone in the Domesday Book was modern Fenny Drayton, on Watling Street, which is the sort of place one would expect to find a cart park. There were two Draycotes in Warwickshire, two other Draitones in Staffordshire, one in Oxfordshire, one in Hampshire, among other examples.

In a way, the word 'drai' (dray) and its equivalents perfectly illustrate the 'hoarding' tendency in the English language. Faced with a choice of the Anglo-Saxon words 'wægn' and 'wægen', the Old Norse word 'kartr' and the Belgic word 'drai', English has adopted all four (although 'wain' and 'wagon' are now rare, surviving in specific contexts like 'haywain' and 'goods wagon', and 'dray' really only appears in 'drayhorse'). 'Kartr' (cart) came to dominate, because it was adopted into Norman French, and possibly because it sounds nicer. But all of these variants were ultimately eclipsed by the 'char' (Picardy: 'car', Wallonia 'châr'), which allegedly derive from the Latin 'carrus'.

In addition to the generic terms discussed above, many rivers in England have names that are probably Belgic:

Colne	probably from 'calonne', meaning river in Belgic
Humber	appears to come from a Belgic word 'umbre', possibly meaning dark, apparently the root of Umbracum, the ancient name of Ombret in Belgium
Itchen	roots unknown ('ichtus' meant 'fish' in Greek)
Ouse	possibly from the root 'is', of unknown meaning, which appears in Oise, a river in the Paris basin and the Yser River in Nieuwpoort.

Thames	Tamise (sometimes Temse) is a town in Belgium. The toponymy is unclear.
Wey	possibly 'wei' meaning marsh or prairie in Belgic

9.4   Belgic Vocabulary

In terms of nouns, the legacy of Belgic is not so rich, but curiously a number of other words in English relating to bodies of water appear to be Belgic, including lake and mere.   I think quite a number of nouns to do with agriculture are also Belgic, although it is difficult to distinguish them from other Germanic sources. Examples are boar, field, tree, hedge, hoe (Old Franconian houwa) and garden (Old Franconian gardo).   Fork is usually said to derive from the Latin furca, and it is said that the Proto-Germanic word furkô comes from the same Latin source, but it is hard to know which is older. The word plough is of obscure Germanic origin. The plough was introduced into Europe, in the area between the Po, the Danube and the Rhine, early in the Christian era (it was described by Pliny the Elder), and it was known in Belgic Gaul from the 2nd century.[13] I suspect that plough is related to the old Walloon word 'ployer', meaning to fold ('plier' in modern French), and is Belgic.

When words in English are found in French or German, and also in their underlying antecedents, it is difficult to discover whether the word came into English from French or German or from an earlier source language. For example, I think that the adjectives 'new' and 'old' are Belgic, but the standard etymology of 'new' is that it comes from a Proto-Germanic word 'newjaz'. It may indeed come ultimately from Proto-Germanic, but I think it came via Belgic. 'Old' is clearly related to the Dutch 'oud' and the German 'alt', and I believe they all derive from a common source. I also think the word 'man' comes from Belgic, but it is hard to distinguish from the other Germanic sources. To illustrate the difficulty, in France scholars have undertaken a similar exercise, postulating a former 'Old Francique' language, the language spoken by the Franks. Some of the words of this long-dead language, and their meanings in English, are said to be as follows:

hatjan	hate
haunjan	honour
hring	ring

13 A Marbach, 'Recherches sur les Instruments Aratoires et le Travail du Sol en Gaule Belgique', 2004.

gris	grey
marisk	marsh
marka	mark (as in boundary post)
trottan	trot
werra	war
wrakkjo	wretch

Assuming that what I call Belgic and Old Francique were related, it is obviously possible that these words came into English from Belgic. But it is also possible that they came into English from French or German, because they are the antecedents of very similar French or German words.

However, the most easily identifiable Belgic words in the English language are verbs, like walk and talk, cough and laugh, shout, wait and learn. The formula for spotting Belgic verbs is a simple process of elimination: in Anglo-Saxon verbs, the root changes in the past tense (I see/saw, I win/won, I sing/sang). In verbs of French, Latin and Belgic origin, the past tense is generally formed by adding 'ed' or 'd' to the root (I march/marched, I create/created). The French verbs are usually easy to spot (partly because they are often long words), and the Latin words all have known origins because Latin was a written language. There are very few Old Norse verbs in English, but they can go either way in terms of the past tense. The list is well-known (are, call, die, run, seem, want etc) and just needs to be checked. And the rest are possibly Belgic.

After the Norman Conquest, the Anglo-Saxon elites were almost entirely dispossessed and many of their nobles were driven into exile (some to Ireland and a considerable number to Byzantium). In the absence of people who spoke good 'Old English', what remained were the commoners and their dialects - about 10% of the population were literally slaves (many of them employed as ploughmen). The new elite spoke French, but since only about 8,000 Normans actually came to England, the common people had no difficulty retaining their own language. Even the Norman aristocracy in England rapidly started to lose their French, especially after they were deprived of their northern French possessions in 1204. But the language of the courts and government remained French, and so the upper classes added a gloss of longer words that became part of the English vocabulary. Today, any word in English with more than two syllables is likely to be of French origin (eg syllable!), but we will return to this subject at the appropriate time.

The language which evolved in England eventually became the language of the Channel Islands, but not until comparatively recent times.

The Islands, which had formed part of the Merovingian, Carolingian and Norman Empires, spoke Gallo-Roman and then Norman French from the end of the Roman Empire until the 19th century. Even in the early 20th century, a majority of the population in rural areas spoke the local Norman French languages, and today there are still a few thousand inhabitants whose first language is Dgèrnésiais or Jèrriais. The transition was driven by the commercial and cultural influence of the UK, and particularly by the enlistment of soldiers from the Channel Islands into the British army in the two World Wars. The evacuation of the children of the Channel Islands to the UK during the Second World War was also a significant factor, because they returned speaking English.

Chapter 10:

The Life of Women in the First Millennium

10.1   Literacy Among Women

As with the male figures of the first millennium, we only read about the elite among women, but there are even fewer mentions of wives and daughters than their male counterparts. No doubt this is partly because women wrote less of the material which survives, but that does not mean that women could not read or write. One of the earliest surviving pieces of writing by a woman (c. AD 100) was found at Vindolanda, near Hadrian's Wall. This is a letter from a Claudia Severa to her friend Sulpicia Lepedina, inviting her to a birthday party:

"To Sulpicia Lepedina (wife) of Cerealis, from Severa:
Claudia Severa, greetings to her Lepedina. On the third day before the ides of September, sister, for the day of my birthday celebration, I give you a warm invitation to make sure that you come to us, to make the day more enjoyable for me by your arrival, if you are present. Give my greetings to your Cerealis. My Aelius and my little son send you their greetings. I shall expect you, sister. Farewell, sister, my dearest soul, as I hope to prosper and hail."

Severa and her friend were Romans, or people who had absorbed Roman culture, in an age when no Celtic or German tribes wrote at all, so we cannot expect to find any texts written by their 'barbarian' contemporaries. The only windows on their lives that literature offers us are the reports made by Romans on the tribes that they encountered, and as we have already seen, these were not in general flattering, and may have been mendacious.

As we move into the era when the Celtic and German tribes started to write, we also need to bear in mind that literacy was determined more by occupation, than by gender or social rank, because the only people who read and wrote for a living were priests and administrators (eg government officials and reeves). The aristocracy no doubt received some schooling, but since they employed people to take care of day-to-day business they did not need to take their studies seriously. Even Charlemagne, the 8th century Frankish Emperor, wrote very badly. It is possible that women were ordained in the early church, at least as deaconesses, but the priesthood was essentially an occupation reserved for men, and we do not hear of female government officials or reeves, so there were few women who needed to read and write for their work.

10.2 The Role of Women in the Preservation of Culture and Language

Clearly the role of women was essentially domestic and child rearing, and the greatest natural hazard they faced was childbirth. However, their role was for the same reason pivotal in the sustenance of cultures, We will see that the later Scandinavian armies arrived without women, and their cultural legacy was soon extinguished as they were absorbed into the host country. Women have always taken the leading role in child-rearing, and it is mainly from women that children learn to speak.

Indeed, it is in the languages of the first millennium that the influence of women is most apparent. The Angle and Saxon migrations into Britain were migrations of peoples, of whole families who arrived in Britain with their own languages. As a result of their success in displacing a significant proportion of the Belgic culture, the country adopted large parts of their language, which eventually became a key component in English. Similarly the migration of Brythonic speaking Celts into Brittany was a migration of whole families, and the western peninsula became entirely Brythonic speaking.

By contrast, the Viking raiders were bands of warriors, who arrived without women, and which left relatively little by way of linguistic legacy. Even when they started to settle in Gaul, we can deduce that the Vikings brought few women with them, because within a couple of generations they were speaking the Gallo-Roman language of the Franks, albeit with a Norman gloss. While their settlements in northern England had some enduring effect on the English language, Old Norse is a small element in the resulting mix.

10.3 Clothing and Lifestyles

In Rome, highborn ladies were able to dress in silks (imported down the Silk

Road from China since c.210 BC), and cotton imported from Egypt. Indeed the cost of importing silk became such a burden on the Roman economy that steps were taken to curb its use. In the early part of the reign of the Emperor Tiberius, the Senate resolved that *"Oriental silks should no longer degrade the male sex".* As to the cost, Pliny the Elder expressed the indignation of husbands down the ages: *"By the lowest reckoning, India, Seres and the Arabian Peninsula take from our Empire 100 millions of sesterces every year; that is how much our luxuries and women cost us."*

Others deplored the sheerness of the fabric. Seneca the Younger wrote *"I can see clothes of silk, if materials that do not hide the body, not even one's decency, can be called clothes...Wretched flocks of maids labour so that the adulteress may be visible through her thin dress, so that her husband has no more acquaintance than any outsider or foreigner with his wife's body."* However, as far as the Romans were concerned, 'barbarians' were notably more modest. While silk and cotton would not have been unknown to the population of Gaul and Britain, clothes made of wool were the lot of the common man and woman. Tacitus described the clothing of the Germans in about AD 98: *"For clothing all wear a cloak, fastened with a clasp, or, in its absence, a thorn: they spend whole days around the fire with no other covering. The richest men are distinguished by the wearing of under-clothes: not loose....but drawn tight, throwing each limb into relief. They wear also the skin of wild beasts....The women have the same dress as the men, except that very often trailing linen garments, striped with purple, are in use for women: the upper half of this costume does not widen into sleeves: their arms and shoulders are therefore bare, as is the adjoining portion of the breast."*

The clasps used to fasten cloaks at the neck are often found in the graves of women, in the Roman period and beyond, and it is clear that the style and quality of the brooch conveyed messages of social and ethnic distinction that are no longer wholly intelligible to us. But by the end of the Western Empire, 'barbarian' dress styles had replaced Roman fashions, even in Rome. Julia Smith writes (in 'Europe After Rome', 2005): *"By c.500, short tunic and trousers had long since lost their opprobrium as 'barbarian' apparel and replaced the classical toga as the dress choice for Roman men; they remained the universal basis of men's clothing throughout the early medieval West, except for clergy and, from c.800 onwards, royal ceremonial. Women, by contrast, always wore a calf- or ankle-length robe"*

In Roman times too, women wore make-up and scents. Maids who were expert in applying make-up were called 'cosmetae', and were highly valued by their mistresses. In general men pretended to disapprove of such artifice as deceitful, and some disliked the smell of the cosmetics then in use. Thomas Aquinas opined that for a woman to use cosmetics to make herself more attractive to her husband was not a sin, but that she should not use them to make herself so beautiful that she might attract other women's husbands.

Jewellery is found in the archaeological record of most nations, made of gold, silver, bronze and copper. Gems of organic origin like amber from the Baltic and jet from Whitby, along with amethyst, garnet and rock crystal feature in pre-Roman and Roman era jewellery. Ladies in Rome had pierced ears and wore finely worked gold earrings. Diamonds from India were known to the Romans, but the material was too hard to be used in jewellery. Instead, diamond splinters were used in the engraving of other gemstones.

The astonishing Staffordshire hoard of more than 3,500 objects found in 2009 has completely altered our view of the craftsmanship of the 7th or 8th centuries. The items are of a martial nature, mainly in gold and red garnet, and the condition of the objects suggests that they were taken from the bodies of a defeated army. But the craftsmen who made these objects for men must have made items of a similar quality for women. Saxon gold and garnet jewellery, for men and women, is known to have been made in England from the 6th century, but the quantity found in Staffordshire, and the quality of the work, is breathtaking.

10.4   Women and Religion

The Christian religion firmly placed women in a position subordinate to men, which no doubt reflected the social norms of most societies at the time. The attitude of the clergy, or at least the Italian clergy, was well illustrated in a sermon delivered by Ambrose, Bishop of Milan (374 – 397): *"But I think one would say it's not so much in clothing as in manners, or habits and behaviour, that one action is fitting for a man and another for a woman. Hence the apostle Paul says, as an interpreter of law, 'Let women keep silence in the churches: for it is not permitted them to speak, but to be subject, as also the law says. But if they would learn anything, let them ask their husbands at home.' And also, 'Let the woman learn in silence with all subjection. But I suffer not a woman to teach, nor to use authority over the man: but to be in silence.' How disgusting it is for a man to perform a woman's work!"*

Perhaps unsurprisingly, some women rejected the life of convention, and lived apart from men. Strabo, writing in AD 24, mentions a tribe called the 'Samnitae', whose women lived on an island in the Loire River (possibly Bouin), which no man was allowed to visit. They ventured to the shore only for the purpose of mating. Other commentators have speculated that the women may have occupied themselves in the production of salt, and some have suggested that 'Samnitae' is a mistaken version of Namnites (the tribe who lived around Nantes).

One aspect of the life of these women, as told by Strabo, is rather disturbing: every year they would re-roof their temple (dedicated to Bacchus), with new straw, and if any woman dropped a bundle of new straw, she was torn to pieces by her colleagues who carried her remains around the temple, chanting as they went.

In the 5th and 6th centuries, several convents were established in Gaul, which proved attractive to many women of the period. One of the early communities was established by Caesarius, Bishop of Arles, who persuaded his sister Caesaria to leave a convent in Marseilles to establish a new order in Arles. Other orders founded at the time were associated with St Genevieve or Clotild, wife of Clovis.

And nunneries were also founded in Britain soon afterwards. St Hilda, was born into the Northumbrian royal family in 614, and after her father was murdered, she was raised at King Edwin of Northumbria's court. Edwin and his entire family were baptised in 627. Hilda's older sister Ereswith was married to Æthelric, the brother of the King of East Anglia, but when she was widowed she decided to retire to the Abbey at Chelles, near Paris. Hilda was on the point of joining her, at the age of 33, when she was persuaded by St Aiden, Bishop of Lindisfarne, to return to Northumbria. She joined a convent on the north bank of the River Wear, where she learned the principles of the monastic lifestyle that Aiden had brought from Iona.

A year later, she was appointed Abbess of Hartlepool Abbey and in 657 she became the founding Abbess of the new Abbey at Whitby. It was at this Abbey, and at her invitation, that the Synod of Whitby was held in 664, which assembly resolved the differences between the Gaelic churches and Rome in favour of the latter. As a pupil, indirectly, of Iona, Hilda's initial sympathies were with the Gaels, but she was persuaded to support the Roman doctrine out of a spirit of unity. Bede said of her *"All who knew her called her mother because of her outstanding devotion and grace."* Despite the six-year illness which eventually resulted in her death in 680, she still had the energy to found another monastery at Hackness, 14 miles from Whitby, in the last year of her life.

Some believe that women were ordained as deaconesses in the early church, but this seems unlikely in view of the doctrine preached by St Paul. However, even if they had no formal role in the church, women played an enormously influential part in the spread of Christianity through the conversion of their husbands and sons. Constantine the Great ended the persecution of Christians, and then became the first Roman Emperor to be baptised, probably under the influence of his mother St Helena, who was a Christian. Clovis became the first king of the Franks to be baptised, under the persuasive influence of his wife Clotild. Æthelbert I became the first of the Saxon kings in England to adopt Christianity, under the influence of his Frankish wife Bertha. Rollo, the first Duke of Normandy, was baptised, at least partly because his wife Poppa was already a Christian. And when a king was baptised, he was invariably followed by thousands of his subjects, so the importance of these women in the spread of the religion should not be underestimated.

10.5   Women in Power

While women had a generally subordinate status, social mobility among women was at least as fluid as it was for men, as women used their charms to gain status. To take an extreme example, during the course of the 7th century, four women rose from slavery to become Merovingian queens. One of them, Balthildis, was a pagan girl from Sussex who entered the household of Clovis II's chief minister in about 640. She was obviously an attractive woman, because Clovis married her, and when he died a few years later, she ruled his kingdom as regent for their son Chlotar III, becoming a campaigner against slavery. So queens did not hesitate to involve themselves in politics. Another of these arrivistes was Fredegund, who came into the household of King Chilperic as the maidservant of his first wife Audovera. She seduced Chilperic, and persuaded him to send Audovera to a convent and divorce her. When Chilperic decided to put Fredegund aside and make a strategic marriage with the Visigothic princess Galswintha in 568, Galswintha was strangled within a year – probably by Fredegund. The marriage had been going badly in any case, because Galswintha objected to Chilperic's mistresses at court, no doubt principally Fredegund. So Fredegund finally got her man, and Chilperic married her.

Galswitha's sister was Brunhilda, born in Toledo in Spain in about 543. In 567, she had married Sigebert I, King of Austrasia, and she was furious at what had happened to her sister. Spurred on by Brunhilde, Sigebert went to war with his brother to avenge the murder of Galswintha, and seized most of his kingdom, forcing Chilperic to retreat to Tournai. But immediately after Sigibert was declared King at Paris by Chilperic's subjects, he was assassinated by men working for Fredegund in 575. Brunhilda was captured and imprisoned at Rouen.

One of Chilperic's sons by an earlier marriage, Merovich, went to Rouen, ostensibly to visit his mother, but decided to take the opportunity to marry his aunt Brunhilda, to strengthen his chances of becoming king (this was an incestuous marriage which was illegal under canon law). Fredegund was appalled, being determined that only her children should succeed (she had already eliminated some of her husband's sons by other women). The errant couple took refuge in a church, being besieged by Chilperic, and when Merovich came out he was tonsured and sent to a monastery. Eventually Merovich asked his servant to kill him, once it became clear that his bid for power had failed.

When Sigebert died in 575, Brunhilda, was determined that her infant son Childebert II should succeed his father, and tried to make herself regent in his name; but she met with resistance from the nobles of the kingdom and she was forced to flee to the court of Gontran of Burgundy (Sigebert and Chilperic's brother). Gontran was newly heirless, and Brunhilda persuaded him to adopt her son Childebert II. This he did in 577, and in 583 Childebert II reached the Frankish age of majority (13) still under the protection of his uncle.

Chilperic died mysteriously in 584, stabbed to death by an unknown assailant while returning from a hunting expedition at his palace at Chelles, and Fredegund seized his treasury and took refuge in Paris, under the protection of Gontran, where she gave birth to a son, Clotaire II of Neustria. Acting as regent, Fredegund immediately made war against her old enemy Brunhilda. In 592 Gontran died and Childebert II, who was already King of Austrasia, succeeded him as King of Burgundy. But he died in 595, aged only 25, to be succeeded by his son Theudebert II, heavily under the influence of Brunhilda.

Clotaire II was 13 when his mother Fredegund died in 597, and she had therefore ruled as regent since 584. Having reached the Frankish age of majority, he was able to rule in his own name, and he made war with his cousins Theudebert II and Theuderic II. They defeated him in 599, but then fought between themselves for the combined kingdoms of Austrasia and Burgundy, allowing Clotaire to take advantage and attack them, defeating Theudebert at Toul in 611 and again at Tolbiac in 612. After the second battle, he captured Theudebert and handed him over to Brunhilda, who had him sent to a monastery, but shortly afterwards had him murdered along with his son Merovech to allow Theuderic to inherit the whole kingdom.

Unfortunately her plan backfired when Theuderic died of dysentery in 613 leaving two illegitimate sons, Sigebert II, aged 12 and Corbo, under the protection of Brunhilda. Clotaire launched an attack against them, and the mayors of the palaces of Austrasia and Burgundy defected to him in a battle on the Aisne, effectively delivering the kingdom into Clotaire's hands. Brunhilda, Sigebert and Corbo were executed, and Clotaire despatched his mother's rival most cruelly.

10.6   Women and the Law

Unlike in many other cultures of the era, such as that of the Romans, it was the custom among the Franks that the husband paid a dowry to the wife's family on marriage. This of course implied a degree of 'ownership', but also made women valuable and gave them a protected status under the law.

The Franks had a complicated scale of fines for various crimes, ranging from touching a freewoman's hand, arm or finger (600 denarii, or 15 solidi – there were 40 denarii in a solidi) to killing a freewoman with children (24,000 denarii or 600 solidi). The fine dropped to 8,000 denarii or 2000 solidi if the woman could no longer bear children, indicating that it was the capacity to bring children into the world that gave women their value. But the sentence for rape, which was originally 2,500 denarii was increased to death (or exile if the perpetrator had sought sanctuary in a church) in 594. Similarly the penalty for a servant who abducted a freewoman was death.

The fine for stealing a slave, maidservant, horse or draft horse was 1,400 denarii in addition to the value of the stolen property. And the fine for seducing a maidservant was 2,880 denarii if the seducer was a swineherd, vinedresser, blacksmith, miller, carpenter, groom or overseer. But the fine was less for a freeman fornicating with a maidservant, who had to pay only 600 denarii to the maidservant's master (1200 denarii if the woman was a maidservant of the king). Calling someone a witch incurred a fine of 2,500 denarii if the accusation could not be proven. And a man who jilted his fiancée would be subject to a fine of 2,500 denarii.

A freewoman who married a slave committed a terrible offence, and all of her property was forfeit to the king. But if her relatives killed her, no penalty would be incurred by them. In fact, if any of her relatives gave her shelter, they would be liable to a fine of 600 denarii. The slave would be broken on the wheel.

It was the custom to allow the hair of young boys as well as girls to grow long. Most adult males wore their hair short, but Frankish kings kept their hair long as a status symbol. Cutting off the long hair of a freeborn boy or girl, without the parent's consent, was a serious offence incurring a fine of 1800 denarii. And untying the hair of a woman, so that her veil fell to the ground, incurred a fine of 600 denarii. Untying her hair-band so that her hair fell to her shoulder was worse, and incurred a fine of 1,200 denarii. A slave doing this could lose his hand.

The law against striking a pregnant woman and causing a miscarriage reveals some interesting value judgements. The basic fine was 600 solidi, or 24,000 denarii. But if the aborted child was female, the fine increased to 2,400 solidi or 96,000 denarii. So we can clearly see that girls were more valuable than boys.

The fines for causing a woman to miscarry by striking her were, however, halved if the woman was a maidservant, a freedwoman or a Roman woman. Since this legal system applied only to people living under Salian law, the rules would not have applied to offences against Bretons, but then Franks and Bretons would not have been living under a common criminal code in the first place.

No similar code for the Bretons survives, but at the end of the 7th century, the Irish Law of Women (the 'Cáin Adamnáin') was promulgated, and this proscribed a range of offences against women and young children. One of these was set out as *"If a woman has been got with child by stealth, without contract, without full rights.without dowry, without betrothal, a full fine for it."*[14] So the dowry was an important part of the marriage contract, and we know from later practice that the wife's family paid it to the husband. No doubt other Celtic cultures had similar customs.

10.7   Marriage and Children

Roman law recognised two levels of commitment between men and women, marriage and concubinage. A marriage could only be concluded between social equals, and concubinage was almost invariably a relationship between a high-status man and a woman of much inferior rank. Marriage was not determined by sexual relationships, but by consent, and children under seven were deemed incapable of giving their consent. Even so, a marriage could not be effective before puberty. The rules related to marriage were essentially set out in church law, and many of the questions which Augustine addressed to Pope Gregory in the correspondence between the two were concerned with marriage and sexual relations.

14 Emilie Amt, 'Women's Lives in Medieval Europe' (1992).

By custom, rather than law, a dowry was paid to the husband on the occasion of the marriage by the wife or her father or family. This was a matter for private negotiation between the families, and the property transferred could include land, movable goods or slaves. As we shall see, the dowry could be returned in the context of a divorce, so it was in the nature of a marriage settlement, and the husband's rights to the property concerned constituted something less than full ownership.

Since consent was the principle that underpinned marriage in Roman law, divorce was the consequence of repudiation. In this, the law was at odds with the teachings of St Paul, which held that marriage was indissoluble, and the resulting tension has never been fully resolved. As a matter of law, the woman was entitled to the return of her dowry, or, if she was under the control of her father, he could sue for it. However, if the divorce was occasioned by the fault of the wife or her father, the husband retained one sixth of the dowry for each child of the marriage (up to a maximum of one half), and the amount returned could be reduced by one sixth for adultery or one eighth for bad behaviour of a lesser degree.

Roman law was most unbalanced, as between the sexes, in relation to adultery, because the Lex Julia prescribed that only men could bring prosecutions for adultery against their wives. If the girl was less than twelve years old when she committed the adultery she could not be accused of it by her husband, for the simple reason that she had not yet reached the marriageable age. Where a married woman committed adultery, her father, but not her husband, had the right to kill her, provided he did so at the same time as killing her lover. Not surprisingly, many married men consorted with a number of sexual partners, and Seneca (1st century AD) refers to *"unchastity, the greatest evil of our time".*

While the Franks had various levels of marriage in terms of formality (determined by factors such as the approval or otherwise of the families concerned), they were noted by the Romans to be very monogamous. Tacitus wrote of the Germans: *"None the less the marriage tie with them is strict: you will find nothing in their character to praise more highly. They are almost the only barbarians who are content with a wife apiece: the very few exceptions have nothing to do with passion, but consist of those with whom polygamous marriage is eagerly sought for the sake of their high birth."*

In Rome, contraception was practised through the use of herbs; and other herbs (such as hellebore), strenuous exercise or physical intervention were used for abortion. It was generally regarded as a female prerogative, though frowned upon if the male partner thought that he was being deprived of a child.

Probably the greatest cause of sadness in early times was the loss of children, because a very significant proportion of all children failed to make it past their fifth birthdays, and many did not survive beyond their first. We know this from the large number of child graves, but children were often buried without grave goods so we do not know very much about their early years. Touchingly, they were sometimes buried with toys, such as a few marbles for boys, and the girls no doubt had dolls which, being made of cloth, have not survived. In Brittany, the grave of one child included a whalebone spreader, which probably formed part of the hammock in which he or she slept.

Tacitus describes life in a Germanic household *"There then they are, the children, in every house, filling out amid nakedness and squalor into that girth of limb and frame which is to our people a marvel. Its own mother suckles each at her breast; they are not passed on to nursemaids or wet-nurses."* With little in the way of academic knowledge available, we can assume that formal education was perfunctory. But the Germans, at least, seem to have treasured childhood: again Tacitus is our source *"The virginity of youth is late treasured and puberty therefore inexhaustible; nor for the girls is there any hot-house forcing; they pass their youth in the same way as the boys; their stature is as tall; when they reach the same height they are mated, and the children reproduce the vigour of the parents."*

Chapter 11:

The Merovingians and Carolingians

11.1 An Overview of the Period

In the 7th and early 8th centuries, the Channel Islands were part of the Merovingian Empire in France, which gave way to the Carolingian dynasty in the second half of the 8th century. As we will see, this period in this region was not merely part of the history of France, but included the events that formed political Europe as we know it today. And other geo-politically significant developments were taking place on the fringes of the Eastern Roman Empire.

The development of the Anglo-Saxon kingdoms in England, while only peripherally relevant to my subject, is not without interest. But it has been so well covered in English language texts that I would prefer to direct the reader interested in this topic elsewhere. I have thought it worthwhile expounding my views on the development of the English language, both because I think I have something new to contribute on the subject and because the English language is profoundly relevant to the history of the Channel Islands, but I will resist the temptation to stray too far into the history of the emergence of England.

However, a few introductory remarks are in order. As we have seen, the Saxons, dominant by 600 over an increasing part of the country we now call England, had formed several 'kingdoms' ranging in size from very small up to the area of a couple of modern counties. At the dawn of this period, some of the Anglo-Saxon kings had accepted Christianity, but some still worshipped pagan gods. The remainder of the millennium in England was dominated by territorial wars between the Anglo-Saxon kingdoms, which resulted in the emergence of Wessex as the pre-eminent power, and the subsequent battles between Wessex in particular and the Vikings.

In Scotland, the Picts ruled the eastern side of the country, and a Gaelic kingdom called the Dál Riata was established in the west. This had additional territories in Northern Ireland. Compressed between the Picts and the Northumbrians were a Celtic British group, living in the Strathclyde region, and similar people occupied Wales (apart from the south-east of the country) and Cornwall.

The compression of the ancient kingdom of Dumnonia in the southwest had resulted in a large-scale migration of Brythonic-speaking Celts to what was now becoming known as Brittany, and some of these may have passed through the Channel Islands on their way. Struggles between the Anglo-Saxons and the Welsh and Cornish continued throughout the period covered by this Chapter, but in 772, the Cornish won the Battle of Hehil, keeping the kingdom of Wessex at bay for a century.

11.2   The 'Principality' of Brittany

As we have seen, Waroch had secured de facto independence for Brittany when he fought the Frankish King Gontran's army to a standstill on the Vilaine River in 590. The Franks were involved in endless internal feuds over successions, in which the Bretons increasingly played a part. But Waroch disappeared from the historical record shortly after his victory, possibly to be succeeded by his son Canao.

The first Breton king that we know of after Waroch is Judicael ap Hoël (c.590 – 658), who may have ruled over the united province of Domnonée and Bro-Waroch. The 11th century 'Life of St Judicaël' tells us that *"he gladly resided in the centre of the peninsula, but in proximity to the Frankish border, on the eastern edge of the present Forest of Paimpont, where without doubt he led a life similar to the Frankish kings who were fond of their villae all around Paris, near the large forests and their hunting grounds."*[15] In 635 Judicael was summoned to attend the court of the Frankish King Dagobert, who was the sole ruler of the Frankish Empire after 632 when his brother Charibert died (or at least, after Dagobert had arranged the assassination of Charibert's son). Judicael attended the Frankish court as demanded, with gifts, but may have offended his host by refusing to dine with Dagobert *"whose life and manners he found too distant from his own"* (according to his biographer, a monk at St Méen Abbey).   However the chronicler puts a diplomatic gloss on the affair, and reports that Dagobert was understanding: *"when he saw the piety of such a man, he deemed himself unworthy of his company".*

The 'Life of St Eloi' was written by St Ouen, who actually met Judicaël. It tells us that St Eloi, who was treasurer to Dagobert, was instructed to prepare a treaty between the Franks and the Bretons, presumably for

15 Pierre-Roland Giot, Philippe Guigon & Bernard Merdrignac, 'The British Settlement of Brittany', 2003

signature at the meeting described above. From the Frankish point of view, the purpose of this treaty was to stop the Bretons forming an alliance with the restive population of Aquitaine, but in practical terms it does not seem to have achieved very much.

After this event, Brittany appears to have gone into decline. Very little pottery of any quality, local or imported, is found in the region, and the only written mention of Brittany between this time and the second half of the 8th century, is a comment in 691 that the Bretons were among the peoples who were formerly submitted to the Franks, but who through the carelessness of the later Merovingians had made themselves independent. But one event of geographical interest is worth noting. In 709, a surge in sea levels cut off the island of Mont St Michel and flooded the Forest of Scissy on the surrounding plain. It is possible that similar inundations took place in the Channel Islands, eg on the west coast of Guernsey, but the cause of this event is unknown. There were several very high tides in March 709, but no reports of earthquakes.

11.3   The Arabs

Arabia had never formed part of the Byzantine, or any other, Empire, due to its remoteness and harsh landscape. Its sparse population followed various pagan creeds, and significant minorities were adherents of Judaism or Christianity. But it was peaceful and the southern provinces were relatively prosperous with advanced systems for water management, including dams and canals to irrigate the land.

But the climatic disaster of the 530s completely destabilised the region, causing floods which burst the largest dam and which resulted in a famine. The last southern Arabian king converted to Judaism and massacred the Christians, provoking an invasion by Abyssinians acting on the orders of the Eastern Roman Emperor, and this in turn provoked a counter-invasion of Persians. The region was left in turmoil.

Muhammed was born in c. 570 in Mecca, and seems to have passed his early years conventionally, possibly as a trader. He was fortunate to marry a wealthy widow in 595, which made him financially independent, and she bore him two sons (who both died) and four daughters. In about 610, he was fasting and praying in a cave near Mecca, when he felt the call of God, either directly or through an angel. He began to preach that there was only one God, and he earned a small following as a prophet. But his activities offended the establishment in Mecca, and in 622 he moved to Medina, where his message was better received. He was followed by 200 families.

He turned warrior and led a successful raid in 624, being wounded when a force from Mecca attacked Medina in 626. When he returned to Mecca in 629, he was acknowledged as a prophet and won respect for the orderly behaviour of his army. He was unsuccessful in an attempt to seize a Byzantine sword factory in the same year, but won his last battle, on the road to Iraq. He died in 632, leaving no provision for his succession.

Those are the bare facts of his life. But the truly remarkable consequence was that, within about 50 years, the Muslims had control over an area that extended from the Atlantic coast of North Africa to the Indus River in India. Muhammed's son-in-law, Abu Bakr, the first Caliph ('successor') and the next two Caliphs, Umar and Uthman, expanded the Arab Empire to the west. Between 636 and 638, they took control of Syria and Palestine; then in 640 the Arabs defeated the Byzantines at Babylon on the Nile Delta, and Egypt was at their mercy. Alexandria was captured after a 14-month siege, and one of the principal sources of wealth in the Byzantine Empire, and its major source of grain, was lost. The Arab army then began its advance along the North African coast.

In 642 the army of the Sassanid Persian Empire was defeated in the Zagros Mountains, and Iran fell to the Arabs by 644. However after the death of Caliph Uthman in 656, a period of civil war followed that saw Islam divided into two factions, the Sunnis and the Shiites, whose mutual antagonism persists to this day. Eventually the second dynasty of Caliphs commenced in c.661, taking its name from the grandfather of the founder of the dynasty, Ummaya ibn Abd Shams. The Umayyad Caliphate made Damascus in Syria its capital city.

Having established control over the coasts of the eastern Mediterranean, the Arabs began constructing a substantial fleet with which to command the sea. In North Africa, Kairouan in Tunisia was taken in 670. The Muslims attacked, but failed to take, Constantinople in the 670s, when they were driven off by 'Greek fire' an incendiary mixture of chemicals, including quicklime, sulphur and petroleum, and further attacks on the city were mounted in 674 to 680.

Uqba ben Nafi led his forces along the coast of North Africa in the period 682 to 683, eventually riding his horse into the waters of the Atlantic to celebrate the completion of this mission. The expansion of the Muslim world was astonishing in the first century of Islam, and it must be said that the Arabs were often well received by the populations they subjected, partly because they were more tolerant in religious matters than the Byzantines, and significantly, because they imposed much lower levels of taxation. Conversion to Islam was initially forced at the point of the sword, but later leaders were more tolerant and respected Jewish and Christian communities. However, property and poll taxes were assessed, and since Muslims were exempt from the property taxes, there was a fiscal incentive to convert.

Thus by the start of the 8th century, Arab Muslims ruled the coast of the eastern Mediterranean and the coast of north Africa, to the doorstep of Europe. And in 711, Târiq, a freed slave, led a force of 7,000 Arabs, Moors and Berbers over the Straights of Gibraltar (which gets its name from 'Jabal Târiq', the 'rock of Târiq') and defeated Roderick, the king of the Visigoths at the Battle of Gaudalete. Although the Visigoth army was larger, a faction of Roderick's forces deserted at a key point in the battle, and the Arabs moved on to take Cordoba and Toledo without a fight. Sidonia and Seville fell in 712 and Merida was taken in 713, as the Visigoth kingdom simply folded without another major battle. Over the next eight years, the Arabs worked their way north until they held the whole of Spain apart from a strip along the northwest coast (defended by, among others, British settlers and the Basques).

At about this time too, the Arab conquest of the Persian Empire, including Bukhara and Samarkand, brought them directly into contact with the Oghuz tribes of Turks in western Central Asia, and they began to recruit Turks into the Arab armies. The Turks were highly mobile fighters from the Steppes, noted for their dexterity as mounted archers, and they were to prove more adept at settling into urban life than their predecessors, the Huns and the Mongols. Such were the martial qualities of these people that by the end of the 9th century, many of the generals and even the political leaders of the Arab Empire were Moslem Turks, who had converted from the shamanist pagan religions of their forefathers.

In 717 the Arabs mounted another unsuccessful attack on Constantinople, but gave up the siege after 13 months because of the cold in winter. In the same year they crossed the Pyrenees to raid monasteries in the Languedoc, capturing Narbonne in 719 and threatening Toulouse. The Emir of Cordoba returned two years later with a far larger army to mount a serious invasion into Aquitaine, and he laid siege to Toulouse. Duke Eudes (or Odo) of Aquitaine fled to get reinforcements, leaving the city besieged, and the Arabs pursued him as far as Tours.

So in the space of a few years, the Arabs had laid siege to Constantinople, the capital of the Roman Empire, had taken control of Portugal and most of Spain and had established themselves in the south of France, with a capital at Narbonne. Christendom was rocking on its heels.

11.4   Charles Martel

Worst of all, the leadership of the Franks had fallen into the hands of the 'Faisnéant' Frankish kings (the 'do nothing' kings of the later Merovingian dynasty). Their indolence was no doubt evidence of a lack of character, but it was partly explained by their shortage of means – more than half of the agricultural land in France was now inalienable property of the church, and the kings had no money to pay for armies. What France badly needed was an injection of martial spirit, and a reduction of the ecclesiastical estate.

"Cometh the hour, cometh the man" as the saying goes, and in this case Christendom found two men to take up leadership of the state and the church respectively in Francia. Charles was born in 688, an illegitimate son of Pepin of Herstal, and his mistress Alpaida. Pepin was Mayor of Austrasia and, in view of the weakness of the monarchy, de facto leader of the Franks. His wife Plectrude had given him two sons, but neither of them survived Pepin. However, one of the sons had left children, including a son called Theodoald, and Plectrude persuaded her husband to disinherit his illegitimate children by Alpaida in favour of Theodoald.

So when Pepin died suddenly in 714, the 8-year-old Theodoald was his named successor as Mayor, but Theodoald's 26-year-old half-brother Charles commanded the support of the Austrasian nobles, owing to the military prowess he had already exhibited. Plectrude had Charles imprisoned to try to prevent unrest over the succession, but the nobles were discontented with the idea of an 8 year old Mayor. There followed a civil war, in which Charles escaped from prison, was acclaimed by the nobles of Austrasia, defeated Plectrude (but showed mercy to her and Theodoald), and declared Clotaire IV to be King.

After taking control of Austrasia, he marched against the Neustrians, who had tried to take advantage of the problems of Austrasia in an alliance with the Frisians. Charles defeated the Neustrians in several battles, thus becoming effectively sole leader of the whole of Francia, and he moved on to defeat the Frisians. Between 718 and 723 he defeated the Bavarians, the Alemanni and the Saxons, and he sent bishops to convert the pagan Frisians and Germans to Christianity. One of these was a British Bishop called Wynfrith (whom the Pope had rechristened Boniface in 718), who worked tirelessly among the pagan Saxons, Thuringians and Hessians.

In return for Charles' support in his missionary work, Boniface supported Charles in the expropriation of church property in Francia. The Pope eventually made Boniface an archbishop, but Charles was never very interested in titles. He was effectively Chief Executive of the Frankish

Kingdom (or in British terms, Prime Minister), and during most of his career he appointed puppet kings to be head of state. But the later Merovingians were so useless that between 737 and 744, he didn't bother to appoint one. Later on he used the title Duke and Prince of the Franks, but when the Pope offered to appoint him Consul in 739, he declined.

After the civil war, and the wars with the Germans that secured his eastern borders, Charles had to turn his attention to the very serious threat of the Arabs in Spain and southern France. When Duke Eudes (or Odo) of Aquitaine returned to Toulouse with reinforcements in 721, he caught the Arabs off guard and dispersed around the walls of the city. He was therefore able to defeat them before the Arab cavalry could assemble or even mount, and the besieging forces were driven away. But his victory brought only temporary respite. In 725 the Arabs launched a massive attack along the Rhône Valley, through Valence and as far as Lyon, but then fell back in the face of resistance, retaining Nîmes, Agde and Béziers. In 731, another assault took them to Châlons, Mâcon, Beaune, Besançon and Auxerre, and the monastery at Luxeuil in Burgundy was sacked. After that the Arabs retained Montfrin, Avignon, Arles and Aix-en-Provence.

Eudes had been forced to make a treaty with the Arabs in 'Cerdanya' (possibly Catalonia) to protect his south-western border, and had married his daughter to the king of that region, Uthman ibn Naissa. In 731 Charles denounced this treaty and invaded Aquitaine from the north, ravaging the countryside and taking Bourges. Eudes confronted him, but was defeated, leaving Charles to return north. In 732, a new Emir of Cordoba, equally unhappy with the treaty, attacked Cerdanya from the south killing Naissa and capturing Eudes' daughter, who was sent to a harem in Damascus. His army then pressed into Aquitaine at great speed and sacked Bordeaux, before confronting Eudes in a battle on the banks of the Garonne. Eudes' forces were heavily defeated, with a massive loss of life, and he fled north to warn Charles of the impending danger, raising a fresh army on the way.

Up until this point the Arabs had only encountered disorganised resistance in the expansion of their empire, and they were unaware of the reputation of the Franks. Attracted by the prospect of a rich haul of loot at Tours, they marched north in October 732 or 733, sacking Poitiers and continuing onwards towards the cathedral city. But there may have been some disunity in their army, which contained large contingents from Syria and the Berber tribes, as well as the troops of the Emir of Cordoba. Apparently, some of the Berbers had insisted on bringing their families with them, which must have impeded the army's progress. Charles positioned his forces south of Tours to protect the city, at a place on the Roman road from Poitiers, to await the Muslim hordes.

The allied army would have been gathered from all parts of the Frankish kingdom, and from among their foreign allies. Of course, after his reconquest of Francia between 715 and 719, many landowners in Neustria owed personal allegiance to Charles. He had bought the loyalty of some nobles with gifts of 'liberated' church properties, and some Austrasian counts had been granted lands in the western part of the empire (eg Roger, who became Duke of Le Mans, and Agatheus who held the counties of Rennes and Nantes). But regardless of personal obligations, the nobles of Francia, as a whole, would have considered it their religious duty to answer Charles' call to arms. And we may suppose that some knights from the Channel Islands would have been among their number.

If the history of the previous century is anything to go by, he probably also had some Saxon support, and we can imagine that he would have called on the Bretons to join the allied forces. He certainly had to accept the offer of assistance from Eudes, who he had so recently been fighting, and the Aquitaine army formed the right flank in his line of battle.

It is said that the two armies faced each other for seven days, with neither side willing to make the first attack. But the Muslims' patience broke first, and they mounted charges to try to break the Frankish lines. Charles countered the Arab cavalry attacks by forming phalanxes of troops in tightly packed squares, with spears pointing outwards to create a 'porcupine' defence. Fighting continued all day, but by nightfall the Arab commander Abdul Rahman al Ghafiqi had been killed. In the morning the Franks returned to their positions on the battlefield, but the Arabs had gone. The Arab Chronicles tell us that the Caliph in Damascus was shocked at the scale of the defeat, and in the 9th century Charles gained the sobriquet 'Martel' ('the hammer') for his achievement.

The absence of contemporary western commentary on the battle has resulted in a debate as to its true significance, ranging from those, like Gibbon, who believed that Charles had saved Christendom, to others who believe that the battle at Tours/Poitiers was merely one in a long line of encounters between Christians and Saracens, and that the Arab invasion would have been stopped somewhere. But there is no doubt that the battle formed a turning point in the war in France, because before then the Arabs were almost always attacking in western Europe, and after it they were basically in retreat.

But Charles knew that this was not a time for complacency. The Franks had won the battle with tactics that would have been familiar to the ancient Greeks or Romans, but he knew he had to counter the threat of the Muslim heavy cavalry. The Arabs thought it would take the Franks a generation to master the new techniques of warfare, but the Franks immediately launched a programme to develop the necessary technology, and to train horsemen to use it.

Meanwhile, Charles reorganised the aristocracy in Burgundy to strengthen that region and to remove his opponents. But in 735 Eudes died, and the nobles of Aquitaine proclaimed his son as the new Duke. Charles, who considered himself their overlord, was not amused. In the same year, Jusuf Ibn 'Abd al-Rahman al-Fihri became governor of the Muslim province in the south of France, and wanted to mark his term of office with a thunderbolt. As it happened, with Charles distracted in a war against the new Duke of Aquitaine and by a revolt in Burgundy, al-Fihri was to get his chance.

The Arabs rampaged over southern France in 736, destroying churches everywhere. Hastily, Charles patched up a treaty with the new Duke of Aquitaine and in 736, in alliance with the Lombards, began a campaign to recover the territory gained by the Arabs. In a series of battles in 737, Charles took Aix-en-Provence, Montfrin, Arles, Nîmes, Agde and Béziers and laid siege to Avignon. When the city finally fell, all of the Arabs defending it were put to the sword.

However, Charles recognised that a full-frontal assault on Narbonne would cost a great many lives, which he could not afford, so he besieged the Muslims in the city. The Arabs decided to send a relief force by sea in 737, which disembarked near Narbonne, and Charles left part of his army to maintain the siege and moved with the rest to intercept the relief force at the mouth of the River Berre. The relief force had not had time to reconnoitre the land, and were therefore at a disadvantage in any case, but worse, very much to their surprise, the Arabs found themselves confronted by enemy heavy cavalry for the first time. The Muslim army was crushed, but Charles decided that he did not have the resources to continue the siege of Narbonne, with winter approaching and with uprisings in Aquitaine and Provence still to be dealt with. He therefore lifted the siege, and Narbonne remained in Arab hands until Pepin the Short took it in 759. By then, the Umayyad Caliphate had been finally destroyed at the Battle of Zab in Iraq, which took place in 750.

A major factor in the decline in Arab power was an outbreak of Bubonic plague in 745, which spread to Africa and over the next seven years killed between 25% and 35% of the populations of the Arab cities. This left the Arab Empire very short of manpower, and by 748 the Arabs had had to resort to the use of slaves, which were supplied to them by the Venetians.

As a footnote, the name 'Martel', applied to Charles many years after his death, refers to the war hammer carried by some soldiers in the Early Middle Ages. It became a well-known surname in France and in England (where a Goisfridus Martel is recorded as an inhabitant of Essex in the Domesday Book). It is also a common surname in the Channel Islands, and a Jean Martell of Jersey founded the oldest of the great cognac houses in France in 1715.

11.5   The Carolingians

Charles died in 741, and left his 'kingdom' to two of his three sons. Carloman inherited Austrasia and Alemannia and Pepin the Short inherited Neustria and Burgundy (with Aquitaine as a vassal kingdom). Pepin, who was also sometimes called Pippin the Younger, therefore became the de facto overlord of the Channel Islands, a king without a title. The third son Grifo, by Charles' second wife, demanded a share of the inheritance, and was banished to a monastery by his half-brothers for his impudence.

Carloman raised the Frankish king Childeric III to the throne in 743, but in 747 Carloman was persuaded to retire to a monastery, leaving Pepin as the sole effective ruler. At about this time Grifo escaped from his imprisonment, and fled to Duke Odilo of Bavaria, who was married to Pepin's sister, which forced Pepin to put down the subsequent revolt. So Pepin emerged as the sole effective ruler of the whole empire, and Grifo was subsequently killed at a battle in 753.

Pepin grew tired of the charade that there was a Frankish 'king' who wielded any real power, and he asked the Pope whether the throne should rest with a nominal hereditary king or with the de facto ruler of the kingdom. The Pope responded that the de facto power should have the throne, and so Childeric was deposed, tonsured and sent to a monastery with his son. The loss of the royal locks was the symbol of the loss of power with the Merovingians. So in about 751, Pepin became King, and in 754 the Pope travelled to Paris to anoint him.

Pepin was not an undistinguished king, finally ridding France of the Arabs for one thing, but he was rather overshadowed by his illustrious father and his still more illustrious son. For the Channel Islands, the most relevant part of the history of his reign was the campaign he launched in 753, to subdue the Bretons, which resulted in the capture of Vannes. After this, he created a military zone, the Breton Marches, from Rennes to Nantes as a 'cordon sanitaire' against incursions from his troublesome neighbours to the west.

When he died, in 768, he was succeeded by his sons Charles and Carloman, but Carloman died in unexplained circumstances in 771 and his family were driven into exile. Charles, who became known as Charlemagne, immediately began preparations for war on several fronts, with the object of establishing a new Christian world order to replace the Western Roman Empire. He launched his first campaign against the pagan Saxons in 772, thus initiating a war that was to last for more than 30 years. And in 774 he attacked and defeated the Lombards in northern Italy, bringing Italy into the Frankish empire.

Spain had been under Arab control since 711, and in 777 Charlemagne was invited by the Moslem governor of Barcelona to take control of the area. However, when he got to Zaragoza, he found the city defended and unwilling to yield. At the same time he heard of developments in the war against the Saxons, which demanded his return to the north, so he took a large tribute in gold and some hostages and marched back through Pamplona. When his army reached Roncevaux Pass, in the Pyrenees, a Basque force ambushed his rearguard and destroyed it, capturing much of the treasure that Charlemagne had just collected. Among the distinguished casualties was Roland, Prefect of the Breton Marches. Although Charlemagne subsequently campaigned in Spain, he did not manage to maintain control over it and the Arabs recovered the territory which he won. Spain, therefore, proved to be a 'bridge too far' in Charlemagne's expansion of Christian Europe, and in fact the Muslims were only finally expelled from their last stronghold, Granada, in 1492 (coincidentally the year of Columbus' first voyage to the Americas).

Charlemagne's career was crowned in 800, when he was acclaimed as 'Holy Roman Emperor' by Pope Leo III at St Peters in Rome, effectively severing the vestigial Western Empire from the Eastern Empire to which it had been subject since the fall of Odoacre. But his wars continued, and he enjoyed more success in Germany, where his 30-year war reached its conclusion when the last of the Saxon resistance was crushed in 804. He offered the defeated Saxons the options of conversion to Christianity or death, and obviously a large number agreed to abandon their pagan gods. But to reduce the scope for uprisings in Saxony, he deported 10,000 of them to Flanders and the Brabant, adding to the growing Saxon presence in what is now Belgium.

As his life drew to a close in 814, tensions mounted on the new border of the Empire with the Kingdom of Denmark, with both sides massing armies to threaten each other.

11.6   Charlemagne in Brittany

Charlemagne's campaigns in Saxony, Italy, Aquitaine, Spain and against the Slavs meant that he had little time to devote to the resolutely independent Bretons, who were in any case already Christian and therefore not a suitable objective for a crusade. But the relationship between the Bretons and the Franks deteriorated markedly. The Breton settlements in Brittany posed a threat to the western borders of the Frankish kingdom, which by the end of the period led to outbreaks of hostilities.

Brittany had become a de-facto independent region by the late 7th century, but was ruled by chiefs of the separate tribal areas until the later part of the 8th century. The peninsula was not very prosperous, and therefore not a tempting target for a full-scale invasion by the Franks, but conflict in the Breton Marches sporadically flared into wider military intervention. In 786, Charlemagne sent his seneschal Audulf with a strong force to Brittany, and Audulf captured Vannes and forced the Bretons of the Vannetais to pledge not to try to recover the city. He took hostages back with him to Charlemagne's court in Worms when he reported the success of his mission. Audulf was replaced in Vannes by Frodald, and Count Guy of Nantes (Wido in Frankish) was made Prefect of the Marches.

The Franks took Alet and there is reason to believe that the castle at Corbénic was razed in the same campaign. Towards the end of the 8th century Charlemagne told the Abbot of Fontenelle to instruct the Channel Islands in the practices of the Roman church, and he placed them in the diocese of Coutances, which may indicate a decline in the status of Dôl.

The Bretons were forced, probably for the first time, to unite under one leader, and they placed their trust in Morvan (c.750 – 818), who was originally from the Morbihan. They seem to have reluctantly accepted the status quo for a decade, but then in 809 they revolted, recapturing Vannes and killing Frodald. In consequence, Guy led an expedition to recover the city in 811, and conquered Brittany *"as had never been done before"*, eventually killing Morvan in about 818. The campaign may have enjoyed unprecedented success against the Bretons, but it did not, in fact, establish an enduring Frankish control over the province.

In part this was because another force intervened at this point in history, which was to completely change the balance of power in northern France. In 799, the Vikings launched their first raid on Aquitaine, sacking the monastery of Saint Philibert on Noirmoutier en route.

Chapter 12:
The Vikings and the Normans

12.1   The Background

The Danes and Norwegians had a long tradition of exacting tribute from the peoples of northern Norway and the Baltic, for example the Finns and Russians. As elsewhere, the status of their rulers depended on the wealth that they could extract from subject populations and the influence that this gave them over their own nobles. They were not Christians, and indeed seem to have had an unusually fatalistic view of the world. Even their gods were doomed to die in a last battle, but the one thing that would never die was the 'word-fame' of each man. And that is what they lived and died for.

During the latter part of the 7th century, they had become increasingly aware of the wealth of Western Europe, with the general expansion of trade in that period, which brought merchants from Frisia and other territories around the North Sea into Danish ports in search of furs, amber, eiderdown and other Baltic products. The port of Dorestad in Frisia became a centre for this trade, communicating with ports in western Denmark, particularly Hedeby.

The Danish kings were especially well placed to exact tribute from the merchants engaged in this commerce, because all shipping from the Baltic to Western Europe had to pass through or around Denmark. But the trade also attracted pirates operating in the Baltic and around the Danish archipelago. The pirates initially used long ships propelled by oars, but their contact with western merchant ships soon made them aware of the use of sails, which they later began to adopt.

On the back of their growing wealth, the Danes began to expand their sphere of influence, and they were particularly keen to gain control over the area called Viken, which controlled the entrance to the Oslo Fjord, thus giving them access to iron from Norway. The inhabitants of Viken who were unwilling to accept Danish hegemony were effectively exiled, and appear to have taken to, or expanded their activities in, piracy. It is believed that this gave rise to the term 'Vikings', which was used in English (but not other languages) to describe all Scandinavian raiders.

As the Danes and Norwegians began to expand their activities into the North Sea, the designs of their ships developed to meet the more turbulent seas they encountered. Their ships traditionally were powered by oars, as seen in the ship buried at Sutton Hoo in about 630. This was about 88 feet (27 metres) long and 15 feet (4.5 metres) wide, and powered by 20 oars on each side. But later they acquired single masts and square sails, with the shipbuilders learning which designs worked by trial-and-error. The Oseberg ship, which dates from about 800, and which was buried with a Norwegian queen, a female attendant, various horses and other animals and many grave goods, had an early design of mast-step. But the mast-step was too short and the partners which supported the mast were too light for the purpose. So the timber of the mast partners had split and it had been repaired with an iron ring. Later designs used a longer mast step and stronger supports, so we can basically assume that effective sailing ships were built by the Vikings from the early 9th century onwards.

The Vikings had numerous designs of ships, including the slender, light and fast troop carriers with which they are most famously associated, but also slower, heavier and more sea-worthy cargo carrying ships. The general theme was a vessel with an oak keel, clinker planking and a flexible hull, which was steered by an oar on the starboard side at the stern. They were double-ended with a curved stem and stern, often decorated to show the status of the owner. But only a king's ship had the dragon ornamentation of the 'drakkars', at its bow.

The ships were measured in terms of the number of pairs of oars employed, with two men at each oar. So for example a '20-seater' would have carried a total complement of about 90 men. Typical 'troop carrier' ships of the period before 1000 would have been 20 – 25 seater ships, of up to 115 feet (35 metres) in length. In later periods the ships grew in size to approaching 230 feet (70 metres). However, it is likely that the size of the crews would have been reduced when the Vikings adopted sail-power as the main motive force. Sailing ships can make longer voyages than galleys, but need more storage on board and fewer hands to man the vessel. So a '20-seater' sailing long ship may have had a crew of half the size of a comparable ship powered mainly by oars.

The 'troop-carrier' type ships had a very high length to beam ratio, typically 6 or 7 to 1, and a shallow draft of less than 3 feet 3 inches (1 metre). They were relatively lightly built with planks less than one inch (2.5 cm) thick, and they could be carried overland (in a 'portage'), if necessary. They were open boats with no shelter and limited provision for stores, so like the earlier Mediterranean galleys they were not designed to make long sea voyages in single stages. The ships could be hauled up on a beach at night, and the crew expected to be able to sustain themselves by raiding and foraging.

12.2   The Pirate Period: c.800 - 833

At the end of the 8th century, Scandinavian pirates began making incursions into the North Sea and beyond, where the richest and easiest of the pickings available were monasteries. The first Viking attacks on England were a raid on the monastery at Lindisfarne in 793, and a raid on the late Bede's monastery at Jarrow-Wearmouth in the following year. The first assault on France was an attack on Aquitaine and the monastery of St Philibert on Noirmoutier in 799. These were 'hit-and-run' operations, conducted by informal gangs of pirates, who never ventured far inland, and whose only motive was robbery. The Scandinavians utterly despised monks, whose personal values were so distant from their own, and they saw them merely as weak and unmanly hoarders of gold.

As in all warfare of early northern European history, the activities of the Vikings were characterised by their seasonality. The Scandinavians launched raids in the summer months, and retired to camps each winter, initially returning to their bases in Denmark or Norway. But as the years went by and they ventured further afield, the effort of returning home every winter became burdensome, and they established raiding bases in the target regions. The Norwegians established bases in the Orkneys, the Shetlands and the Hebrides, from which to raid Ireland, and the Danes based themselves on islands in the Seine and the Loire, to enable them to penetrate inland. The 12th century Orkneyinga Saga describes the life of a Viking living in Orkney in a bye-gone age:

"In the spring he had more than enough to occupy him, with a great deal of seed to sow which he saw to carefully himself. Then when the job was done, he would go off plundering in the Hebrides and in Ireland on what he called his 'spring trip', then back home just after midsummer where he stayed until the cornfields had been reaped and the grain was safely in. After that he would go off raiding again, and never came back until the first month of winter was ended. This he used to call his autumn trip."

Charlemagne responded to the first raids on the coasts of his Empire by ordering coastal defences to be constructed in Aquitaine in 800, and he was as alert as anyone to the threat posed by King Godfred of Denmark to the northern regions of his Empire. He set up systems of watches along the North Sea coast and patrols in the River Scheldt, and in 808 he had a fleet based at the mouth of the River Elbe, just south of the Danish border. The measures taken by the Franks seem to have been at least partially successful, because Viking raids occurred only sporadically and on a small scale for several decades.

However, Charlemagne died in 814 and was succeeded by his son Louis the Pious. Louis' reign was characterised by civil wars involving his sons, which resulted in his being deposed for a year in 833/834. Independently minded regions on the fringes of the Empire were not slow to take advantage of the internal schisms of the Franks, and the Bretons in particular fought hard to maintain their independence. Louis' initial approach to the Breton problem was to use force, and he ordered campaigns against them from Rennes and Nantes in 818, 822, 824 and 825. But when he returned to Paris from another campaign in Brittany in 830, Louis found that civil war had broken out, and he himself was captured by his son Pepin, King of Aquitaine. Louis bought his freedom by promising Pepin and one of his brothers a bigger share of his estate, and soon restored order, but he realised that the Breton wars were a distraction that he could no longer afford.

So he then decided to accept the de facto independence of Brittany, and to try to install leaders of the Bretons who would be more compliant. In about 831 he made a Breton leader, Nominoë, the Duke of Brittany, in return for Nominoë's acknowledgement of Louis' suzerainty.

12.3   Organised Extortion: c.833 - 862

Meanwhile the Scandinavians, who had watched the disintegration of the Carolingian Empire with interest, had seen Louis deposed in 833 and restored in 834, and decided to profit from the chaos. The activities of the Scandinavians took on a different character. Large-scale raids were mounted with royal sponsorship, still mainly for robbery, but also with a view to destabilising the German states across the Danish border and profiting from the discord in the Empire generally.

The first of the large operations began with Danish forces making repeated attacks on Frisia each summer, and then returning to their bases in Denmark for the winter. Dorestad was raided in 834, and again in each of the following three years. Consistent with their policy of establishing bases for further raiding, the Isle of Sheppey was attacked in 835, and the following year a Viking army landed in north Somerset and defeated the forces of Wessex. This marked a change in tactics, with the objectives moving beyond robbery into extortion. By demonstrating that they could overthrow the ruling power, the Vikings hoped to be paid to go away.

Annual raids into Frisia from bases in Denmark were one thing, but returning to Denmark from northern or western France at the end of every season involved too long a sea journey, so the Vikings began to establish bases for over-wintering at the mouths of the rivers they used. The monks of Noirmoutier were forced to abandon their monastery, as the island was taken over as a base for further Scandinavian raids in the Loire Valley, and the Scandinavians began to use islands in the Seine like Jeufosse. The next thirty years saw large scale fleets attacking Britain and France, but without any intention to settle beyond the establishment of military bases.

In 840 Louis the Pious died and his Empire was divided between his sons. His youngest son, Charles the Bald inherited most of what is now France. In 841 Charles appointed Renaud d'Hebauges to the title of Count of Nantes, but the city was coveted by a rebel Count Lambert, who was an ally of the Bretons. Lambert invited a fleet of Norwegians to attack Nantes, and they struck on St John's Day, June 22 in 842, when the city was full of visitors. The slaughter was indiscriminate, and Bishop Gunhard and all his clergy were killed. The Vikings raided further up the Loire, sacking the monasteries at Indres and Vertue, northern Poitou, and then sailed down the coast of Aquitaine, returning to winter at Noirmoutier.

Renaud attacked the Bretons under Nominoë in 843, but was killed at the battle of Messac by Nominoë's son Erispoë. Nominoë then launched an attack on Le Mans in 844, but had to return to the Loire when he received reports that the Viking fleet had arrived in the river once more. The Viking fleet withdrew, sailing up the Garonne and destroying everything as far as Toulouse. They turned south towards Galicia but were driven off by missile throwing war machines and wintered on the coastal islands off Poitou.

In 845 the Scandinavian fleet that had sailed up the Seine four years earlier sent 120 ships up to Paris under the command of Ragnar and extracted an extortion payment of 7000 pounds of silver from the Emperor. It was clear to all that Charles the Bald was incapable of defending even the most important Frankish cities, and he began to lose his grip on his subjects. Ragnar returned to the court of King Horik in Denmark, displaying the riches he had stolen or extorted, coincidentally while an embassy from King Louis the German was at the court, so we know what Ragnar told the king. *"Never had he seen, he said, lands so fertile and rich, nor ever a people so cowardly."* But Ragnar returned from Paris with more than he bargained for, because he immediately fell ill with the plague, and died.

Taking advantage of Charles' weakness, in 845 the Breton Duke Nominoë defeated a large Carolingian army at the Battle of Ballon. Faced with Scandinavian raiding all along the French coast, Charles had no option but to make peace with the Bretons, which was cemented in a treaty of 846 marking the independence of Brittany. Nominoë took Rennes and Nantes in the same year, but was unable to keep possession of them for long and when Charles recovered Rennes and Nantes he created a military zone called the Breton Marches running north-south along the axis of the two cities, and appointed Amaury to be Count of Nantes and Prefect of the Marches.

Meanwhile, a Viking voyage to Spain which ended in Seville was less successful, as the Arabs succeeded in driving away the fleet, killing a thousand Vikings in battle and hanging 400 prisoners. In 847 the Vikings based on the coastal islands near the Loire launched a major offensive against Brittany. Nominoë and the Breton army resisted, fighting three battles, but eventually they succumbed. Nominoë himself had to flee for a short time, and in the end had to buy the Vikings off, one of only two occasions when the Bretons paid extortion money. The Viking fleet then moved south to ravage the coast of Aquitaine. Breton discontent with Frankish rule extended to the authority of the metropolitan Bishops of Tours, and in 848 Nominoë expelled four Frankish bishops and replaced them with Bretons. Nominoë apparently purported to set up an Archbishopric at Dôl, although the See was not recognised by Rome for several centuries.

In 849, hostilities resumed between the Franks and Bretons, and Nominoë seized Rennes and Nantes, raiding deep into France. The Frankish bishops wrote him a letter in 850, reproaching him for having crossed the frontiers of his ancestors, which illustrates the point that Brittany had not historically included Rennes and Nantes. In 851 Nominoë was killed near Vendôme and his son Erispoë took command of the Breton forces, but this brought no respite for the Franks. Erispoë wiped out the army of the Franks at the Battle of Jengland, the same year, killing several thousand Franks with minimal Breton losses. At the subsequent Treaty of Angers, Charles the Bald, who needed Breton support against the Vikings on Noirmoutier, ceded Nantes and Rennes, along with the area around Pornic to Erispoë. So the Breton Marches were totally incorporated into Brittany.

Viking attacks in the Seine and Loire were by now virtually annual events, aimed at pillaging and extorting ransoms. In an age where violence and cruelty were commonplace, the Vikings were considered by everyone they encountered the worst and most barbaric of all. But it is worth noting that their attacks were focused on centres of commerce and wealth, including monasteries, and that it was not in the interests of an army that depended on locally sourced agricultural products to wipe out the peasant farmers who produced them. As a result, the aftermath of Viking raids in a region like Brittany was typically an area devoid of Frankish overlords and monks, who had fled to safer locations further inland, leaving a leaderless peasantry to cultivate the land.

The Vikings also developed a side-line as mercenaries, and were available to assist anyone in the warring clans of the Frankish kingdoms who would pay for their services. Sometimes this brought Vikings into conflict with other Vikings, as each party had agreed to support opposing sides in a local war, but in practice they usually found a way of avoiding battles against each other (normally by betraying one or both of their employers).

In the 850s Godfrid, son of the Harald who had led the Viking raids on Frisia in 830 (Harald Klak), sailed up the Seine and besieged Paris, forcing Charles the Bald to come to terms with him. To complicate matters further, Charles began to conspire against Nominoë with his cousin Salomon, and in 852 Charles went so far as to grant Salomon one third of Brittany.

Erispoë, who was several times in contemporary documents described as a prince, tried to counter Salomon's machinations, and in 856 negotiations took place to marry his daughter to Charles the Bald's son Louis the Stammerer. In consideration for this prospective alliance, Erispoë returned the Duchy of Le Mans to Louis. But the marriage never took place, and Erispoë was murdered by Salomon in 857, on the altar of the church at Talensac, 12 miles to the west of Rennes. Although Salomon seized control of Brittany ostensibly as Charles' vassal, he immediately began to ally himself with anyone who would oppose Charles, notably Louis the Stammerer and Robert the Strong of Neustria.

In 857 a Viking army led by Björn Ironside and a fellow commander Hastein began an epic four-year cruise with another assault on Paris, destroying virtually the whole city. The priests at the four churches that were left standing had paid the Vikings to spare their buildings. The Scandinavians then decided that having plundered Paris, they might as well go one better, and they set off with 62 ships with the object of sacking Rome. After raiding along the coast of France they reached Spain. The Arabs were prepared this time, and captured two of the Viking ships off the mouth of the Guadalquivir, so the fleet pressed on through the Straits of Gibraltar. They crossed the Straits to the coast of Africa to pick up some black slaves (who ended up in Ireland), and then headed back to the coast of Spain. After raiding the Balearic Islands, they attacked the south of France, including Narbonne and then sailed (or more probably rowed) up the Rhône. They reached Valence before being forced to return down the river and then worked their way along the coast to Italy, where they raped a town, which may have been Luna, in the evident belief that they had reached Rome.

On his return journey, Hastein's fleet was attacked by the Arabs in Spain, with many casualties, but the residue of his fleet assaulted Pamplona and ransomed the governor for a princely sum, after which they eventually reached the Loire in 862. Just 20 of the original 62 ships survived, and the Vikings never again raided Spain, or sailed into the Mediterranean from the western end.

In 859 the Seine Vikings continued to raid widely, destroying Noyon and Beauvais, and a new Danish army arrived on the Somme under the command of Weland. Weland's fleet laid waste to Amiens and Saint-Valéry-sur-Somme and wintered at the mouth of the river. The following year this Somme fleet campaigned in England, but Weland offered to return and fight the Seine Vikings for Charles provided he was paid 3000 pounds of silver and supplied with food and wine. Charles agreed and paid up, but any relief in one area was quickly matched by new threats in another, as an endless stream of Scandinavians pillaged at will.

Weland returned from England with 200 ships, in 861, being later joined by a further 60, and he besieged the Seine Vikings at Oscelles. However, after being paid 6000 pounds of silver by them, he allowed the Seine Vikings to sail away and winter elsewhere on the river, so Weland had then taken 9000 pounds of silver from the two sides, and Charles had effectively been duped. Paris was again burned by a Danish fleet.

12.4   The Vikings in the Channel Islands

In their various voyages up and down the Channel, the Vikings obviously passed within a few miles of the Channel Islands, and we are told by Wace that all the islands were raided by *"la gent Sanrazine"* ('the Saracens') causing much destruction. ('Sarrazin', or Saracen was a term used at that time to describe any barbarian, not merely Arabs). Wace (c.1100 to 1180) was born in Jersey but partly educated at Caen, and therefore may have known of the history from both sides.

We do not know if any Vikings stayed for prolonged periods, but in Guernsey the castle at the site of the present Castel Church was known in ancient times as 'Le Chastel du Grand Sarrazin' (Castle of the Great Saracen), and it has sometimes been suggested that 'the Great Saracen' was Hastein. The castle was also sometimes referred to as 'Le Chastel du Grand Jeflfroi or Geffroi', and local historians have assumed that 'le Grand Geffroi' was the same person as 'le Grand Sarrazin'.

This assumption seems to derive from the 'Histoire du Cotentin et de ses Îles' written by Gustave Jules Dupont in 1870 – 1885. Dupont claims that Geoffroi must have been the 'Godefrid' or 'Godefroy', whose father Harald *"destroyed the church of Mont St Michel"*, incurring the wrath of the Frankish counts, who killed him.[16] He tells us that, in revenge, 'Godefrid' ravaged the lands of the Franks for three years, forcing Charles the Bald to pay him off in 850. Dupont then makes the extraordinary assumption that this tribute included Guernsey.

It is impossible to reconcile this account with known history. The 'Annales Bertiniani' tell us that there was a Danish king Godfrid Haraldsson (c.820 – c.856), who was a son of Harald Klak. After raiding in Frisia, Flanders and the Rhine, he sailed up to Ghent in 851 and attacked the Abbey of Drongen. In 853, he sailed up the Seine, and camped for the winter on an island near Les Andelys, where he was besieged by Charles the Bald. However, Charles had no boats with which to assault the island, and the standoff was resolved in the spring when Godfrid simply sailed off, probably with tribute. Nothing in this history suggests that Godfrid ever came near the Channel Islands, so the idea that Guernsey belonged to this Danish king can be safely dismissed.

Incidentally, it should be mentioned in passing that there was also a 'Tombeau du Grand Sarrazin' (tomb of the Great Saracen) and an 'Autel du Grand Sarrazin' (altar of the Great Saracen) in Guernsey, which were both megalithic monuments and which therefore clearly had nothing to do with the Dark Ages. The tomb was destroyed by quarrying in 1872.

So who was 'Geffroi'? At a guess, he may have been Geoffroi de Montbray, who was Bishop of Coutances (in which diocese Guernsey lay) from 1048 to 1093. He was a loyal servant of William the Conqueror, and was given command of the Norman forces in England when William was obliged to make a return visit to Normandy. The Abbé Lecanu described him, in his 'Histoire des Eveques de Coutances' as a man of immense wealth, vast possessions and a munificence corresponding to his large means. It is known that William gave him 280 manors in England, and lands in the Channel Islands.

John Le Patourel writes (in ' Feudal Empires: Norman and Plantagenet',

16 Godfrid, or 'God's peace' was an extraordinarily inappropriate name for a Viking!

1984): *"There is clear evidence that the churches and parishes of Guernsey and Jersey existed in some form before he was made bishop, so that he cannot be responsible for their foundation; but we may reasonably infer from an apparently contemporary account of his episcopate that he brought them fully into the organization of the diocese and that by the time of his death the Islands were integrated into the ecclesiastical as they were into the secular structure of the duchy."* Very possibly his work included the construction or renovation of St Marie du Castel, the church now standing on the site of the Castel du Grand Sarazzin.

It appears that from the early 10th century, Guernsey was partly owned by the Néel family of St Sauveur in Normandy, one member of which gave some woods in Guernsey to the Priory of Mont St Michel in 942. By the end of the century Guernsey was owned by two noble Norman families, the Néels and the Anslechs, who founded the house of Bricquebec. The Néels of St Sauveur owned the parishes of St Sampson, St Peter Port, St Andrew, St Martin, the Forest and Torteval, and the Bricquebecs owned the parishes of the Vale, the Castel, St Saviour, and St Peter in the Wood.

The most enduring legacy of the Vikings in the Channel Islands is the names of some of the islands and rocks around them, but it is not clear whether this influence arrived at this time or later during the Norman era. The –sey name endings are probably of Norse origin, because 'ey' meant island in Old Norse and the Germanic languages. It is therefore assumed that Jer is a contraction of a Viking personal name, so Jersey is 'Jer's island'. The ending of the name of Guernsey changed from 'ri' to 'ey', as we have seen, at the end of the 11th century, possibly to match Jersey. And the names of islands ending in 'hou' (from 'hólmr', meaning small island as in 'Stockholm') are all of Norse origins. Brecqhou was 'brenk hólmr', the 'steep island', and 'hólmr' is found in Guernsey's Houmet (in the Vale) and Houmet Paradis as well as elsewhere in the Islands. In the evolution of the name of Brecqhou, the transition of 'brenk' to 'brekk' was complete by 850, and I think we can assume that most of the Channel Islands had acquired their modern names by that time, apart from Guernsey, which went through one more evolution at the end of the 11th century. The Norse name for a type of rock shaped like a cup, 'stakkr', is found in Jersey's L'Etacq (recorded as Stakus in 1274) and also in a place of the same name in Sark.

While it is certain that many place names in the Channel Islands have an origin in old Norse, it is not clear when this influence arrived. The Islands were under Norman rule from 933, and it is therefore entirely possible that the Norse influence did not arrive before that time. Without any archaeological evidence of earlier contact, the question will probably never be resolved.

12.5   The Expansion of Brittany

In 857, Charles found himself unable to deal with a raid by the Loire Vikings on Tours and the surrounding area, being simultaneously faced with a Danish attack on Chartres during which Bishop Frotbald was killed. When Robert the Strong, Marquis of Neustria and his supporters rebelled in 858, Charles was in desperate straits, and he realised that he had to settle the Breton wars to enable him to cope with his other problems. As usual, his instinct was to buy Robert off with additional lands.

In 861, to contain the Bretons, Charles created a new Marche de Bretagne, further to the east than the old one, comprising the counties of Touraine, Angers and Maine, and placed it under the command of Robert. He then turned his attention to trying to stem the endless flood of raiders from Scandinavia, and the following year he initiated a programme of river defences. The Marne was blockaded at several points trapping Weland's ships at Trimaldon Bridge and forcing them into Jumièges for repairs. Weland was obliged to formally submit to Charles, who then ordered the construction of fortifications on the Seine.

A part of Weland's fleet split from him and joined a small group of Vikings on the Loire. This combined fleet was hired for a reported 6000 pounds of silver by Robert the Strong for a campaign against Salomon. But Salomon responded by hiring 12 Loire Viking ships which had been troubling southern Brittany, and the resulting standoff produced a short period of relative peace. Weland was killed in a duel in 863, which helped to relieve some of the pressure on the Franks, and Salomon made peace with Charles, receiving grants of land between the Mayenne and the Sarthe in return.

The Vikings had by now become so embroiled in the politics of France that Pippin II of Aquitaine had actually joined them and renounced Christianity. In Brittany, the Vikings were increasingly acting as allies of the Bretons against the Franks, and the Bretons took advantage of the situation to expand their 'kingdom' into the new Breton Marches.

In 865 Salomon had attacked Le Mans, and in the following year he allied himself with the Danish Hastein for an expedition against Anjou, Maine and Touraine. Le Mans, the traditional seat of the Franks in north-west France, was sacked again. Robert the Strong joined forces with Ranulf, Count of Poitiers, Gauzfrid and Hervé of Maine to repulse the invaders, but the Franks were unable to save Le Mans. Robert decided to intercept the retreating Vikings, who he knew would have to return to the Loire via Brissarthe ('passage over the Sarthe'), one of the few places where it was possible to cross the river. The ambushed Vikings were forced to take refuge in a church, surrounded by a much larger Frankish force, where they held out until nightfall.

Robert posted sentries and sent part of his force to pillage the Viking longboats, but during the night, Hastein attempted a sortie. Robert, without protection, was in the first line of the Franks who met this attack, and he was killed by an axe blow, the Vikings dragging his body back into the church. The Count of Poitiers was also gravely wounded by an arrow and subsequently died of his wounds, and Hervé was injured. So in the morning, being virtually leaderless, the Franks melted away and allowed the Vikings to escape.

866 saw a dramatic victory for the Seine Vikings. After defeating Robert and Odo at Melun, a large host not only forced Charles to pay a tribute of 4000 pounds of silver and wergild for dead Vikings, but also to release all Scandinavian prisoners. An attempt to block the Seine at Pîtres failed and the Seine fleet reached the open sea. Charles was now desperate to stop the Bretons and the Loire Vikings from entering into an alliance with the Seine Vikings, which would have been fatal for his share of the Empire. So Charles entered into a treaty with Salomon conceding him not only the whole of the larger Brittany, but also the land as far west as the base of the Côtentin peninsula, which had never formed part of the province. Salomon was granted the abbeys, villae and fiscs of Coutances and thereafter styled himself 'rex'.

Not only did this treaty represent the high-water mark of Breton hegemony, it may also have meant that for the first time the Channel Islands came under Breton control, although the details of the treaty in respect of the Islands are unclear. It was also successful, from Charles' point of view, in driving a wedge between the Bretons and the Loire Vikings, because by 869 Salomon was fighting against Hastein in the Vilaine.

12.6   The Great Army

England had suffered raids during the first half of the century, but not on the scale of the assaults on Francia. The raids had at an early stage moved on from the smash-and-grab attacks on monasteries to attempts to destabilise the ruling Anglo-Saxon regimes, and the Vikings identified the schism between the Celtic Britons and the Anglo-Saxons as a key fault line to be exploited, exactly as they were later to play off the Franks and the Bretons. In 807 they formed an alliance with the Cornish, but in 814, Egbert of Wessex was able to conquer the whole western peninsula for the first time.

However the Cornish persistently rebelled, with Viking support, and a Scandinavian army fought the Saxons in Somerset in 835. Nevertheless, a combined Viking-Cornish army was defeated by Egbert's Wessex army at the Battle of Hingston Down in 838, and Cornwall was thereafter incorporated into Wessex.

By the middle of the century, the Viking tactic was to establish bases in the Thames Estuary, at Thanet and Sheppey, from which to conduct their assaults on London. In 851, a very large fleet attacked Canterbury and London, and drove away the Mercian army, but attempts to overthrow the Kingdom of Wessex met with failure. An invasion force took Winchester in 860 but was subsequently beaten off and returned to the Continent.

After Charles the Bald began to improve the Frankish defences against the fleets in the Seine and the Loire, in 862, more of the Vikings in those rivers began to look to England for easier pickings, but they had by now realised that Wessex was the toughest nut to crack. In 865 a 'Great Army' landed in Essex, and over the next five years this force of several thousand men conquered the Anglo-Saxon kingdoms of East Anglia and Northumbria, and seized part of Mercia. The Great Army marched north to York in 866, and found the city undefended because the Northumbrian King Ælle was away fighting a usurper called Osbert. The two Northumbrians patched up their differences to mount an attempt to retake the city in 867, but both of them were killed in the ensuing battle, along with a great many of their army.

In 870, the Vikings defeated and killed King Edmund of East Anglia, and in 871 the Great Army was reinforced by new arrivals, called the Great Summer Army. For the rest of that year the Vikings fought a series of skirmishes against the Kingdom of Wessex, which was ruled by King Alfred. At the end of the year, Alfred made peace, no doubt with a payment of Danegeld, to buy time to regroup while the Scandinavians turned their attention to Mercia. The combined Viking army attacked the Mercians in Repton and drove their King Burgred abroad. But around this time, it appears that the plague struck the Danes, because a large grave containing the remains of a king and about 250 followers was found in Repton in the 19th century, and apparently none of the dead had battle injuries. Most of the deceased were from Scandinavia, and about 50 were women, which gives us an idea of the ratio of the sexes in the camp.

The character of this invasion was different, because the Scandinavian raids in Francia, despite being sponsored by the Danish kings, were not designed to seize territory. But in England, having brought down whole kingdoms, the Vikings made themselves at home and started to distribute the land of the defeated Anglo-Saxons among themselves. In 876, the Viking leader *"Hálfdan shared out the lands of Northumbria, and they started to plough and make a living for themselves."* ('The Anglo-Saxon Chronicle')

Nevertheless, the Vikings continued to make intensive efforts in the late 870s, to conquer the kingdom of Wessex. A planned combined operation against Wessex by East Anglian and Irish Vikings was aborted after the fleet sailing from Ireland was wrecked by a storm, and the East Anglian Vikings withdrew to Mercia, no doubt having collected Danegeld. And an attempt to capture Alfred at Chippenham just after Christmas 878 narrowly failed, because Alfred escaped into the Somerset marshes. Later that year, he was able to assemble a force large enough to defeat the Danes at Edington, just outside Chippenham. The Vikings sued for peace, their leaders accepted Christianity and they withdrew to East Anglia where they settled down.

In 885-886, a new treaty formalised the boundary of the Danelaw, running along the Thames to London, then up the River Lea to its source, then in a straight line to Bedford and then up the River Ouse to Watling Street. For a period, peace reigned in England.

12.7   The Settlement of Normandy

The main focus of attention reverted to the Seine in the late 870s, because the deaths of both Charles the Bald, in 877, and his oldest son Louis the Stammerer, in 879, left the Carolingian Empire in chaos, and the Vikings virtually unopposed. Widespread destruction in Neustria forced the monks at Evreux, Lisieux, Bayeux and Avranches to flee. The inability of Charles the Bald to fight the Vikings had led to the promotion of those who could, such as Baldwin II of Flanders, but these local leaders frequently made alliances with the Vikings for their own ends, resulting in anarchy.

When Louis the Stammerer died, he was succeeded by his sons, who divided up the Empire, his second son Louis III inheriting Neustria. After the customary civil war, Louis achieved a major success against the Vikings at the Battle of Saucourt-en-Vimeu in 881, when 8,000 Vikings were killed. But Louis then died in 882, after falling off a horse while pursuing a young lady, and his brother Carloman II only lasted two more years.

The crown of West Francia then passed to Charles the Fat, who continued with the strategy that the Franks had by then adopted, of building fortified bridges across the Seine and the Loire. In November 885, another huge Danish fleet sailed up the Seine under the command of Sigfrid, but with another Viking commander among their number who was to have a much greater effect on the history of France and ultimately Britain. Rollo (Gangu-Hrolfr - 'Ganger Rolf' or 'Walker Rolf') was a Viking so large that it was said no horse could carry him, hence his name. According to Norman legends, Rollo had earlier tried his luck in England, but having found the Kingdom of Wessex, under Alfred the Great, too robust for his liking, he looked to the Seine for better opportunities. For a whole year the defenders of the bridges and the riverbank walls of Paris held out against a horde estimated by the Abbot of Fleury at forty thousand men, and by 886 Charles the Fat had assembled an army large enough to besiege the Danes. However, much to the horror of the people of Paris, he promised to pay the Vikings 600 pounds of silver if they would remove themselves and attack Burgundy, where Charles had other problems with the locals, thus killing two birds with one stone. And when the Vikings decided to ignore Burgundy completely, and instead raided elsewhere in northern France, Charles still paid over the silver.

Events started to go badly wrong for the Franks. Scandinavians had now been in Francia continuously for over six years, and in one of the worst years of raiding in the ninth century the whole eastern Empire was flooded with Vikings. In 886 the Franks were defeated near Paris and Abbots Hugh and Gozelin were killed. In July of the same year, Heinrich, the defender of the eastern frontiers, was slain by the Viking Sigtred, forcing the Frankish Emperor to pay a tribute and retreat. In 887, an ailing Charles was deposed by local chieftains in Eastern Francia and Lotharia, and he was incapable of responding to the usurpers. He then lost all of his remaining kingdoms at the end of the year, and when he died six weeks later in January 888, without a legitimate heir, the Empire broke up. Each of the provinces elected their own 'kings', and West Francia elected Odo, the hero of the siege of Paris; but the other kings refused to recognise him.   The Frankish Empire was not reunited until Odo died in 898, after which Charles the Simple took the combined throne.

In the meantime, the Vikings under Rollo started to settle in the Seine valley, in the area around Rouen. There is no record of his activities after the siege of Paris, but in 911 Rollo laid siege to Chartres unsuccessfully. He was forced to retreat, and Charles the Simple decided to negotiate a settlement with him. They met at St Clair-sur-Epte, on the eastern border of the areas occupied by the Vikings in Normandy, and Charles offered to make Rollo the Count of Normandy (nowadays he is described as the first Duke of Normandy), with power over the territory occupied by the Vikings, in return for an oath of allegiance to Charles as King.

The Treaty no longer exists, if it ever did, but it was referred to in a grant of land in 918, which stated that the land had been granted to *"the Northmen of the Seine, namely Rollo and his followers, for the defence of the kingdom".* Gustave Jules Dupont is sceptical that any agreement was reduced to writing; *"The fictitious treaty of Saint Claire-sur-Epte, which was never written, did nothing but recognise the fact, and convert it into law, that Charles the Simple was no longer the master of, to give or not to give, the lands over which he had lost control."*[17]   Rollo seems to have been given the title of Count and charged with the defence of the region. He was granted the districts of Talon, Caux, Roumois, and parts of the Vexin and Evrecin. Legend has it that Rollo was supposed to kiss the King's foot at the ensuing ceremony, but he ordered one of his henchmen to do the job for him; the Dane duly picked up the King's foot and drew it to his mouth, dropping the King unceremoniously on his back! In the same treaty, the 'northmen' also agreed to become Christians, and Rollo appears to have accepted this part of the deal with rather more sincerity than the commitment to pay homage to the King! No doubt his decision was influenced by his Christian wife, but his piety did not run so deep as to cause him to endow any churches or monasteries during the remainder of his life.

The Vikings in Normandy must have arrived without women, because they very soon adopted the language and customs of the Franks.   Rollo probably only spoke Norse, but he first married a Frankish Christian woman, Poppa of Bayeux, and was subsequently married to Charles the Simple's daughter Giselle. His son by Poppa, William Longsword, married Luitgarde, another Frankish noblewoman. And when William succeeded his father (who retired in old age) in 927, he faced a revolt from his Norman subjects who considered he had become too Gallic and 'soft'. It is inconceivable that William did not speak Norman French. He had no children by Luitgarde, but had a son, Richard the Fearless, by his Breton concubine Sprota. Richard's first marriage was to Emma, daughter of Hugh the Great of France, but this union produced no children and she died eight years later. He did however have several children by his concubine, Gunnor, who he later married to legitimise the children. Gunnor was the daughter of a local forester, but a

---

17 *"Le prétendu traité de Saint-Claire-sur-Epte, qui jamais ne fut écrit, ne fit que reconnaitre un fait, et le convertir en droit; car Charles le Simple n'était pas plus le maître de ne pas donner à Roll le pays dont il s'était emparé."*

Dane by descent, so we cannot know what her native language was. But Richard had children by numerous other mistresses, and it seems probable that his court spoke French. He may even have learned some Breton from his mother.

The new Dukes of Normandy (who were probably called counts at the time) also modelled their government in Normandy on the Frankish system, where power was concentrated at the top. Rollo and his descendants established a stable regime, which flourished to the extent that they were able, 150 years later, to overthrow the King of England. And the establishment of a Norman duchy around the mouth of the Seine had the prophylactic effect that Charles the Simple had hoped to achieve – Vikings stopped raiding up the Seine valley. But all this meant was that the Viking pirates merely moved to other areas - by 925 the coasts around Normandy and northern Brittany were so infested with Vikings that the Bishops of Coutances removed themselves to Rouen for safety. The abbey of St Gildas de Rhuys (in Quiberon Bay, outside the Morbihan) was subject to two attacks, in 914 and again more severely in 919, and we may suppose that raids on the Channel Islands were not uncommon in this period.

In 933, William Longsword came to an agreement with Raoul, the King of Western Francia, whereby, in return for William's support, Raoul gave William *"all territory of the Bretons at the edge of the sea"*, ie the lands of the Côtentin Peninsula and adjacent islands, and at that point the Channel Islands became incorporated into the Duchy of Normandy. Essentially they have remained a part of that Duchy ever since, though the Duke has long since renounced the title (Henry III abandoned it in the Treaty of Paris in 1259).

12.8   Viking Rule in Brittany

After Salomon had been given the Avranchin by Charles the Bald in 865, Viking activity in Brittany intensified in the period 866 – 873, with the Vikings as often raiding in alliance with the Bretons as against them. The three powers interested in the western peninsula were engaged in a deadly political game, playing each opponent off against the other, and in 868 Salomon agreed to lead a joint Breton/Frankish force against the Loire Vikings. But he found himself fighting alone against the Danes when the Carolingian force that he had been promised ignored the Scandinavians and launched raids into Neustria instead. In the end it was the militia in Poitiers that drove the Vikings off.

However Hastein remained secure in his base at Noirmoutier, and in 869 he was again raiding the Vilaine, where he was checked by Salomon *"and all the Bretons"*. This contest came to an end with a peace treaty between the parties, the terms of which included an exchange of hostages, 500 head of cattle for the Vikings, and a share of the Anjou wine harvest for the Bretons. Again, this illustrates the point that the armies on both sides were dependent on peasant farmers for their sustenance, and were very unlikely to attack them. There were probably few people in the Loire valley safer, during this period, than a peasant tending his vines (although he could certainly have expected to have a large proportion of his produce stolen).

The Loire Vikings were now attacking smaller and less valuable targets, because the main centres of commerce and the richest monasteries had already been plundered. The list of possible targets was becoming restricted, because Charles the Bald was improving the defences of the Frankish cities of the Loire Valley, and Le Mans and Tours were fortified. Raids against smaller centres of population around the coast of Brittany became more common, with Alet suffering an attack before 872, and it is possible that Hastein's devastation of the Channel Islands dates to this period. However Hastein then pulled off a coup, by taking Angers in 872. The citizens had evacuated the city at the news of his approach, and Hastein simply sailed up the Maine and entered through the open gates. Moreover, having taken over occupation, he did not simply pillage and burn the city, and then leave, as the inhabitants must have expected. He decided to stay. In 873, the Carolingians dislodged him with an ingenious tactic: Charles had besieged the city with little effect, but the Franks then diverted the course of the river, and left the Viking fleet literally stranded. Hastein was forced to agree to leave the region, but in fact merely returned to Noirmoutier.

In 877, Charles the Bald died, being succeeded by Charles the Fat, son of Louis the German, and the focus of Viking activity switched back to the Seine. This was the campaign which led to the siege of Paris in 885 – 886, which is discussed above. After Charles the Fat was deposed, the Bretons and Vikings faced rather more formidable opposition in Odo, the King of Neustria, and Charles the Simple, a grandson of Charles the Bald, who became King of Aquitaine. Odo defeated Hastein at Montfaucon in 888, but the Vikings again attacked Paris the following year, and had to be paid to leave.

In 874 a civil war in Brittany broke out, after the murder of Salomon by a rival, but this was eventually resolved with an agreement between the rival heirs, Judicael and Alain, to rule jointly. And when Judicael was killed fighting the Vikings in a victory at the Battle of Questembert in 888 or 889, Alain became sole ruler of the whole of Salomon's Brittany, which extended to include Coutances, the Avranchin, Anjou and the western parts of Poitou. It seems very likely that he would also have ruled the Channel Islands, but there is no documentary evidence for this. Alain the Great, as he became known, was probably the only Breton leader to hold the title of 'king' by a grant of a Frankish Emperor (Charles the Fat). He defeated the *"Northmen who had come from the Seine"* at Saint-Lô in Normandy in 890, and during the rest of his reign Brittany was relatively free of invaders.

As Alain cleared Brittany of Vikings, the Scandinavian stranglehold on the Empire was also coming to an end. King Arnulf of Carinthia, the king of East Francia, destroyed the Great Army camped at Louvain, in September 891, killing Sigfred and capturing sixteen Viking standards. And the attacks also lessened in Flanders after the strengthening of its cities' walls. By the end of 892, when there was a great famine in France, Hastein and the Great Army had left mainland Europe and sailed for England, where they landed in two groups, one by the River Lymne in Kent and the other in London. However Alfred's defences were equal to the task, and the invaders marched around England fruitlessly, before eventually returning to the Seine where they appear to have settled. Hastein disappeared from the record in about 896.

When Alain the Great died in 907, the Bretons were left without a strong leader, and the Vikings who had not settled in the lower Seine area, having exhausted the opportunities elsewhere, turned their attention to Brittany (and also to Ireland). These were piratical Vikings, for whom settlement and domestication held no appeal, and they probably started out with no territorial ambitions, but, as Breton resistance collapsed, they were able to take control of the whole province for twenty years, a reign of terror which left hardly any archaeological footprint.

By about 910, the whole of the Breton court had evacuated to England, and taken refuge at the court of King Æthelstan. The Chronicle of Nantes records that: *"... Among the nobles who fled for fear for the Danes, Mathuedoi, the count of Poher, put to sea with a great multitude of Bretons, and went to Athelstan, king of the English, taking with him his son, called Alan, who was afterwards surnamed "Crooked Beard". ['Barbetorte'] - He had had this Alan by the daughter of Alan the Great, duke of the Bretons, and the same Athelstan, king of England, had lifted him from the holy font. This king had great trust in him because of this friendship and the alliance of this baptism."* Other Breton leaders went to Burgundy and Aquitaine, and Brittany was abandoned to Viking misrule.

In 912 the monastery of Saint Guénolé at Landevennec was sacked and in 914, as documented in the Anglo-Saxon Chronicle, a large Danish fleet sailed south from the Severn to launch a four-year assault on Brittany before returning to attack England and Wales. In 914 the Abbey of St Gildas de Rhuys was sacked, and the Abbey of St Tudy at Loctudy was destroyed at about the same time.

In 919, a massive fleet of Loire Vikings under a Norwegian commander called Rognvald attacked the Abbey of St Gildas again, sacked Nantes and then seized the whole of Brittany. And by 925, the coasts around Normandy and Brittany were so infested with Viking pirates that the Bishop of Coutances removed himself to Rouen for safety. In 927, a Viking force raided the Limousin, but was driven out by twelve squadrons of cavalry led by Raoul I, King of Western Francia.

The leaderless Bretons occasionally put up some resistance to their Scandinavian overlords, and in 931, when the Vikings from all over Brittany had gathered to launch an attack on the Franks, the Bretons took their opportunity to rise up, killing many Vikings in the region. The assembled Viking army immediately diverted to deal with the problem and the revolt was quickly and brutally suppressed. It was the growing threat to the Franks from the Vikings in Brittany which forced Raoul to make a new alliance with William Longsword in 933, under which William was given *"all the territory of the Bretons at the edge of the sea",* probably including the Channel Islands.

In 935 Hugh the Great, the Frankish ruler of the parts of Neustria not under the control of the Northmen, made an alliance with Rollo's son, William Longsword, effectively isolating the Vikings in Brittany. The Seine Vikings had long since given up raiding, and indeed had become as French as the Franks through inter-marriage, so they had little in common with the unreformed freebooters who were now living parasitically in the western peninsula.

Abbot John of Landevennec, appealed to Alain Barbetorte in 936 to return home from England, where, as we have seen, he was a guest at the court of Æthelstan, and where he had been raised as the King's godson. Æthelstan spent a great deal of time at Malmesbury in Wiltshire, and some have claimed that he made the town his capital city, although this is disputed by others who believe that Winchester retained that honour. Alain responded by raising a force for the liberation of Brittany composed of Bretons and their English allies. His journey to the River Rance would have taken him past the Channel Islands, and very likely involved a stay at Guernsey to catch the tide into the Bay of St Malo, so he may even have picked up some reinforcements there. Alain landed at Dôl with an army of Bretons, catching the Vikings unprepared and quickly defeating those who were revelling in the monastery. He met a second small force at St Brieuc where the Vikings had built one of only two Viking fortified encampments in Brittany that survive today, and he found himself temporarily unable to take this stronghold. He returned along the coast to Plourivo where he fought and beat another small Viking force, his army gathering strength as it went. The following year he resumed his campaign against the Scandinavians, fighting many battles and accumulating force as his army liberated more and more of the region. Eventually the Vikings were forced back to Nantes.

The Scandinavians had built a camp at Saint-Aignan at the junction of the Loire and the Erdre, just outside Nantes. Alain surrounded the camp with his army, and led a charge against the ramparts, which was repelled. After defeating a Viking sortie, the Bretons rested and then attacked again, and after a battle that lasted a whole day in stifling weather, Alain's army eventually stormed the fort. The surviving Vikings retreated down the Loire.

We are given a picture of the complete devastation of Nantes as the Bretons found it, in the 'Chronicle of Nantes'. Alain's army walked through weed-covered streets, past ruined buildings and Alain was forced to cut his way through thick brambles to reach the basilica of St Felix, empty and disused for nineteen years. Duke Alain now established Nantes as his capital, restored the city and built a rampart around the cathedral.

In 938 the scattered remnants of the Loire Vikings had moved north-east, and they built a large fortification at Trans la Forêt. In the following year they resumed raiding in the vicinity of Rennes, where they were opposed by Judicael (alias Berengar), the Count of Rennes. In August 939 Judicael was joined by an army under the joint leadership of Alain and Hugh the Great; and after a brief siege, a combined assault on the Viking camp finally eliminated the last of the Scandinavians who had occupied Brittany. Their enduring legacy in Brittany was minimal – no place names, no contribution to the language and a negligible genetic footprint – but they had caused decades of suffering and terror.

As we have seen, the present day boundaries of Brittany had been broadly established in 933, when Raoul had given William Longsword the Côtentin and Avranchin, so Brittany then comprised what are now the five Departments of the Côtes d'Armor, Finisterre, Île-et-Vilaine, Morbihan and the Loire Atlantique. But Alain was able to cement the independence of the region through his relationship with King Louis IV of West Francia. The two men were friends, both having been exiled as boys at the court of King Æthelstan in England[18]. In 936, shortly before Alain expelled the Vikings from Brittany, Louis had returned to France and had been crowned King at Laon. Alain paid homage to Louis in 945, in return for which Louis recognised that Brittany had never formed part of his kingdom. Alain had in fact by then augmented his territory with some lands to the south of the Loire, as a result of an alliance with the Duke of Aquitaine in 942, but these lands subsequently reverted to Aquitaine.

Alain Barbetorte died in 952, having made remarkable progress in repairing the damage caused by the Viking invaders, including the restoration of most of the monasteries in the province. His son Drogo was still a child at the date of his father's death, and inevitably there followed a period of civil war from which Conan I of Rennes eventually emerged as the victor. Richard I of Normandy spent the early part of his reign defending Normandy from the predations of Franks, like the Count of Blois, but preferred diplomacy to war. He built a network of alliances by arranging strategic marriages for his children, including that of his daughter Emma to Æthelred, King of England (and subsequently to King Canute, after Æthelred's death). He promoted the interests of the monastery (and former convent) at Fécamp, and in 966 he expelled the occupants of Mont St Michel, and replaced them with about 30 Benedictine monks. According to Guernsey legend, the displaced community moved to Guernsey and established a priory of St Michel in the Vale, at the north end of the island. Relations between the Bretons and Normans were cemented in 966 by two marriages. Richard I's daughter Hawise married Geoffrey I, Duke of Brittany, and shortly afterwards her brother Richard II married Geoffrey's sister Judith. The Bretons and Normans thereafter formed an alliance, with the Bretons in the junior role. Peace between the two Duchies was largely maintained until c. 1030 when friction between Alain III of Brittany and Duke Robert of Normandy erupted into war. Alain had inherited the Duchy of Brittany when he was a minor in 1008. His mother Hawise was a Norman, the sister of Richard II, Duke of Normandy, who had acted as regent during his minority with Richard acting as guardian. But when Richard died in 1026, Alain tried to break free of Norman control, and the overlordship of Duke Robert, Richard's successor. War broke out between the two duchies, and, with Duke Robert threatening Brittany with an army that he had raised for an aborted invasion of England, peace was eventually brokered by the

---

18 Louis IV was a son of Charles III and an English mother who had removed him to England for safty at the age of three, when his father, who had been deposed a year earlier, was taken into captivity by an ally of Raoul, Duke of Burgundy and subsequently King of France.

uncle of the two Dukes, Robert the Archbishop of Rouen. In the resulting settlement, Duke Alain paid homage to Duke Robert, and the status quo was preserved.

12.9   The End of the Anglo-Saxons

Alfred the Great's heroics did not end the Viking incursions into England, and we have already seen that in the period 892 to 896, almost to the end of his life, he was still successfully battling very large invasion forces. He died in 899, but he and his immediate heirs enjoyed a great deal of success until the end of the millennium, against various combinations of Vikings, Scots and the Irish.

However, in 978 the throne passed to Æthelred the Unready (whose name would have been more accurately translated as Æthelred the Ill-advised), who was no more than 13 years old. Æthelred took the throne in unfortunate circumstances, after the murder of his half-brother, an event that had left the nation divided. The Vikings were always quick to spot internal dissention, as an opportunity to be exploited, and Danish raids on England recommenced. Unable to command forces sufficient to defeat the intruders, Æthelred was forced to pay Danegeld to preserve his kingdom from 991 onwards. Æthelred seems to have believed that the Viking incursions were being encouraged by the Normans, and may have felt that he had a claim to the Duchy of Normandy through his wife Emma. So in about 1000, he launched an invasion of Normandy, in a fleet which sailed from Portsmouth to Barfleur. This force was repulsed by Norman forces led by Count Neliou, a descendant of Nécl de Saint Sauveur, who owned half of Guernsey. In 1002 Æthelred tried genocide to relieve the pressure from Scandinavian immigrants, and he ordered a massacre of Danes settled in England on St Brices Day. The resulting slaughter is believed to have killed many in the areas dominated by the Anglo-Saxons, for example in Oxford, but it would have had little impact in the former Danelaw regions. This atrocity provoked a reaction from the Danes, and in 1003 the Danish King Sweyn Forkbeard invaded. Sweyn faced unexpected opposition in Norfolk, and retreated to Denmark in 1005. But he returned in 1013, conquered England and deposed Æthelred in 1013, forcing him into exile in Normandy.

Sweyn died the following year, so Æthelred returned to England from Normandy, to take up the throne once more, but war then broke out between Æthelred and Sweyn's son Canute (Knut), resulting in a victory for Canute in 1016, which led to his enthronement as England's first Danish king. Æthelred died shortly afterwards.

The devastation caused to the Anglo-Saxons at this time is vividly recorded in several sources. Wulfstan II, the Archbishop of York, writing between 1010 and 1016, said *"Therefore it is clear and well seen in all of us that we have previously more often transgressed than we have amended, and therefore much is greatly assailing this nation. Nothing has prospered now for a long time either at home or abroad, but there has been military devastation and hunger, burning and bloodshed in nearly every district time and again. And stealing and slaying, plague and pestilence, murrain and disease, malice and hate, and robbery by robbers have injured us very terribly."*

The casualties among the Anglo-Saxon nobility, fighting the Vikings, mounted year by year. The Anglo-Saxon Chronicle reports one of several battles in the year 1016 in the following terms: *"When the king [Edmund] understood that the army was up, then collected he the fifth time all the English nation, and went behind them, and overtook them in Essex, on the down called Assingdon; where they fiercely came together. Then did Alderman Edric as he often did before – he first began the flight with the Maisevethions, and so betrayed his natural lord and all the people of England. There had Knute his victory, though all England fought against him! There was then slain Bishop Ednoth, and Abbot Wulsy, and Alderman Elfrie, and Alderman Godfrey of Lindsey, and Ulfkytel of East Anglia and Ethelward the son of Alderman Ethelsy. And all the nobility of the English nation was undone!"* The grip of the Anglo-Saxons on England was being steadily loosened by a war of attrition with the Danes – a war that they were inexorably losing. And it was not just the aristocracy who were suffering; the Anglo-Saxon thegns (knights) and ceorls (freemen) were being cut down in their thousands. The ceorl was the lowest social rank entitled to bear arms, so the large numbers of slaves or bondsmen, and all those who lived outside the areas under effective Anglo-Saxon rule, did not fight.

The result was that, after 1016, England was ruled by Danes, but to some extent they intermarried with the Anglo-Saxons and Normans. Canute (1016 – 1035) had a Mercian mistress, Ælfgifu of Northampton, by whom he had two sons, Svein and Harold Harefoot. He then married Æthelred's widow, Emma, daughter of Richard I of Normandy, who already had a son called Edward (later the Confessor) by Æthelred. And she gave Canute another son called Harthacnut, who was his legitimate heir. Svein and Ælfgifu were sent to Norway in 1030, to act as joint regents, but their regime was unpopular and Svein was driven out of Norway and died in 1035, after which the danish royal family abandoned their claim to the Norwegian crown.

When Canute died in 1035, Harthacnut was heir to the kingdoms of Denmark and England. But Harold Harefoot contested the throne of England, and initially there was a standoff during which Harold had effective control of the country north of the Thames, while Harthacnut, supported by his mother Queen Emma and Earl Godwin of Wessex, ruled the south. Earl Godwin ('the King Maker') was a son of a Danish Viking, who had amassed immense wealth and power in the south of England, with estates from Cornwall to Kent. However when Harthacnut was obliged to spend a prolonged period in Denmark, defending his claim to the Danish throne, Godwin decided to switch allegiances, with the result that Harold's rule became accepted throughout England – and Emma was forced to take refuge in Bruges.

Harold Harefoot only lived for five more years (so he reigned from 1035 to 1040) and when he died, Harthacnut finally took the throne to which he was entitled, albeit for a brief period (1040 to 1042). When he died, Earl Godwin promoted the interests of Edward, Æthelred's son by Emma, and helped to put him on the throne – as the last monarch from the House of Wessex. Edward had been exiled in Normandy for large parts of his youth, and had many friends at the Norman court. Indeed, according to the Norman Chronicles, Robert, Duke of Normandy had attempted to mount an invasion of England in the period 1029 to 1034 to install him on the English throne, and had thereby became inadvertently the first and only Duke of Normandy to visit the Channel Islands.

His fleet, which had set sail from Fécamp in Normandy had been assailed by a great storm when within sight of the coast of Sussex, and, somewhat puzzlingly, had been blown around the Côtentin peninsula and landed up in Guernsey or Jersey, or both. The various accounts in the Norman histories tell us that he arrived in Gersus, Gersy, Gersui, Gèresy or Grénésy, and partisans of each island have long debated which island was referred to. Textual analysis would support the claim of Jersey, but a landing there would have been even more off-course than a landfall in Guernsey, and local legend in Guernsey maintains that Duke Robert was brought into the bay at L'Ancresse by a local pilot, and that the bay derives its name from this event.

Be that as it may, whichever island may have been favoured with the Duke's visit, his stay there was unexpectedly prolonged, as the weather prevented him from leaving for about two weeks, and the Duke became very bored. He decided to abandon his attempted invasion of Britain and to send part of his force to attack the Bretons under Alain III.

When Harthacnut died in 1042, Earl Godwin probably viewed Edward as a suitably compliant candidate for the throne. But Edward filled his court with Norman favorites, inciting Godwin's jealousy, and then provoked Godwin into an act of disobedience for which he had him exiled in 1051. This did not last long, because the following year Godwin returned to England with a force sufficiently large to intimidate Edward, forcing him to restore Godwin's position and expel his Norman courtiers. Godwin died shortly afterwards, and was succeeded by his son Harold Godwinsson, who became the effective ruler of England in all but name during the last ten years of Edward's reign. Edward died childless.

12.10   The Invasion of England

In 1064, Harold Godwinsson visited the Norman court, according to the Bayeux Tapestry at Edward's instruction, to advise William, Duke of Normandy, that Edward was appointing him as his heir. Edward then died in January 1066, but on the following day Harold had himself proclaimed King of England. His claim to the throne was disputed by William and also by Harald Hardrada, king of Norway, who claimed that Harthacnut and Harald Hardrada's nephew Magnus, with whom Harald had initially shared the Norwegian throne, had an agreement that if either of them died, he would leave his kingdom to the other.

Harald Hardrada invaded England with 300 long ships, but Harold Godwinsson rushed north to York and then defeated the Norwegian at the Battle of Stamford Bridge, beating him so badly that it required only 24 ships to take the survivors of his army home. That was the last Viking invasion of England, although a fleet led by King Sweyn II of Denmark had to be bought off with a payment of Danegeld in 1070. But the battle, and a subsequent forced march to the south coast, took so much out of the forces of Harold Godwinsson, that when they reached Hastings to confront a second invasion force led by Duke William, they were much weakened.

William set off with an army of about 10,000 including archers and heavy cavalry. His army may have included men from the Channel Islands, but would certainly have included the Normans who held title to land in the Islands. It also included a number of Bretons, among them Judhael of Totnes, Alan of Richmond, Eudo of Tattershall and Alfred of Lincoln, who thus completed a circuit of north-western Europe commenced by their ancestors, possibly in the 6th century. A community of Bretons was eventually established in Richmondshire.

William's landing at Pevensey on 28th September was unopposed, because he had arrived, fortuitously, only two days after the Battle of

Stamford Bridge; so his troops had time to gather and make camp in good order. Harold, meanwhile, had heard the news of the invasion and rushed south, reaching London on 5ᵗʰ October, where he stayed five days gathering reinforcements. He then headed south to meet William with a force of about equal size, but mainly comprised of foot soldiers, arriving on 14ᵗʰ October. William received notice of Harold's pending arrival and marched out to meet him at Seniac Hill, near what is now Battle in Sussex. There the two armies drew up in battle order, with Harold holding the higher ground. The reports of the ensuing engagement are confusing, but the outcome is clear: Harold and many of his nobles were killed, and the Normans won the day.

However the battle did not conclude the war, because Edgar Atheling was proclaimed king by the nobles and archbishops of England, and William marched north to London to eliminate this new challenge. Fighting at Southwark but finding himself unable to cross London Bridge, he moved upriver to cross the Thames at Wallingford in Berkshire, and defeated Edgar's supporters at Berkhamsted in Hertfordshire. Even after he was crowned at Westminster Abbey in December 1066, resistance continued for many years, until the last of the rebels were crushed at Ely in 1071.

The consequences for the ruling nobility of England, much of it still Anglo-Saxon, were far reaching. William had promised rich rewards for his supporters, and 95% of the land in England changed hands as a result of his redistributions. The confiscations led to further revolts, which were brutally suppressed, and the Anglo-Saxon and Viking nobility were driven into exile, some, like Harold's sons, to Ireland. In the 1070s a large group of Anglo-Saxons sailed to Constantinople in 235 ships, where they became mercenaries in the service of the Emperor and established towns called New London and New York. William's repression was so successful that by 1072 he was able to return to France and thereafter spent no more than a quarter of his time in England.

About 8,000 Normans settled in England to replace the Anglo-Saxon and Viking aristocracies, and the new regime proved significantly different from the old. When William landed, about 10% of the population of England were literally slaves of the Anglo-Saxons or Vikings, but within a few years there were hardly any slaves in the country. The English peasants probably found rule by absentee Norman landlords much more convenient than the oppression of the Anglo-Saxons. And the language of the country changed profoundly: Old English, the language of the Anglo-Saxons, disappeared to be rapidly replaced by Middle English, a language influenced by the Normans, certainly, but equally reflective of the language of the common people. In fact, we can say that the real winners of the Battle of Hastings were the wealas.

Hastings also marked a watershed for the Channel Islands, because the Islands acquired a new relationship with the English Crown. However, the Kings of England ruled in the Islands not in that capacity, but as Dukes of Normandy, as they had done since 933. (The monarch was a Duke, whether he was a king or she was a queen). The relationship survived the loss of Normandy by King John in 1204, since when the Channel Islands have been the only part of the ancient Duchy to remain in the hands of the Dukes.

The Channel Islands have remained possessions of the English Crown for a thousand years.[19] Strictly speaking, since the monarchs of England abandoned their claim to the Duchy of Normandy in 1259, they have ruled in the Islands as successors to the Dukes, but old habits die hard: the loyal toast in the Channel Islands still celebrates the historic relationship: 'The Queen, our Duke".

---

19 Apart from a few intervals such as Cromwell's Protectorate, which followed the English Civil War in the 17th century, and the brief occupations of the Islands by the French in the 13th and 14th centuries (and on one occasion by a force of Spanish mercenaries led by a Welsh commander). The most recent disruption of the relationship was the occupation of the Islands by the Germans during the Second World War.

SELECT BIBLIOGRAPHY

Amt, Emilie (Editor)	*Women's Lives in Medieval Europe*, 1992
Arnold, Martin	*The Vikings; a short history*, 2008
Ashley, Mike	*A Brief History of King Arthur*, 2005
Barbero, Alessandro	*Charlemagne; Father of a Continent*, 2004
Bede	*Ecclesiastical History of the English People* (Penguin Classics)
Bradbury, James	*The Routledge Companion to Medieval Warfare*, 2004
Casson, Lionel	*Ships and Seamanship in the Ancient World*, 1995
Clark Hall, JRA	*Concise Anglo-Saxon Dictionary*, 1894
Clarkson, James	*Indo-European Linguistics: An Introduction*, 2007
Coates, Richard	*The Ancient and Modern Names of the Channel Islands*, 1991
Cunliffe, Barry	*Armorica and Britain: Cross-Channel Relationships in the late first millennium BC*, 1997
	Europe Between the Oceans, 2008
	Hengistbury Head, 1978
	The Ancient Celts, 1997
De Beaurepaire, François	*Les Noms des Communes et Anciennes Paroisses de la Manche*, 1986
De la Bédoyère, Guy	*Roman Britain; A New History*, 2006
Deegan, Alison Foard, Glenn	*Mapping Ancient Landscapes in Northamptonshire*, 2008
Delamarre, Xavier	*Dictionnaire de la Langue Galoise, 2nd Edition*, 2003
Driscoll, Paul	*The Past in the Prehistoric Channel Islands*, 2010
Dupont, Gustave Jules	*Le Côtentin et ses Îles*, 1870
Fleming, Robin	*Britain after Rome*, 2010
Fouracre, Paul (Editor)	*The New Cambridge Medieval History, Volume 1*, 2005
Fowler, Peter	*The Past in Contemporary Society: The, Now*, 1992
Fowler, Robert James	*Metallurgy in Antiquity*, 1950

Giles, J A	*History of the Britons*, 1838
Giot, Pierre-Roland	*The British Settlement of Brittany*, 2003
Guignon, Philippe	
Merdrignac, Bernard	
Geoffrey of Monmouth	*The History of the Kings of Britain* (Penguin Classics)
Gregory of Tours	*The History of the Franks* (Penguin Classics)
Härke, Heinrich	*Anglo-Saxon Immigration and Ethnogenesis*, 2011
Hatt, Jean-Jacques	*Celts and Gallo Romans*, 1970
Hayes, JW	*Late Roman pottery*, 1972
Hindley, Geoffrey	*A Brief History of The Anglo-Saxons*, 2006
Kristiansen, Kristian	*Europe Before History*, 2000
Le Patourel, John	*Feudal Empires: Norman and Plantagenet*, 1984
Magnusson, Magnus	*The Vikings*, 1980
Mallory, JP	*Bronze Age Languages of the Tarim Basin, Expedition, Volume 52, No 3*
	In search of the Indo-Europeans, 2005
Mallory, JP	*The Oxford Introduction to Proto-Indo-*
Adams, DQ	*European and the Proto-Indo-European World, 2006*
Murphy, JP (Editor)	*The Ora Maritima*, 1977
Olmer, Fabienne	*Amphores en Gaul aux IIer et Ier siècles avant notre ère. Aspects épigraphiques, quantatifs et economiques*, 2008
Oppenheimer, Stephen	*The Origins of the British: a genetic detective story*, 2006
Papworth, Martin	*The Search for the Durotriges*, 2011
Pattison, JE	*Integration versus apartheid in post-Roman Britain: a response to Thomas et al, 2008*
Renfrew, Colin	*Archaeology & Language. The Puzzle of the Indo-European Origins*, 1987
Riddle, John M	*A History of the Middle Ages, 300 – 1500*, 2008
Sawyer, Peter	*The Oxford Illustrated History of the Vikings*, 1997
Smith, Julia M H	*Europe after Rome*, 2005
Sykes, Brian	*Blood of the Isles: exploring the genetic roots of our tribal history*, 2006
Talbert, Richard	*The Peutinger Map; Rome's World Reconsidered*, 2010
Venning, Timothy	*The Anglo-Saxon Kings*, 2011
Warner, Philip	*British Battlefields; The Midlands*, 1972

Wiseman,
Anne and Peter   *The Battle for Gaul,* 1992
Wickham, Chris   *Framing the Early Middle Ages,* 2005
Wilson, Derek   *Charlemagne; The Great Adventure,* 2005

INDEX OF ISLANDS, CITIES AND TOWNS

INDEX OF PEOPLE